Pentaho Reporting 3.5 for Java Developers

Create advanced reports, including cross tabs, sub-reports, and charts that connect to practically any data source using open source Pentaho Reporting

Will Gorman

BIRMINGHAM - MUMBAI

Pentaho Reporting 3.5 for Java Developers

First published: September 2009

Production Reference: 1310809

Published by Packt Publishing Ltd.
32 Lincoln Road
Olton
Birmingham, B27 6PA, UK.

ISBN 978-1-847193-19-3

www.packtpub.com

Cover Image by Vinayak Chittar (vinayak.chittar@gmail.com)

Credits

Author
Will Gorman

Reviewers
Jem Matzan

Kurtis Cruzada

Acquisition Editor
James Lumsden

Development Editor
Dhiraj Chandiramani

Technical Editor
Gaurav Datar

Indexer
Rekha Nair

Editorial Team Leader
Gagandeep Singh

Project Team Leader
Priya Mukherji

Project Coordinators
Zainab Bagasrawala

Lata Basantani

Proofreader
Laura Booth

Production Coordinator
Adline Swetha Jesuthas

Cover Work
Adline Swetha Jesuthas

Drawing Coordinator
Nilesh R. Mohite

Foreword

During the course of the last 8000 years, no other invention has driven the course of human development more than the ancient art of business reporting. In the ancient city states of Mesopotamia, the rulers of the fast growing states carved inventory lists and tax records into stone plates. For the first time in human history this enabled the management of large distributed empires, armies, and organizations.

Fast-forward a few thousand years, and the art reporting is still in fashion. Even today reporting drives empires, not ones rules by kings, but empires created by entrepreneurs as well as large-scale public traded companies. Carving lists and numbers in stones has been replaced by electrons traveling at the speed of light to deliver critical information to the leaders of today's business world.

When I first came to JFreeReport, I did not care about the big players. All I needed was a printing system to create long and boring printouts at reasonable speed and cost. None of the commercial vendors were able or willing to solve my needs, and hence I stumbled (quite accidentally) over JFreeReport. After some time extending, optimizing, and debugging in the reporting engine, I was addicted to it. Eight years later, the project has changed radically from its early roots. As we grew from simple printing to fully featured BI-reporting, we left the name "JFreeReport" behind and became known as "Pentaho Reporting". But this original love has never diminished and all these years later, the project has grown stronger to now challenge even the age-old commercial offerings in their own space.

The book you're holding in your hand right now marks an important milestone in Pentaho Reporting's history. For the very first time, we are now able to point our users, developers, and partners to a professionally written document that covers all aspects of the Pentaho reporting engine. After eight years of sending developers into the Java code to learn how a feature is working, this is a remarkable and welcome change.

If you want to understand the concepts used in Pentaho Reporting or want to add reporting capabilities to your own application, you will find this book an invaluable companion on your journey. As the book guides you from the very simple examples, to the fully embedded reporting scenarios, the knowledge in the book will guide you safely through all your tasks so that you can become productive very fast.

Business Reporting should be available for everyone who has a need for it, so take control of your data.

Thomas Morgner
Chief Architect, Pentaho Reporting

About the Author

Will Gorman is an Engineering Team Lead at Pentaho. He works on a variety of Pentaho's products, including Reporting, Analysis, Dashboards, Metadata, and the BI Server. Will started his career at GE Research, and earned his Masters degree in Computer Science at Rensselaer Polytechnic Institute in Troy, New York. Over the years, Will has given many speeches, including topics at local Java User Groups and has also published technical papers in journals such as Neurology. Will is originally from Cincinnati, Ohio and now lives in Orlando, Florida, the headquarters of Pentaho.

This book was possible thanks to all the great help from Pentaho's Reporting team, including Thomas Morgner, the lead architect and founder of Pentaho Reporting, Kurtis Cruzada, Pentaho Reporting's Product Manager, Jem Matzan, documentation lead for Pentaho Reporting, and many of the Pentaho engineers who work on Pentaho Reporting and Pentaho Report Designer, including David Kincade, Mike D'Amour, Ezequiel Cuellar, and Bill Seyler. I'd also like to thank all those in the open source community who have contributed to Pentaho Reporting.

I also want to thank the founders of Pentaho, Doug Moran, James Dixon, Marc Bachelor, and Richard Daley, who make every day at Pentaho entertaining and enlightening. Finally, I want to give special thanks to my patient wife Laura and our wonderful son Luke, who both gave me their full support during the many weekends and holidays of book writing.

About the Reviewers

Jem Matzan is the author of hundreds of information technology articles and reviews. Apart from being an author, he is a ghostwriter, editor of several technology-oriented books, and a software documentation specialist.

Kurtis Cruzada is a graduate of the University of Central Florida majoring in Accounting and minoring in Computer Science, and also holds an MBA with a focus in Accounting Information Systems. Kurtis began his career in the Business Intelligence field in the early 1990s. In late 1990s, Kurtis joined Arbor Software/ Hyperion Solutions where he managed Wired for OLAP (Hyperion Analyzer and Web Analytics) and Hyperion's BI Workspace, which later became the collective front-end framework for all the web-based Hyperion products. In late 2005, Kurtis joined Pentaho as a Senior Product Manager primarily focusing on Reporting and the BI Platform.

I would like to thank my wife, Tracy and my kids, Riley, Mallory and Kai for supporting me throughout my career and endeavors.

Table of Contents

Preface

Pentaho Reporting lets you create, generate, and distribute rich and sophisticated report content from different data sources. Knowing how to use it quickly and efficiently gives you the edge in producing reports from your database. If you have been looking for a book that has plenty of easy-to-understand instructions and also contains lots of examples and screenshots, this is where your search ends.

This book shows you how to replace or build your enterprise reporting solution from scratch with Pentaho's Reporting Suite. Through detailed examples, it dives deeply into all aspects of Pentaho's reporting functionalities, providing you with the knowledge you need to master report creation.

What this book covers

Chapter 1 — An Introduction to Pentaho Reporting provides a quick overview of Pentaho Reporting, including a feature summary and architectural summary, as well as a history of the product.

Chapter 2 — Pentaho Reporting Client and Enterprise Examples tells how to install and create reports, and how to embed reports in your J2EE and client Java applications.

Chapter 3 — Pentaho Reporting Examples in the Real World tells how to connect to a JDBC data source and create realistic inventory, balance, and invoice reports, including charts and sub-reports.

Chapter 4 — Design and Layout in Pentaho's Report Designer takes a deep dive into Pentaho's Report Designer, learning how to create great-looking reports.

Chapter 5 — Working with Data Sources teaches the various ways to connect your report to live data, including JDBC, Hibernate, Java Beans, OLAP, and many other data sources.

Chapter 6 – Including Charts and Graphics in Reports is about incorporating Pie, Bar, Line, and many other chart types in your reports, as well as including dynamic images in your report.

Chapter 7 – Parameterization, Functions, Formulas, and Internationalization in Reports defines parameters for dynamic report generation. It helps you write formulas and use available functions for rich summary and calculated values in your reports, along with dynamically adjusting colors and styles using expressions in your report.

Chapter 8 – Adding Sub-Reports and Cross Tabs to Reports gives an overview of how to build reports that include side-by-side sub-reports and cross tabs.

Chapter 9 – Building Interactive Reports teaches how to add dynamic interaction to HTML and Swing reports, for immediate feedback and dashboard-like functionality.

Chapter 10 – API-based Report Generation is about building reports from XML and by using Pentaho Reporting's Java Bean API.

Chapter 11 – Extending Pentaho Reporting teaches how to write custom functions and elements within Pentaho Reporting.

Chapter 12 – Additional Pentaho Reporting Topics discovers how to use Pentaho Reporting with the Pentaho BI Server, including Pentaho Metadata. It aids in learning more about Pentaho Reporting's open source approach, and how you can contribute to the free software movement.

Who this book is for

This book is primarily written for Java developers who want to assemble custom reporting solutions with Pentaho Reporting. Their main interest is in the technical details of creating reports. They want to see how to solve common report problems with a minimum of fuss and don't need an overview of BI or the importance of reporting.

Secondary audiences of this book are information technologists who need to install a reporting solution in their environment, and want to learn advanced concepts within Pentaho Reporting such as sub-reports, cross tabs, data source configuration, and metadata-based reporting.

Conventions

In this book, you will find a number of styles of text that distinguish between different kinds of information. Here are some examples of these styles, and an explanation of their meaning.

Code words in text are shown as follows: "Copy the servlet file `chapter2\src\Chapter2Servlet.java` to `chapter3\src\Chapter3Servlet.java`, and rename the class to `Chapter3Servlet`."

A block of code will be set as follows:

```
String reportName = request.getParameter("reportName");
if (reportName == null) {
    response.getWriter().println("No report parameter specified");
    return;
}
```

Any command-line input or output is written as follows:

```
ant restart_tomcat
```

New terms and **important words** are shown in bold. Words that you see on the screen, in menus or dialog boxes for example, appear in our text like this: "Right-click on the sub-report element in the canvas and select **Edit SubReport**".

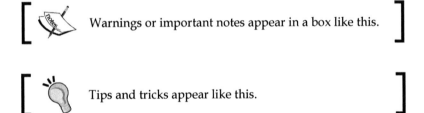

Warnings or important notes appear in a box like this.

Tips and tricks appear like this.

Reader feedback

Feedback from our readers is always welcome. Let us know what you think about this book—what you liked or may have disliked. Reader feedback is important for us to develop titles that you really get the most out of.

To send us general feedback, simply drop an email to feedback@packtpub.com, and mention the book title in the subject of your message.

If there is a book that you need and would like to see us publish, please send us a note in the **SUGGEST A TITLE** form on www.packtpub.com or email suggest@packtpub.com.

If there is a topic that you have expertise in and you are interested in either writing or contributing to a book, see our author guide on www.packtpub.com/authors.

Customer support

Now that you are the proud owner of a Packt book, we have a number of things to help you to get the most from your purchase.

Downloading the example code for the book

Visit http://www.packtpub.com/files/code/3193_Code.zip to directly download the example code.

[The downloadable files contain instructions on how to use them.]

Errata

Although we have taken every care to ensure the accuracy of our contents, mistakes do happen. If you find a mistake in one of our books—maybe a mistake in text or code—we would be grateful if you would report this to us. By doing so, you can save other readers from frustration, and help us to improve subsequent versions of this book. If you find any errata, please report them by visiting http://www.packtpub.com/support, selecting your book, clicking on the **let us know** link, and entering the details of your errata. Once your errata are verified, your submission will be accepted and the errata added to any list of existing errata. Any existing errata can be viewed by selecting your title from http://www.packtpub.com/support.

Piracy

Piracy of copyright material on the Internet is an ongoing problem across all media. At Packt, we take the protection of our copyright and licenses very seriously. If you come across any illegal copies of our works in any form on the Internet, please provide us with the location address or website name immediately so that we can pursue a remedy.

Please contact us at copyright@packtpub.com with a link to the suspected pirated material.

We appreciate your help in protecting our authors, and our ability to bring you valuable content.

Questions

You can contact us at questions@packtpub.com if you are having a problem with any aspect of the book, and we will do our best to address it.

1
An Introduction to Pentaho Reporting

Pentaho Reporting is an easy-to-use, open source, lightweight suite of Java projects built for one purpose—report generation. In this book, you'll discover how easy it is to embed Pentaho Reporting into your Java projects, or use it as a standalone reporting platform. Pentaho Reporting's open source license—the **GNU Lesser General Public License (LGPL)**—gives developers the freedom to embed Pentaho Reporting into their open source and proprietary applications at no cost. An active community participates in the development and use of Pentaho Reporting, answering forum questions, fixing bugs, and implementing new features. While many proprietary reporting options are available, none can offer the openness and flexibility that Pentaho Reporting provides its users with.

As with most successful open source projects, Pentaho Reporting has a proven track record, along with a long list of features. Most of this history has been documented in open forums and in email threads, which are still available for folks to browse through and glean ideas from. Starting as a side hobby and turning into an enterprise reporting suite over the course of seven years, the **Pentaho Reporting Engine** and its suite of tools such as the Report Designer, Report Design Wizard, and Pentaho's web-based Ad Hoc Reporting user interface, are used as critical components in countless corporate, educational, governmental, and community-based information technology solutions.

In most business software applications, a reporting component is necessary, be it for summarizing data, generating large numbers of customized documents, or simply for making it easier to print information that would be useful in various output formats. With a complete set of features, including PDF, Excel, HTML, and RTF report generation, along with advanced reporting capabilities such as sub-reports and cross tabs, Pentaho Reporting can crack the simplest of problems quickly, along with solving the more advanced challenges when designing, generating and deploying reports.

Read on in this chapter to learn more about the typical uses, history and origins of Pentaho Reporting, along with a more detailed overview of the reporting functionality that Pentaho Reporting provides.

Typical uses of Pentaho Reporting

Business users need access to information in many different forms for many different reasons. Pentaho Reporting addresses the following typical uses of reporting, along with many other types that will be covered in this book.

Operational reporting

One of the most commonly used forms of reporting is **operational reporting**. When a developer or an IT organization decides to generate reports directly from their operational data sources for the purpose of detailed transaction level reporting, this is referred to as operational reporting. In this scenario, the database is designed to solve an operational problem, and usually contains live data supporting critical business functions. Users of Pentaho Reporting can point directly to this data source and start generating reports.

Some examples of operational reporting include building custom reports directly based on a third-party software vendor's database schema such as Bugzilla's bug tracking system or SugarCRM's Customer Relationship Management system. These reports might include summaries of daily activity, or detailed views into particular projects or users in the system. Reports might also be generated from data originating from an in-house custom application. These reports are typically based on a SQL backend, but could be generated from flat log files or directly from in-memory Java objects.

Pentaho Reporting's parameterization capabilities provide a powerful mechanism to render up-to-the-minute customized operational reports. With features such as cross tabs and interactive reporting, business users can quickly view their operational data and drill back into operational systems that might require attention.

There are limitations when developing reports based on live operational data. Developers need to be careful to make sure that queries in the operational system do not impact the performance of regular operations. An extremely CPU-intensive query could delay a transaction from taking place. Also, certain historical questions — for example, state transitions or changes to particular informational fields such as address — aren't traditionally captured in an operational schema design.

Business intelligence reporting

When you've reached the limits of operational reporting, the next logical step is to move your data into a data warehouse. This move is often referred to as **business intelligence reporting**. Reporting alone does not provide the necessary tools to make this transition. You will need an **Extract**, **Transform**, and **Load (ETL)** tool such as Pentaho Data Integration, along with a sensible warehouse design such as a snow flake schema, in order to enable business intelligence reporting.

This type of use allows business users to monitor changes over time. It also helps gain performance benefits by pre-calculating aggregations and defining schemas that are built in mind for summarized reporting. Until recently, data warehousing and business intelligence have been limited to large enterprises due to the cost of software and limited expertise. With open source tools becoming more widely available, a large number of small and medium size businesses are deploying data warehouses, in order to get solutions for the critical questions in their business domain. Common examples of data warehouse reporting include combining sales and inventory data into a single location for reporting, or combining internal proprietary sales data with publicly available market trends and analysis.

Pentaho Reporting's flexible data source support makes it easy to incorporate reports into your business intelligence solutions. Also, with Pentaho Reporting's speed and scalability, you can deploy Pentaho Reporting with confidence that reports will be executed efficiently.

As with all approaches, there are limitations to this approach. In traditional warehousing, data is usually batched nightly, weekly, or monthly. Therefore, business users rarely get to see up-to-the-minute reports on business operations. Also, when designing a warehouse, it is important to ask the correct business questions. Unfortunately, it is possible to build a data warehouse and still not address business users' needs, if not investigated ahead of time.

Financial reporting

Financial reporting is a very specific, but very common form of reporting, geared towards generating financial summaries for accountants, managers, and business investors. Standard reports that fall into this category include balance sheets, income statements, retained earning statements, and cash flow statements. Unlike business intelligence or operational reporting, many of these reports are required by law, with regulations around their content and presentation. Financial reports often include computations for assets, liabilities, revenues, and expenses.

Following is the screenshot showing one such report:

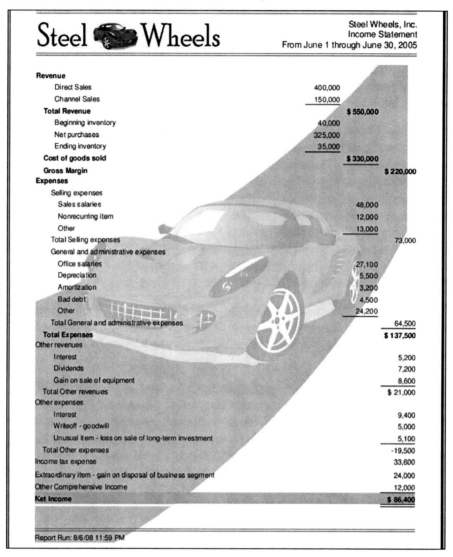

With features such as group summary aggregations, Pentaho Reporting makes it very easy for developers to implement custom financial reports that business managers and owners require.

Typically, this type of data exists in a controlled form, be it in a proprietary system such as QuickBooks or SAP, or in a secure database system such as Oracle or MySQL. Due to the sensitivity of this data, developers will need to be conscious of who has access to reports and may want to implement features such as audit logging.

Production reporting

Another typical use of Pentaho Reporting includes production reporting. This type of reporting includes reports such as a customized form letter, invoice, or postcard for a large audience, as well as automated mail merging. Normally, batch processing is involved in this form of reporting. However, custom reports generated for individuals based on a standard template can also fall under this category.

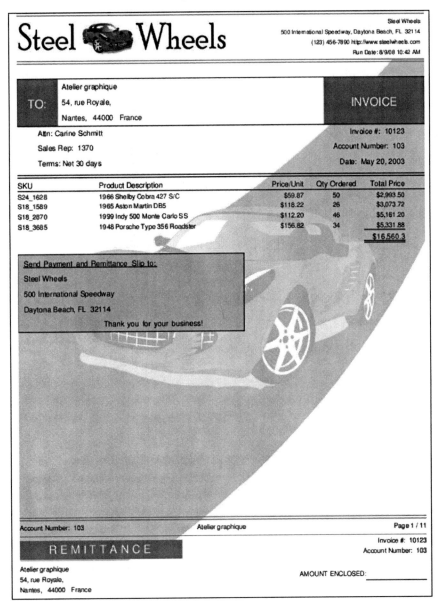

There are certain specific features in Pentaho Reporting such as dynamically incorporating images from a data source, as well as pixel accurate formatting, which can be of real help when implementing production reporting.

Pentaho Reporting history

Pentaho Reporting began as **JFreeReport**, a Java-based reporting engine and Swing widget, back in 2002. David Gilbert, author of JFreeChart, implemented the initial version of JFreeReport to address report rendering needs. Soon after launching the project, Thomas Morgner, standing to the right of Will Gorman in the following picture, became the primary developer. He added critical functionality such as report functions and XML report definitions, launching JFreeReport into a successful open source Java project.

Since the beginning, Pentaho Reporting has been an international project. David is located in Hertfordshire, United Kingdom, and Thomas is located in Frankfurt, Germany. Many others from all over the world have contributed translations and code to Pentaho Reporting.

From 2002 to 2006, Thomas continued to develop JFreeReport into an enterprise-worthy reporting engine. While working as a consultant, Thomas added support for a variety of outputs, including Excel and RTF. At the beginning of 2006, Thomas and JFreeReport joined Pentaho, an open source business intelligence company, and JFreeReport officially became Pentaho Reporting. At this time, Thomas transitioned from a full-time consultant to a full-time developer, on the Pentaho Reporting Engine and suite of tools.

In January 2006, along with the acquisition of Pentaho Reporting, Pentaho announced the general availability of the Pentaho Report Design Wizard, which walks business users through a set of simple instructions for building sophisticated template-based reports. Mike D'Amour, a Senior Engineer at Pentaho, was the initial author of this wizard, which is now used in many Pentaho applications.

Another important milestone in Pentaho Reporting's history was the introduction of Pentaho Report Designer. In 2006, Martin Schmid contributed the first version of the Pentaho Report Designer to the community. Since its introduction, the Report Designer has evolved with the reporting engine.

In 2007, Pentaho teamed up with Sun's OpenOffice.org, to deliver a reporting solution for OpenOffice.org's database tool set. This project was headed by Thomas Morgner, and is now known as the **Pentaho Reporting Flow Engine**. While this engine shares many of the concepts from the classic engine discussed in this book, it is a separate project with dramatically different features and functionality than Pentaho's classic reporting project.

Beginning in Pentaho **Business Intelligence (BI)** Platform release 1.6, Pentaho Reporting also tightly integrates with Pentaho's Metadata Engine, allowing easy-to-use web-based ad hoc reporting by business users who may not have SQL expertise, data driven formatting in reports, as well as column and row level data security. The same functionality is available inside **Pentaho Report Designer** for query and report building, allowing business users to go from a quick template-based report to a full-fledged custom report.

Pentaho Reporting timeline

The following is a timeline of the major events in Pentaho Reporting over the past several years:

- **April 2002**: David Gilbert and Thomas Morgner start the JFreeReport project.
- **September 2003**: Version 0.8.3 of JFreeReport is released, refining PDF, HTML, and Excel rendering, along with many additional enhancements.
- **March 2005**: Version 0.8.5 of JFreeReport is released, with enhancements to function and expression building, along with new features such as Barcode support.
- **January 2006**: Pentaho acquires JFreeReport and hires Thomas Morgner as Pentaho's Chief Reporting Engineer. In the same month, Pentaho Reporting Wizard is released.
- **June 2006**: Martin Schmid releases the first version of Pentaho Report Designer.

- **November 2006**: Web-based Ad hoc Reporting Support is added to Pentaho's BI Platform.
- **April 2007**: Pentaho teams up with OpenOffice.org to deliver Pentaho Reporting's Flow Engine, embedded in OpenOffice.org.
- **August 2009:** Pentaho releases version 3.5 of Pentaho Reporting.

Feature overview

In this quick introduction to the various features available in Pentaho Reporting 3.5, you'll have an executive summary of how Pentaho Reporting works and what it can accomplish for your reporting needs. The topics that will follow are covered in more depth in later chapters of the book.

An advanced reporting algorithm

The reporting algorithm is at the heart of Pentaho Reporting. This algorithm manages the layout and rendering of the entire report, no matter which output format is being rendered. This algorithm combines a reporting template, along with a dataset on the fly, in order to generate the final report. There is no unnecessary compilation step. All other Pentaho Reporting features can be described in the context of the overall reporting algorithm.

This algorithm allows reports to render with a page header and footer, a report header and footer, group headers and footers, as well as a details band. The reporting algorithm traverses the dataset multiple times to render the report. In the first pass, the algorithm performs calculations and determines how to separate the data into groups, along with calculating the height and width of text and images. After the initial pass, the algorithm traverses the dataset a second time, in order to render the output.

A multitude of available data sources

Pentaho Reporting defines a standard Java API for accessing data. Many data source implementations are made available with Pentaho Reporting. The most commonly used implementations include JDBC Database Connectivity, XML XPATH capability, Multidimensional OLAP Data Access using MDX, and simple Plain Old Java Object (POJO) support.

Additional data sources that are available include a Pentaho Data Integration data source, a Hibernate Query Language (HQL) data source, and a Pentaho Metadata data source. With Pentaho's Data Integration data source it is easy to use Excel, Logs, or other file formats as inputs to a report without the need to write any code.

All of these data sources interact with the reporting engine through a standard API, which is easy to extend.

The following data sources are available with Pentaho Reporting:

- Swing TableModel
- Java Reflection (POJO)
- Hibernate HQL
- JDBC SQL
- OLAP MDX
- XML XPATH
- Pentaho Data Integration
- Pentaho Metadata

By combining Pentaho Reporting's data source functionality with Pentaho's Data Integration engine, most known data formats and systems are available for input. This includes combining data sources into a single report. An example might include a Microsoft Excel file, on a remote shared drive, with a plain text log file from an HTTP server.

A wide variety of output formats

Pentaho Reporting has the ability to render to the most widely used output formats, including Adobe's PDF standard using the iText Library, Microsoft's Excel standard using the POI Library, and HTML, all highlighted in the following image. Other formats available include XML, plain text, Rich Text Format (RTF), and Comma-separated values (CSV). In addition to these output formats, a Pentaho Report can be rendered in Swing and directly printed using PostScript formatting, allowing print previewing capabilities.

Following is the screenshot showing one such report obtained using Report Designer.

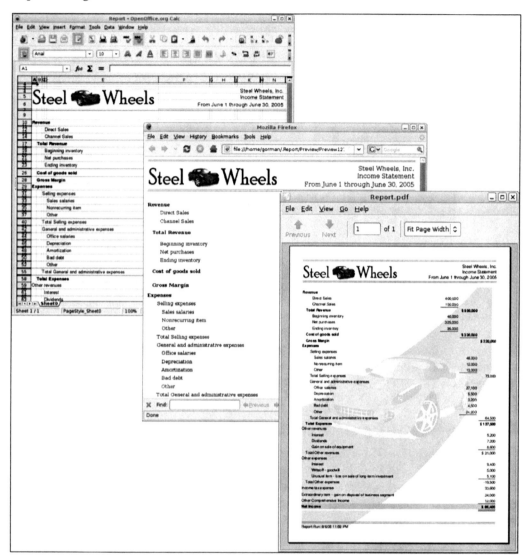

Pixel accurate rich formatting

Reports defined in Pentaho Reporting can specify at the pixel level where objects such as text or images should render. Using Pentaho Report Designer, it is easy to align fields and group items that need to stay aligned. While not always possible due to different format types such as XML, CSV, and plain text, the three main graphical outputs—HTML, PDF, and Excel—strive to look as similar as possible.

Rich formatting includes TrueType system font selection, the ability to render geometrical shapes and lines, along with the ability to include images and other objects in a report. This rich formatting is specified under the covers through styles similar to **Cascading Style Sheets** (**CSS**), separating out the format from the report detail. This makes it easier to modify and maintain reports, and also to apply corporate styles through the report wizard.

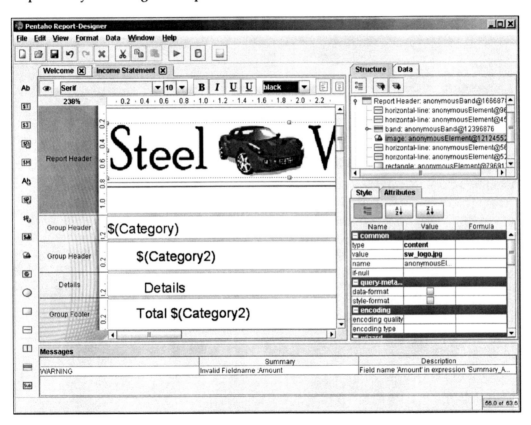

Embedded charts

The Pentaho Reporting Engine and suite of tools make it easy to embed charts in reports, using the **JFreeChart engine**. Many chart types are available, including Bar, Histogram, Pie, and Line charts.

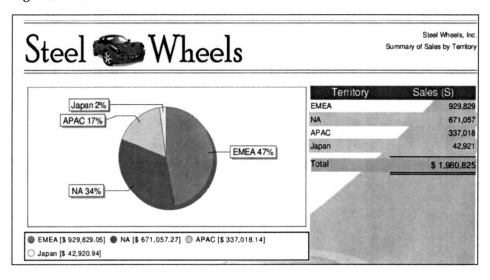

Report parameterization

Pentaho Reporting provides easy-to-use tools to parameterize a report, allowing users to specify ranges and other values that customize the output of a report. Parameter values can be selected from a list of hardcoded values or driven from a query. With parameterization, end users may control the amount of information that is displayed on a report. The following screenshot is an example of parameter input from within Pentaho's Business Intelligence Server:

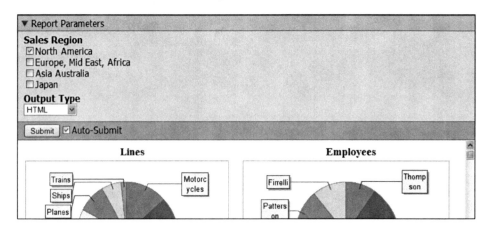

Formulas and style expressions

Report builders may define custom formulas and style expressions, using the OpenFormula standard, allowing for calculated values and dynamic formatting in their reports, such as aggregations, number formatting, as well as traffic lighting.

Sub-reports

Pentaho Reporting allows report developers to include sub-reports within a master report. This provides a powerful capability, which allows reports to contain different smaller reports, both side-by-side and within the various bands of a report. These sub-reports may be based on different data sources.

This capability makes it possible to reuse detailed reports within multiple primary reports, as well as enabling a single report template to render multiple times in a single PDF document, allowing painless printing of a large number of reports. The following screenshot is an example of a report that includes a separate chart sub-report:

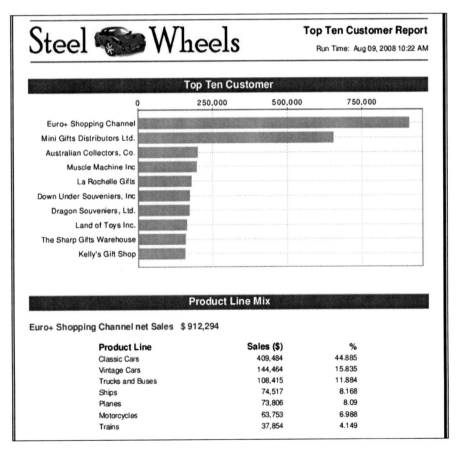

Cross Tab Reports

Cross Tab Reports present data in a spreadsheet-like format, making it easier to view summaries of data. Cross Tab Reports present both row and column headers, as well as cells of data, all of which can be customized through report elements.

Product Line	Years	Quarters	Markets All Markets APAC	EMEA	Japan		NA
Classic Cars	2003		1,052	5,853	898	12,762	4,959
Classic Cars	2004		1,785	8,976	307	16,085	5,017
Classic Cars	2005		1,015	3,463	122	6,705	2,105
Motorcycles	2003		654	1,428	205	4,031	1,744
Motorcycles	2004		540	2,177	380	5,906	2,809
Motorcycles	2005		658	1,501	44	2,771	568
Planes	2003		456	1,723	677	3,833	977
Planes	2004		723	2,326	547	5,820	2,224
Planes	2004	QTR1	318		322	971	331
Planes	2004	QTR2		311		1,113	802
Planes	2004	QTR3		977		1,178	201
Planes	2004	QTR4	405	1,038	225	2,558	890
Planes	2005		151	1,464		2,207	592
Ships	2003			1,968	174	2,844	702
Ships	2004		396	2,144	127	4,309	1,642
Ships	2005		32	696	81	1,346	537
Trains	2003		33	384	174	1,000	409
Trains	2004		106	977		1,409	326
Trains	2005			183	49	409	177
Trucks and Buses	2003		91	2,261	415	4,056	1,289
Trucks and Buses	2004		801	1,558	102	5,024	2,563
Trucks and Buses	2005		488	836		1,921	597
Vintage Cars	2003		1,243	3,094	308	7,913	3,268
Vintage Cars	2004		1,587	5,472	229	10,864	3,576
Vintage Cars	2005		1,067	1,094	84	4,116	1,871

Interactive reporting

While most reports are static after being rendered, a subset of reporting includes functionality such as drill through, pivoting, and other interactivity. Pentaho Reporting provides a straightforward Java and JavaScript API for manipulating a report after it has been rendered, allowing report builders to create very interactive reports. Pentaho Reporting's Interactive functionality is available when rendering a report in HTML, Excel or Swing. Links to external documents can also be added to PDF documents.

The following screenshot shows a report with links, that when clicked launches a more detailed report:

Steel **Wheels**

Steel Wheels, Inc.
Summary of Sales by Customer
From 2005-01-01 through 2005-06-01

All Territories · All Product Lines · All Employees · All Products

Euro+ Shopping Channel	326,798
Mini Gifts Distributors Ltd.	213,256
La Rochelle Gifts	103,402
The Sharp Gifts Warehouse	95,410
Down Under Souveniers, Inc	87,698
Anna's Decorations, Ltd	65,012
Salzburg Collectables	59,475
Corporate Gift Ideas Co.	54,204
Reims Collectables	
Suominen Souveniers	
Oulu Toy Supplies, Inc.	
Gifts4AllAges.com	
Tekni Collectables Inc.	
Toys4GrownUps.com	
Souveniers And Things Co.	
L'ordine Souveniers	
UK Collectables, Ltd.	
GiftsForHim.com	
Tokyo Collectables, Ltd	
FunGiftIdeas.com	
Mini Caravy	
Kelly's Gift Shop	
Québec Home Shopping Network	
Gift Depot Inc.	
Scandinavian Gift Ideas	
Collectables For Less Inc.	
Toys of Finland, Co.	
Extreme Desk Decorations, Ltd	
Danish Wholesale Imports	
Australian Gift Network, Co	
Lyon Souveniers	
Royale Belge	
Alpha Cognac	
Australian Collectables, Ltd	
Auto Canal+ Petit	
Technics Stores Inc.	
Mini Creations Ltd.	
Mini Auto Werke	
Petit Auto	
Diecast Classics Inc.	
Dragon Souveniers, Ltd.	
Boards & Toys Co.	
Handji Gifts& Co	

As of 8/9/08 10:45 AM

Steel **Wheels**

Steel Wheels, Inc.
Order Details
The Sharp Gifts Warehouse

The Sharp Gifts Warehouse
Account Number: 450

San Jose, CA
4085553659

Order#: 10400   Status: Shipped   Order Date: 2005-Apr-01

Line #	SKU	Product Description	Price/Unit	Qty Ordered	Total Price
1	S18_1662	1980s Black Hawk Helicopter	$189.23	34	$6,433.82
2	S24_2841	1900s Vintage Bi-Plane	$61.66	24	$1,479.84
3	S24_3420	1937 Horch 930V Limousine	$57.20	38	$2,173.60
4	S72_1253	Boeing X-32A JSF	$56.12	20	$1,122.40
5	S700_2047	HMS Bounty	$87.80	46	$4,038.80
6	S18_3856	1941 Chevrolet Special Deluxe Cabriolet	$125.99	58	$7,307.42
7	S18_3029	1999 Yamaha Speed Boat	$74.84	30	$2,245.20
8	S24_3816	1940 Ford Delivery Sedan	$72.96	42	$3,064.32
9	S10_4757	1972 Alfa Romeo GTA	$150.96	64	$9,661.44

* Order 10400 contains 9 line items and shipped on Apr 04, 2005. $37,526.84

Order#: 10407   Status: On Hold   Order Date: 2005-Apr-22

Line #	SKU	Product Description	Price/Unit	Qty Ordered	Total Price
1	S18_2248	1911 Ford Town Car	$72.65	42	$3,051.30
2	S18_1749	1917 Grand Touring Sedan	$185.30	76	$14,082.80
3	S18_4409	1932 Alfa Romeo 8C2300 Spider Sport	$90.19	6	$541.14
4	S18_4933	1957 Ford Thunderbird	$66.99	66	$4,421.34
5	S24_2887	1952 Citroen-15CV	$98.65	59	$5,820.35
6	S24_2766	1949 Jaguar XK 120	$94.50	76	$7,182.00
7	S24_3191	1969 Chevrolet Camaro Z28	$81.33	13	$1,057.29
8	S24_1046	1970 Chevy Chevelle SS 454	$76.43	26	$1,987.18
9	S24_3432	2002 Chevy Corvette	$86.73	43	$3,729.39
10	S24_1628	1966 Shelby Cobra 427 S/C	$40.25	64	$2,576.00
11	S18_1589	1965 Aston Martin DB5	$119.46	59	$7,048.14
12	S18_2870	1999 Indy 500 Monte Carlo SS	$155.76	41	$6,386.16

* Order 10407 contains 12 line items and shipped on null. $57,883.09

Total Number of Orders for The Sharp Gifts Warehouse is 2.

1 / 1

Rich authoring tools

While it is possible to build Pentaho reports using either XML or a Java API, most reports begin as templates built by the Pentaho Report Designer. Pentaho Report Designer is a **What-You-See-Is-What-You-Get (WYSIWYG)** report editor that exposes the rich set of features provided by the Pentaho Reporting Engine. In addition to building a report from scratch, the Report Design Wizard, included as a part of the Pentaho Report Designer, walks a report author through building a report, which will then be displayed in the Report Designer for further customization.

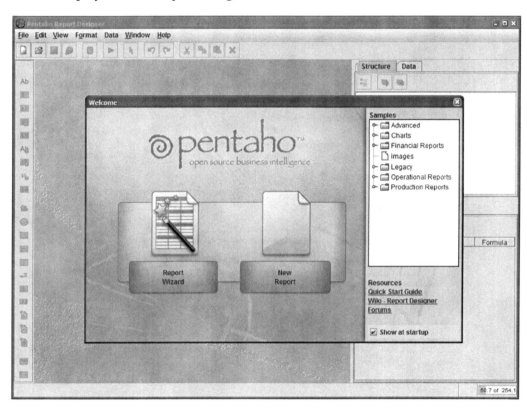

Reporting server

As a part of the Pentaho suite, reports created by Pentaho Reporting may be published, executed, and scheduled on Pentaho's Business Intelligence Server. The BI Server offers authentication and authorization, as well as a central repository, to manage your business reports. The BI Server also hosts the web-based Ad Hoc Reporting user interface for creating Pentaho Metadata-based reports. By combining the use of Pentaho Report Designer and Pentaho's BI Server, there is no need to write any code to get your business up and running with Pentaho Reporting.

Java API for building reports

Pentaho Reporting comes with a well-documented Java API for building reports from the ground up, so developers can stick with the Java programming language when customizing existing report templates or building reports from scratch. This Java API allows developers to create and modify the various sections of a report, including the various header, footer, group and detail bands, along with creating and modifying objects within each section of a report.

Extensibility

Pentaho Reporting is designed from the ground up in pure Java, exposing many interfaces for extension. From implementing basic formulas and functions that can be embedded in reports, to writing a custom data source or output format, Pentaho Reporting's source code and API interfaces are well documented and easy to work with.

A business friendly open source license

One very attractive feature of Pentaho Reporting is its license. Pentaho Reporting is available for free under the GNU Lesser General Public License. This license allows other open source and proprietary projects to embed Pentaho Reporting without fear of large license fees or viral open source limitations. As an open source project, developers also have unprecedented access to the engine and to a large group of software developers within the Pentaho Reporting community. This community includes open discussion forums, **Internet Relay Chat (IRC)** along with commercial support and licensing, if required.

Pentaho reporting roadmap

In addition to these features, Pentaho Reporting is in active development. Please visit http://reporting.pentaho.org to learn more about what additional features and functionality are being considered for development, or to access early release versions of the product.

Pentaho Reporting architecture

The Pentaho Reporting Engine is broken up into eleven main Java projects, which are then combined to author and render reports. The Pentaho Reporting Engine is backward compatible to Java 1.2.2, making certain that it stays as lightweight and as useful as possible. Most of the eleven libraries are independently useful for Java developers, outside of using them strictly for reporting purposes. The following diagram describes the various dependencies between each of the reporting projects:

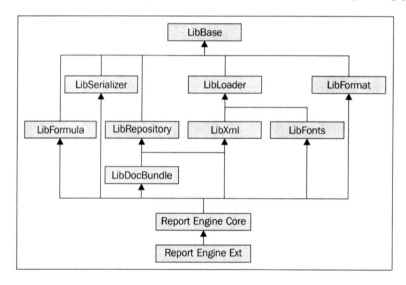

LibBase

LibBase is the root library for all other Pentaho Reporting libraries. This library contains common capabilities, such as debug and error logging utilities, library configuration, along with library initialization APIs, for consistent startup and shutdown management of the reporting engine.

LibDocBundle

LibDocBundle abstracts the management of Pentaho Reporting file bundles, which are by default stored as ZIP files, and implements the **OpenDocument format** (**ODF**). This makes it simpler for other parts of the reporting engine to work with and manipulate Pentaho Reporting's file formats.

LibFonts

LibFonts allows Pentaho Reporting to work with TrueType system fonts, extracting the necessary metadata from font types, populating an abstract interface to allow appropriate rendering in various contexts, including PDF and Excel views.

LibFormat

LibFormat is a string formatting library, which can render dates and numbers appropriately based on format strings. This library is focused on memory and CPU efficiency for high performance report rendering.

LibFormula

LibFormula is a formula parsing and execution library based on the OpenFormula standard. You can learn more about OpenFormula by visiting `http://wiki.oasis-open.org/office/About_OpenFormula`. This library is similar in function to Excel-based formula definitions. LibFormula is a very general library, and is used outside Pentaho Reporting in other projects that require OpenFormula style parsing and execution.

LibLoader

LibLoader manages the loading and caching of all necessary resources required for generating reports in a generic way, providing a simple API for other parts of the reporting engine that control static and dynamic content, including data sources and images.

LibRepository

LibRepository abstracts the input and output of hierarchical storage systems, such as file systems, that Pentaho Reporting interacts with. This makes it possible for a custom storage system such as FTP, to be implemented and to be mapped to the API, giving Pentaho Reporting access to the system.

LibSerializer

LibSerializer provides helper methods for serializing non-serializable objects. This is necessary so that the reporting engine can serialize standard Java classes that don't implement Java's Serializable interface.

LibXml

LibXml provides utility classes for SAX (Simple API for XML) parsing and XML writing, based on Java's JAXP (Java API for XML Parsing) API. This library assures the speedy loading and validation of Pentaho Reporting XML template files.

Report Engine Core

The Report Engine Core project contains the main reporting algorithm for rendering reports, along with the necessary functionality to support styling. This project also contains the algorithms for rendering specific outputs, including PDF, Excel, CSV, XML, and more. The engine relies on the already mentioned Lib libraries for managing the loading, parsing, formatting, rendering, and archiving of generated reports.

Report Engine Extensions

The Report Engine Extensions project contains third-party extensions to the reporting engine, which are very useful, but increase dependencies. Extensions in this project include JavaScript Expression support using the Rhino project, a Hibernate data source factory, Barcode support using Barbecue, Sparkline support, along with additional JDK 1.4 support for configuration and printing. Additional extension projects exist that include charting and many of the data sources discussed in this book.

When combined, these libraries form the Pentaho Reporting Engine. In addition to these libraries, there are also other related open source tools and projects in the Pentaho Reporting landscape, including the Report Engine Demo, Report Design Wizard, Report Designer, and the web-based Ad Hoc Reporting user interface.

Summary

In this chapter, we've highlighted some typical uses of Pentaho Reporting, providing you with baseline ideas for implementing your own solutions. Typical uses for embedded reporting include operational, business intelligence, financial, and production reporting.

We've covered the unique history of Pentaho Reporting, from its JFreeReport roots to its current status as Pentaho Reporting. We've learned about the individuals who have built Pentaho Reporting from a spare time open source project into an enterprise level reporting engine, competing with proprietary reporting engines.

We've also learned a great deal about the rich features of Pentaho Reporting. Core features include a wide variety of data source integration, along with PDF, HTML, and Excel rendering. On the other hand, more advanced features include sub-reports and cross tab reports. Additionally, developer-oriented features such as open Java APIs, along with the available source code and a business-friendly LGPL open source license gives Pentaho Reporting a leg up on all other Java Reporting toolkits.

The architecture of Pentaho Reporting is also covered in this chapter, providing developers with a twenty thousand foot view of where they might be able to modify or contribute to the Pentaho Reporting Engine, along with giving them the ultimate flexibility of access to source code.

You'll soon be able to apply the rich feature set of Pentaho Reporting to your use case. In the following chapters, we'll introduce you to Pentaho Reporting's easy to use Report Designer and Java API, making it fun and easy to embed reporting into your Java application.

2
Pentaho Reporting Client and Enterprise Examples

This chapter is focused on getting up and running with Pentaho Reporting. You'll begin by setting up an environment for building and embedding reports. From there, you will walk through creating a report. After creating the report, you'll walk through embedding the report into a Java Swing Client application, and finally you'll walk through embedding the same report into a Java Enterprise J2EE application. Along the way you'll receive an introduction on building a report, getting data into the report, along with generating PDF, Excel, and RTF output documents.

This chapter is written as a tutorial. The best way to learn is to follow the instructions on your PC while reading. At the end of this chapter, you'll feel comfortable with the basics of building and embedding a Pentaho Report. Later chapters will assume that your environment is configured appropriately and that you've retained the knowledge that you gained in this chapter, so pay attention!

Pentaho Reporting and example prerequisites

Pentaho Reporting and Pentaho Report Designer are written in pure Java, allowing any operating system that supports the Java Runtime Environment to run the application. This tutorial requires the use of JDK 5.0 or later. Pentaho Reporting is a cross-platform application and will run in Linux, Windows, Mac, and other Java-supported environments. The reporting engine is backward compatible to JDK 1.4, and the core engine component is backward compatible to JDK 1.2.2. The Report Designer is compatible with JDK 5.0 and above.

The only prerequisites needed before starting the examples in this chapter are Sun's Java Development Kit, Apache Ant for builds, and Apache Tomcat to host the example J2EE application.

To get started, please visit http://java.sun.com/ and download the latest patch release of the J2SE 6.0 JDK. Verify your install by running java -version on the command line.

Download the binary distribution of Apache Ant 1.7 from http://ant.apache.org. Verify that Ant 1.7 is accessible in your system path by typing ant -version on the command line.

Finally, download the binary distribution of Apache Tomcat 5.5 from http://tomcat.apache.org. To verify that you've installed Tomcat correctly, start up the server by running bin/startup.bat on command line, and verify that you can access http://localhost:8080/.

One common issue when running Apache Tomcat is a port conflict with 8080. You can adjust the default ports Tomcat uses by modifying the Connector element in conf/server.xml.

Setting up Pentaho Reporting

To install Pentaho Reporting, your first task is to download Pentaho Report Designer. Visit http://reporting.pentaho.org, and follow the link to download the Report Designer, under the **Report Creation Tools** section of the webpage. Follow the link to download the latest stable binary distribution.

When downloading Pentaho Report Designer, three packages are available. The first two packages, prd-ce-*.zip and prd-ce-*.tar.gz, contain the binary distribution archived in their preferred archive formats. The third package, prd-ce-src-*.zip, contains the entire source code of the Pentaho Report Designer. If modifications are necessary, if you would like to build the project yourself, or if you would like to take a look at the source, download the source distribution. Otherwise, stick with the binary distributions.

Once you've downloaded the binary distribution of the Report Designer, create a directory on your machine and unzip the contents of the package into that directory. Once the contents are unzipped, you will see report-designer.exe in the main directory. Double-click the executable to start Pentaho Report Designer. You should see the Report Designer welcome screen as shown next:

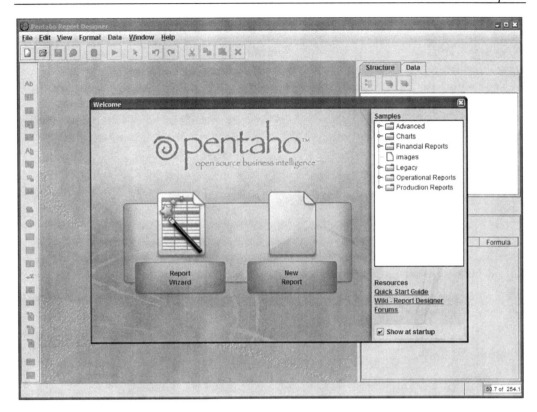

 When running Linux, start Pentaho Report Designer by running `report-designer.sh`. If you are running on a Macintosh, use `report-designer.app`.

At this point, you may want to create a shortcut to your desktop or to your start menu. Simply right-click on `report-designer.exe` and select **Create Shortcut**. Rename the shortcut to the name of your choice and then drag the shortcut to your start menu or desktop.

You've successfully installed Pentaho Report Designer! Pentaho Report Designer comes packaged with the core Pentaho Reporting Engine libraries, so you now have the necessary reporting components to complete the examples in this chapter.

If you've experienced difficulties installing Pentaho Report Designer, there are some common troubleshooting issues that you will want to verify. The most common issue is related to the Java Virtual Machine and SDK that you've installed on Windows. The `report-designer.exe` uses the first Java command found on the system path. Therefore, you will want to verify that your path is configured correctly. You can do this by executing `java -version` in a command window, in order to see which version of Java you are using.

Building your first report

Now that you've successfully installed Pentaho Report Designer, this example will walk you through building a very simple report, along with embedding it into a simple Swing application. This simple report will display the eleven Java libraries involved in Pentaho Reporting, along with the size of each library. At the bottom of the report, you'll have a summary that shows the total size of the libraries. Before you begin, create a directory called chapter2 on your machine, to manage the files you create in this chapter.

Report Designer introduction

When you first start Report Designer, you are taken to a welcome screen. From this start page, you can create a new report, or browse example reports to help you learn the various capabilities of Pentaho Reporting. Get started by clicking the **New Report** button on the welcome page.

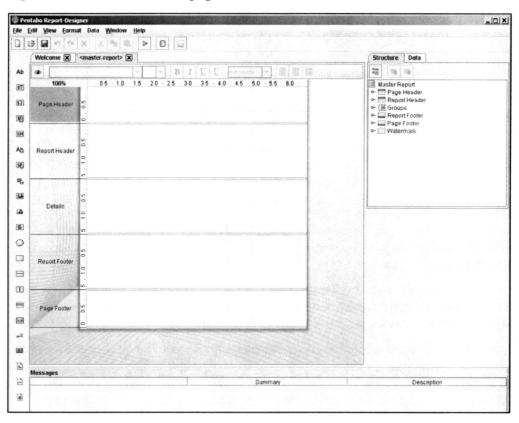

The report canvas, shown in the center of the previous screenshot, is where you define the look of your report. Note that at this point you haven't decided if the report will be rendered as PDF, RTF, or Excel. In fact, any report definition can be rendered in all of those formats. Therefore, at this point, you do not have to worry about that.

The report canvas contains a set of bands that together make up a report. Bands include the **Report Header** and **Report Footer**, individual **Group Header** and **Group Footer** bands, as well as a **Details** band that is rendered for each row of data. Reports may also contain a page header and footer.

To the left of the canvas is a palette where you can choose the various report elements you would like to include in your report, such as labels, fields, and graphics. You can drag-and-drop these report elements into the various sections of the report canvas.

To the right of the canvas is the **Structure** tab and **Data** tab. Below these tabs, the details of the currently selected structure or data item are displayed. The **Master Report** structure tree includes details about every report object displayed on the report canvas, while the report data tree includes details about the report's data source information, parameters, and functions.

Below the canvas is an optional messages panel that displays help, warning, and error messages that help you understand what might be wrong with your report. An example message might be an undefined field warning.

You can hide any of the panels around the canvas by changing their visibility within the Window menu. This can help manage your screen while designing reports.

You'll now begin to create a very basic report with the Report Designer.

Creating and configuring your first data source

First, you need to define a dataset that you want to report on. To keep things simple, this example will have you enter some example data into a table dataset. Click on the **Data** tab on the righthand side of Report Designer. Now, right-click on the **Data Sets** tree item and select **Table**. The following dialog will appear:

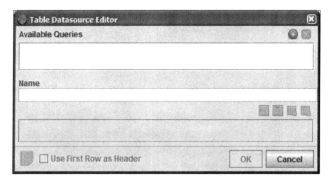

Click the add query image button, and then enter the **Name** as default for the table. This name will be referenced in your report as the main source of data. Click the add column image button to add a third column. Double-click and edit the column headers to be **Library Name**, **Library Description**, and **Library Size**. Double-click on the **Library Size** column header table cell and select java.lang.Integer as the data type for this column. Enter the following data into the table cells, clicking the add row image button to add additional rows of data. An empty report titled chapter2_tabledata.prpt is available with this book, in order to avoid the need to type this data.

Library Name	Library Description	Library Size
LibBase	Library containing common functions	121745
LibLoader	Loading and caching library	122900
LibSerializer	Java serialization utility library	25689
LibRepository	Hierarchical storage library	63655
LibXml	XML utility library	72896
LibFormula	Implementation of OpenFormula	368263
LibFonts	Font utility library	248320
LibDocBundle	ZIP bundle library	71186
LibFormat	String formatting library	69464
Report Engine Core	Base report engine	3375047
Report Engine Extensions	Group of common extensions	92335

The library sizes shown here may vary between releases of Pentaho Reporting, so they might not actually match the current size of the JAR files.

Once you've entered data in your table, the **Table Datasource Editor** dialog should look similar to this:

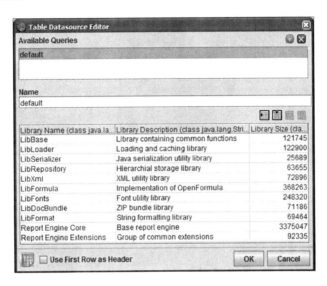

Now click the **OK** button. You should see the expanded **Data Sets** tree with the three new columns, as shown in the following screenshot:

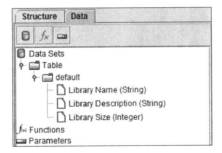

Report layout

With the dataset defined, it's now time to build a very simple report. In this report, you'll include a report title, column headings, and a details band for the reporting libraries. You will also include a summary section displaying the total number of libraries, as well as the sum of their sizes.

Creating the report title

From the palette on the left, drag a **Label** report element over to the upper left of the report's **Report Header**. Edit the label by either double-clicking directly on it, or by selecting the **value** property on the right side in the **Attributes** tab panel. Enter **Pentaho Report Engine Library Report** as the title of the report. Also, adjust the font and size of this label. Making sure you have the label selected, change the font size in the top toolbar from **10pt** to **16pt**. Also, select the bold font option. At this point, you may need to resize the label to display the entire report title. Move the mouse to the bottom right of the label and drag the label to accommodate the size of the title.

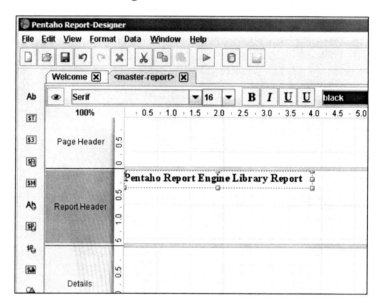

Creating column headings

Below the report title, add three more labels that will represent the column headings for the details data. The three labels should be **Library Name**, **Library Description**, and **Library Size**. You may want to enable **Snap Guides**, which renders a rectangle around the labels, making it easier to view their alignments. To do this, select the **View | Guides | Snap** option in the main menu.

Also, add a horizontal-line report element below the labels to distinguish the header row from the data. You may adjust the line width and color by editing the **stroke** and **text-color** style attributes of the line in the **Style** tab panel appearing on the right side of the window.

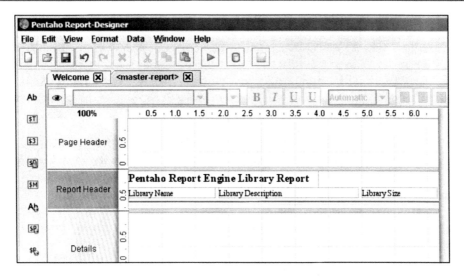

Populating the details band

The details band of the report will repeat itself for each row of data, provided by the dataset in the report. The example dataset includes eleven libraries, so there will be eleven individual rows represented by the objects placed in the details band.

To place the dataset fields in the details band, select the **Data** tab, and then drag-and-drop the **Library Name, Library Description,** and **Library Size** fields into the details band, resizing them appropriately to fit the report.

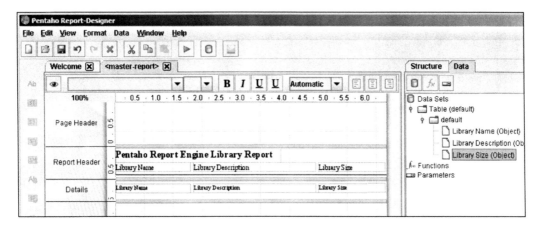

Creating a report summary

As the final step in completing the report, add a summary section that includes the total number of libraries in the report, along with a total of space needed for all the libraries. First, place a line element at the top of the **Report Footer** band. Also, place two labels—**Library Count:** and **Total Library Size:**—close to the right side of the report.

It's now time to create the functions necessary to calculate the total number of libraries and their size. Click on the **Data** tab and right-click on the **Functions** item in the tree. Click the **Add Function...** menu item. Select the **Count (Running)** function within the **Running** functions group and click **Add**. Name the function **Library Count**. Also add a **Sum (Running)** function, which is located in the **Running** functions group. Name the function **Total Library Size**. Set the **Field Name** to **Library Size**.

Finally, drag-and-drop the **Library Count** and **Total Library Size** functions into the **Report Footer** band. Feel free to adjust the style of these labels and fields.

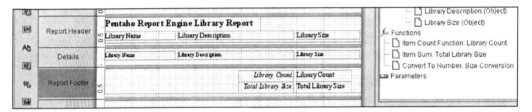

Previewing and saving your report

The Report Designer allows you to preview your report by clicking on the **Preview** icon in the toolbar above the canvas. Alternatively, you may preview the report in various output formats by clicking on the menu **File | Preview As**. Take a look at the example report to make sure all fields appear and render appropriately.

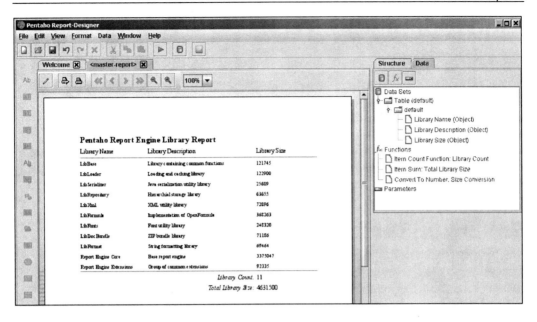

Once you are satisfied with the look of your report, save the report for later access by the Swing and J2EE examples. Go to **File | Save As**, and save this report as `chapter2/data/chapter2_report.prpt`, in order to access it later.

The `prpt` file generated by the Report Designer is similar to OpenOffice.orgs's OpenDocument format. This file is a ZIP bundle that includes a main report XML file, along with other supporting files, including any necessary images, data source information, sub-reports, and more. If you are interested in viewing the contents of the file, use your favorite unzip utility and extract the included files.

You've successfully built your first report with Pentaho Reporting! Now you'll need a place to execute your report. For non-developers, Pentaho provides an open source business intelligence reporting server, discussed in the last chapter of this book. The next two examples demonstrate embedding your report into a custom Swing and J2EE application.

Embedding your report in a Swing application

You're now going to leave the world of what-you-see-is-what-you-get report building and enter Java land. This example includes defining a simple Swing application that will include Pentaho Reporting's Swing preview dialog, affectionately named `PreviewDialog`. The example application will simply render a report. With the help of the `PreviewDialog` helper widget, you'll be able to save the report in a variety of formats, along with being able to preview and print right from the application.

Setting up the Swing example application

The first step in building the application is to define a Swing application shell. This example shell is an extremely simple Swing application that is only a few lines of Java code. You'll start adding to it once you've got the initial application defined and once it is successfully compiled. In the chapter2 directory, create two new subdirectories called `src` and `lib`. The `src` subdirectory will contain the entire example source, and the `lib` subdirectory will contain all the necessary JAR dependencies. Create the file `Chapter2SwingApp.java` in the `src` directory with the following Java code:

```java
import java.awt.*;
import java.awt.event.*;
import javax.swing.*;

public class Chapter2SwingApp extends JFrame {

    // constructor which displays the simple
    // application shell

    public Chapter2SwingApp() {
        super("Chapter 2");

        // exit the JVM when the window is closed

        this.addWindowStateListener(new WindowAdapter() {
            public void windowClosed(WindowEvent e) {
                System.exit(0);
            }
        });
        // display a preview and exit button in the
        // main window of the example application.

        add(new JLabel("Chapter 2 Swing Application"));

        JPanel buttonPanel = new JPanel();
        JButton previewButton = new JButton("Preview");
```

```
JButton exitButton = new JButton("Exit");

buttonPanel.add(previewButton);
buttonPanel.add(exitButton);

add(buttonPanel, BorderLayout.SOUTH);

previewButton.addActionListener(new ActionListener() {
        public void actionPerformed(ActionEvent e) {
                onPreview();
        }
});


exitButton.addActionListener(new ActionListener() {
        public void actionPerformed(ActionEvent e) {
                System.exit(0);
        }
});
    }

// The onPreview method is called when the preview
// button is pressed
public void onPreview() {
        // TODO: Load Report and Launch the Preview Dialog
}
// the main method is the entry point into our application
public static void main(String args[]) {
        // TODO: Initialize the Reporting Engine
        Chapter2SwingApp app = new Chapter2SwingApp();
        app.pack();
        app.setVisible(true);
    }
}
```

For now, the code contains two TODO comments where Pentaho Reporting Engine integration code will go. To compile and run this application, you'll need to define a simple Ant `build.xml` file, located in the `chapter2` folder. This file includes all the necessary targets and classpath entries for building the complete Swing application.

```
<?xml version="1.0" encoding="UTF-8"?>
<project name="Chapter 2 Examples" default="run">

    <path id="classpath">
            <fileset dir="lib">
                    <include name="*.jar" />
            </fileset>
```

```
        </path>
        <path id="runtime_classpath">
                <fileset dir="lib">
                        <include name="*.jar" />
                </fileset>
                <dirset dir="classes"/>
        </path>
        <target name="clean">
                <delete dir="classes"/>
        </target>
        <target name="compile">
                <mkdir dir="classes"/>
                <javac classpathref="classpath" destdir="classes"
                        fork="true" srcdir="src"/>
        </target>
        <target name="run" depends="compile">
                <java fork="true" classpathref="runtime_classpath"
                        classname="Chapter2SwingApp"/>
        </target>
</project>
```

The first Ant build target, clean, clears out the compiled class files from the classes directory. The second Ant build target, compile, generates the class files and places them in the classes directory. The final Ant build target, run, executes the Chapter2SwingApp Java application.

You've now set up the Java application shell and build script. Verify that you can run the Swing application by typing ant in the chapter2 project directory. You should see a window appear with a **Preview** and an **Exit** Button.

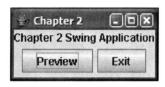

Incorporating Pentaho Reporting into the application

As the first step towards integrating Pentaho Reporting into your example application, you need to copy the necessary reporting engine JAR files. These JAR files are already a part of the Pentaho Report Designer located in the designer's `lib` directory. You simply need to copy them into the `chapter2/lib` directory. Each JAR file appears with a version number in the Report Designer. Because the version numbers may vary, they are not included in this list. Following is the list of the JAR files that you must copy into `chapter2/lib` for the examples to compile and run successfully:

- `commons-logging-api.jar`
- `itext.jar`
- `poi.jar`
- `libbase.jar`
- `libdocbundle.jar`
- `libfonts.jar`
- `libformat.jar`
- `libformula.jar`
- `libloader.jar`
- `librepository.jar`
- `libserializer.jar`
- `libxml.jar`
- `pentaho-reporting-engine-classic-core.jar`
- `pentaho-reporting-engine-classic-extensions.jar`

In addition to the eleven libraries discussed in the first chapter, you must also include three external libraries. Pentaho Reporting uses Apache Commons Logging for logging, iText for rendering PDF documents, and POI for rendering Excel documents. Additional libraries are required when working with charts and other extensions to the reporting engine.

Now that the JAR files have been copied, you can begin writing the necessary integration code, embedding Pentaho Reporting into your sample `Chapter2SwingApp.java` source file. First, start off by initializing the reporting engine within the application's main method:

```
public static void main (String args[]) {

    // TODO: Initialize the Reporting Engine

    ClassicEngineBoot.getInstance().start();

    Chapter2SwingApp app = new Chapter2SwingApp();
```

This single line of code allows the Pentaho Reporting Engine to boot up. The boot up process includes loading system fonts and initializing the engine, based on configuration properties. In this first example, you do not need to adjust any of the default initialization behavior of the engine. In future chapters, you'll explore the startup process in more detail. To compile, you must also add the following import to the beginning of the file:

```
import org.pentaho.reporting.engine.classic.core.ClassicEngineBoot;
```

You are now ready to write the code to render the report using the reporting engine's Swing `PreviewDialog` helper widget. There are two steps to this process, loading the report and launching the preview dialog. First, add the following lines to the preview button's `ActionListener.handleAction()` method to load the report definition:

```
public void handleAction() {

    // TODO: Load Report and Launch the Preview Dialog

    try {
        // load report definition
        ResourceManager manager = new ResourceManager();
        manager.registerDefaults();
        Resource res = manager.createDirectly(
            new URL("file:data/chapter2_report.prpt"),
            MasterReport.class);
        MasterReport report = (MasterReport) res.getResource();
```

To load the report, use LibLoader's `ResourceManager` to generate a `MasterReport` object. The `ResourceManager.createDirectly()` API call may throw a `ResourceException`, if the resource is not available or fails to load. In addition to this code, you must also add the following Java imports:

```
import java.net.URL;
import org.pentaho.reporting.engine.classic.core.MasterReport;
import org.pentaho.reporting.libraries.resourceloader.Resource;
import org.pentaho.reporting.libraries.resourceloader.ResourceManager;
```

Now that the report is loaded, you can launch the preview dialog:

```
// launch the preview dialog
final PreviewDialog preview = new PreviewDialog(report);
preview.addWindowListener(new WindowAdapter() {
        public void windowClosing (final WindowEvent event) {
                preview.setVisible(false);
        }
});
preview.pack();
preview.setVisible(true);
```

The only parameter provided to the preview dialog is the `MasterReport` object. The `setVisible(true)` call renders the dialog on screen.

The following import must also be added:

```
import org.pentaho.reporting.engine.classic.core.modules.gui.base.
PreviewDialog;
```

To finish the `onPreview()` method, you need to handle the exceptions thrown by the three sections you just wrote. The two types of exceptions thrown, `ResourceException`, which is thrown when loading the report, and the `IOException`, which may be thrown when parsing the URL string, both need to be caught:

```
} catch (ResourceException e) {
        e.printStackTrace();
} catch (IOException e) {
        e.printStackTrace();
}
}
```

The following two imports must be added to complete the `handleAction()` method:

```
import java.io.IOException;
import org.pentaho.reporting.libraries.resourceloader.
ResourceException;
```

In this example application, any thrown exceptions are printed to standard error. In production applications that you build, you may want to present the error in a dialog, or handle the exception differently.

With this final set of code, you've now completed the first example of embedding Pentaho Reporting into a Swing application. In just 19 lines of code and 8 imports, you've added reporting capabilities to your application! Run the ant command again and see the results:

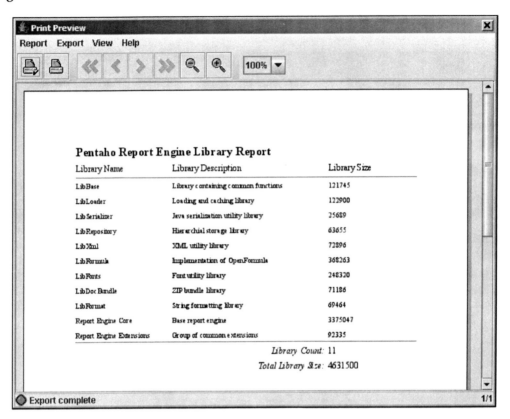

You can now see a preview of the report in your Swing application. From the preview dialog, you can export the report to the HTML, Excel, PDF, RTF, or CSV format by clicking on the **Export** menu. Or you can click the print icon to send the report directly to the printer. Here are a few example screenshots of rendered output formats:

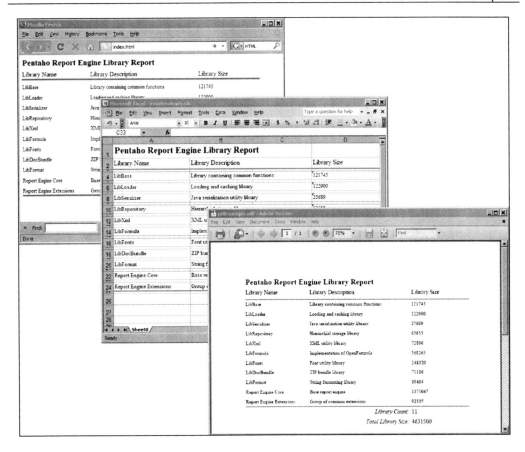

Embedding your report in an enterprise web application

To take this example one step further, the following steps demonstrate how to embed your report into a simple Tomcat J2EE application.

Setting up the example Tomcat application

To begin, you must define your Tomcat web application. This includes building a **Web Application Archive (WAR)**. The first step is to create a few directories in the existing `chapter2` example project. Create the following directories:

- `war`
- `war/WEB-INF`
- `war/WEB-INF/lib`

Once you've defined those directories, you need to define a `web.xml` file in the `war/WEB-INF` directory as follows:

```
<?xml version="1.0" encoding="UTF-8"?>
<web-app>
</web-app>
```

This file will eventually include a very basic reporting servlet.

You also need to define an `index.html` file in the `war` directory:

```
<html>
<body>
<h1>Example Application</h1>
<p>This is an example application demonstrating how to embed Pentaho
Reporting into your web application.</p>
</body>
</html>
```

Now, you need to update the project's Ant `build.xml` file with additional properties and a `war` target. First, add the following property and update the classpath reference with a pointer to the `servlet-api.jar` file, necessary for compiling the servlet class:

```
<property name="tomcat.home" value="c:/apache-tomcat-5.5.25"/>
<path id="classpath">
    <fileset dir="lib">
            <include name="*.jar" />
    </fileset>
    <fileset file="${tomcat.home}/common/lib/servlet-api.jar"/>
</path>
```

Make sure to replace the example `tomcat.home` value with the reference to your Tomcat installation location. Also, add the following `war` and `start_tomcat` targets at the end of the file:

```
<target name="war" depends="compile">
        <delete file="chapter2.war"/>
        <war basedir="war" destfile="chapter2.war" webxml="war/WEB-
                INF/web.xml">
            <classes dir="classes"/>
            <zipfileset dir="data" prefix="data"/>
            <zipfileset dir="lib" prefix="WEB-INF/lib"/>
        </war>
        <delete dir="${tomcat.home}/webapps/chapter2"/>
        <delete file="${tomcat.home}/webapps/chapter2.war"/>
        <copy file="chapter2.war" todir="${tomcat.home}/webapps"/>
```

```
        </target>

    <target name="start_tomcat" depends="war">
        <exec timeout="1000" dir="${tomcat.home}/bin"
        executable="${tomcat.home}/bin/shutdown.bat"/>
        <sleep seconds="2"/>
        <exec dir="${tomcat.home}/bin"
    executable="${tomcat.home}/bin/startup.bat"/>
    </target>
```

Now, run the `ant war` command from the command line. The `war` target clears out the existing `chapter2` web application and deploys a new project. To restart your Tomcat server, run `ant start_tomcat`. Once you've started the server, you should be able to visit `http://localhost:8080/chapter2/` and see the following screen:

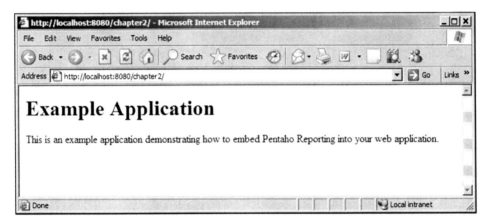

Incorporating Pentaho Reporting into the web application

Now that you have a basic web application configured, you can start writing code. Start off by writing a simple servlet that serves up reports based on user requests.

Begin with the skeleton of an `HttpServlet`. Place the following code into `Chapter2Servlet.java`, located in the project's `src` directory:

```java
import java.io.IOException;
import javax.servlet.*;
import javax.servlet.http.*;
public class Chapter2Servlet extends HttpServlet {

    // servlet initialization method
    public void init(ServletConfig config) throws
```

```
                    ServletException {
        super.init(config);
        // TODO: Initialize the Reporting Engine
    }
    // the doGet method handles all the requests
    // received by this servlet
    public void doGet(HttpServletRequest request, HttpServletResponse
                    response)
            throws ServletException, IOException {
        // TODO: Handle Pentaho Report Request

    }
    // the doPost method simply calls the doGet method
    public void doPost(HttpServletRequest request, HttpServletResponse
                    response)
            throws ServletException, IOException {
        doGet(request, response);
    }
}
```

Now that you have a baseline `HttpServlet` to work with, you can start to add the
necessary initialization and service code to generate a report. Add the following code
to the `init()` method of the `Chapter2Servlet` class. Notice that this is identical to
the initialization code seen earlier in the Swing example application.

```
public void init(ServletConfig config) throws ServletException {
    super.init(config);
    // TODO: Initialize the Reporting Engine
    ClassicEngineBoot.getInstance().start();
}
```

Now, you'll add the necessary code to the `doGet()` method for serving up PDF files.
The following two steps are similar to the two steps in the Swing client example
code. First, load the report definition from disk:

```
// TODO: Handle Pentaho Report Request
try {
    // load report definition
    ResourceManager manager = new ResourceManager();
    manager.registerDefaults();
    String reportPath = "file:" +
    this.getServletContext().getRealPath("data/chapter2_report.prpt");
    Resource res = manager.createDirectly(new URL(reportPath),
                MasterReport.class);
    MasterReport report = (MasterReport) res.getResource();
```

Notice that the only difference between the Swing example code and the servlet code is the use of a `ServletContext` object to locate the report definition. Now that you've loaded the report, you need to generate and return the PDF to the requesting client:

```
// render the pdf
response.setContentType("application/pdf");
PdfReportUtil.createPDF(report, response.getOutputStream());
```

This step is the significant difference between the Swing and the servlet example. In the Swing example, a print preview dialog is rendered. On the other hand, in the servlet example, a direct call is made into the `PdfReportUtil` to write the PDF to the `HttpServletResponse` object's `OutputStream`. Notice that before writing the binary data, the response's content type is set to `application/pdf`. This notifies the browser that the server is transferring a PDF file to the client.

The final change to the `doGet()` method is catching any potential exceptions being thrown:

```
} catch (ResourceException e) {
    e.printStackTrace();
}
```

In writing your enterprise applications, you should handle the exceptions appropriately. Now that you've completed the `doGet()` method, you need to make sure and include the necessary Java imports:

```
import java.net.URL;
import org.pentaho.reporting.engine.classic.core.MasterReport;
import org.pentaho.reporting.engine.classic.core.ClassicEngineBoot;
import org.pentaho.reporting.engine.classic.core.modules.output.
pageable.pdf.PdfReportUtil;
import org.pentaho.reporting.libraries.resourceloader.Resource;
import org.pentaho.reporting.libraries.resourceloader.
ResourceException;
import org.pentaho.reporting.libraries.resourceloader.ResourceManager;
```

Most of these imports were included in the Swing client example. You've now successfully built a complete servlet that generates a Pentaho Report in PDF format. In just a few short lines of code, you can generate a report!

Once you've completed updating the servlet code, you need to update the `web.xml` and `index.html` to serve the report. Add the following XML to the `web-app` parent element in the `web.xml` file. This makes sure that the servlet gets initialized and mapped to the correct URL.

```
<servlet>
    <servlet-name>Chapter2Servlet</servlet-name>
    <servlet-class>Chapter2Servlet</servlet-class>
</servlet>
<servlet-mapping>
    <servlet-name>Chapter2Servlet</servlet-name>
    <url-pattern>/report</url-pattern>
</servlet-mapping>
```

The final update involves providing a link to the report from the `index.html` file. Right below the `</p>` tag, add the following HTML:

```
<a href="report">Generate PDF Report</a>
```

You are now ready to deploy the fully functional example `chapter2` web application. Run the `ant start_tomcat` target command, which stops Tomcat, builds a new WAR, and then restarts Tomcat. You should now be able to visit `http://localhost:8080/chapter2/` and view the example PDF!

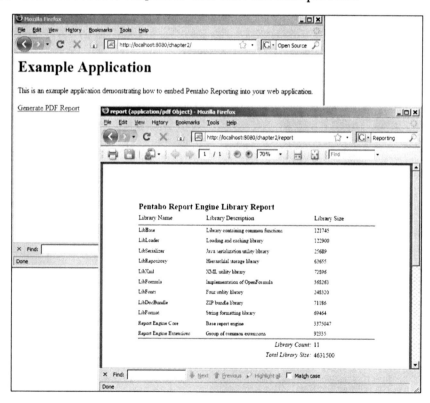

Adding additional output formats

In the initial implementation of the reporting servlet, a PDF file was generated by default. Adding output support for other formats is just as easy. Continue the example by updating the servlet with Excel and RTF output format options. The first step will be to detect the requested output format type. Once the report is loaded, the following code should be placed within the `Chapter2Servlet` class, replacing the existing PDF rendering code:

```
// determine the output format and render accordingly
String outputFormat = request.getParameter("outputFormat");
```

Based on the request, the servlet will check the parameter and generate output. First, it will check to see if it should render PDF output from earlier:

```
if ("pdf".equals(outputFormat)) {
    // render in pdf
    response.setContentType("application/pdf");
    PdfReportUtil.createPDF(report, response.getOutputStream());
```

Next, it will check to see if it should render Excel output:

```
} else if ("xls".equals(outputFormat)) {
    // render in excel
    response.setContentType("application/vnd.ms-excel");
    ExcelReportUtil.createXLS(report, response.getOutputStream());
```

And for any other `outputFormat` request, the servlet will render the report in the RTF format:

```
} else {
    // render in rtf
    response.setContentType("application/rtf");
    RTFReportUtil.createRTF(report, response.getOutputStream());
}
```

> While you might think that a report rendered as HTML would be less complicated than PDF or Excel, in fact, it is more complicated from a Reporting API perspective. These initial examples do not include HTML rendering because HTML requires multiple files to render, such as images and CSS. You'll see an example in the interactive reporting chapter that demonstrates rendering an HTML formatted report.

One last modification necessary to the `doGet()` method is to catch the `ReportProcessingException` exception that `RTFReportUtil` and `ExcelReportUtil` throw:

```
    } catch (ResourceException e) {
        e.printStackTrace();
    } catch (ReportProcessingException e) {
        e.printStackTrace();
    }
```

The final code change to the servlet is to make sure that you import the necessary Java classes related to the additional output formats:

```
    import org.pentaho.reporting.engine.classic.core.
    ReportProcessingException;
    import org.pentaho.reporting.engine.classic.core.modules.output.table.
    rtf.RTFReportUtil;
    import org.pentaho.reporting.engine.classic.core.modules.output.table.
    xls.ExcelReportUtil;
```

Update the `index.html` file to include links to the new formats. Replace the anchor tag added earlier with the following HTML:

```
    <a href="report?outputFormat=pdf">Generate PDF Report</a>
    <a href="report?outputFormat=xls">Generate Excel Report</a>
    <a href="report?outputFormat=rtf">Generate RTF Report</a>
```

After making the necessary modifications, run the Ant `start_tomcat` target again. Reload `http://localhost:8080/chapter2`. You should see three new links. Verify that all three formats are rendering as expected. Congratulations! You've built your first enterprise application that embeds Pentaho Reporting!

Summary

In this chapter, you've walked all the way through a complete reporting example, with step-by-step instructions on how to embed Pentaho Reporting into both Java Swing and J2EE Applications. You started off learning the basics of Pentaho Report Designer, including building a simple report that displayed details regarding Pentaho Reporting's libraries. You then learned the basics of how to include aggregate report values, such as counts and sums, within the report footer.

After completing the report in Report Designer, you started a new example Java Swing project from scratch, including the source code and build file.

Finally, you completed the chapter working with Tomcat. You learned how to deploy a simple, but powerful web application that can serve your Pentaho Reports not only as a PDF, but also as Excel and RTF documents.

3
Pentaho Reporting Examples in the Real World

In the previous chapter, you learned from scratch about how to get reports to render in both client and enterprise environments. In this chapter, you'll go one step further and learn the most commonly used features of Pentaho Reporting through real world examples.

To get started, you'll first set up a SQL data source that will provide all the data for the examples. From there, you'll create an "Inventory" report, where you will use additional functions and embed charts in your report. You'll then create an "End of the Day Cashier Balance" report, defining report parameters, conditional reporting, and traffic lighting. Finally, you'll learn how to create an "Invoice" report, creating an inline sub-report, along with building report bursting capabilities.

When you've completed this chapter, you will have seen a breadth of features that Pentaho Reporting has to offer, and how they aid report developers in creating highly useful and attractive looking reports.

Setting up the example data source

In most cases, you'll be using Pentaho Reporting with an already existing dataset—be it CSV, a relational database, or another form of data. To demonstrate the capabilities of Pentaho Reporting, a reasonably believable data source is included with this book, which will allow you to learn Pentaho Reporting's capabilities.

Included is a dataset for a fictional retail company called ElectroBarn that sells computer and electronics supplies. This dataset includes inventory, purchases, invoices, and customer relational tables, which are used for the three reporting examples in this chapter.

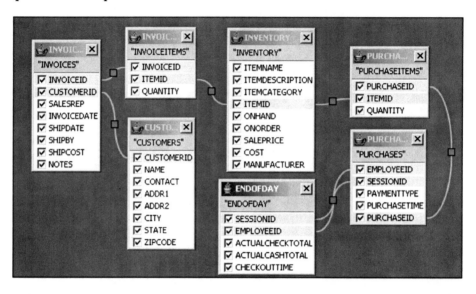

The examples that will follow use HSQLDB's file-based embedded database option to access the JDBC database without the need to start a separate server. HSQLDB is a lightweight Java database. To learn more about HSQLDB, visit `http://www.hsqldb.org`. As long as the `hsqldb.jar` library is included in your classpath, you will be able to execute SQL queries. In the examples that will follow, you'll use the HSQLDB JAR file distributed with Report Designer.

To configure HSQLDB with the ElectroBarn Schema, you need a script that defines the database tables. The script defines the tables and associates each table with a CSV file. Create a new directory called `chapter3`, along with a sub-directory called `data`. Within the `data` directory, create a new text file `electrobarn.script` with the following script:

```
// electrobarn.script

CREATE SCHEMA PUBLIC AUTHORIZATION DBA

// INVENTORY Table Definition

CREATE TEXT TABLE INVENTORY(ITEMNAME VARCHAR,ITEMDESCRIPTION
VARCHAR,ITEMCATEGORY VARCHAR,ITEMID INTEGER,ONHAND INTEGER,ONORDER
INTEGER,SALEPRICE DOUBLE,COST DOUBLE,MANUFACTURER VARCHAR)

SET TABLE INVENTORY SOURCE "inventory.csv;ignore_first=true"

// PURCHASE Table Definition
```

```
CREATE TEXT TABLE PURCHASES(EMPLOYEEID INTEGER,SESSIONID
INTEGER,PAYMENTTYPE VARCHAR,PURCHASETIME TIMESTAMP,PURCHASEID INTEGER)
SET TABLE PURCHASES SOURCE "purchases.csv;ignore_first=true"

// PURCHASEITEMS Table Definition

CREATE TEXT TABLE PURCHASEITEMS(PURCHASEID INTEGER,ITEMID
INTEGER,QUANTITY INTEGER)
SET TABLE PURCHASEITEMS SOURCE "purchaseitems.csv;ignore_first=true"

// ENDOFDAY Table Definition

CREATE TEXT TABLE ENDOFDAY(SESSIONID INTEGER,EMPLOYEEID
INTEGER,ACTUALCHECKTOTAL DOUBLE,ACTUALCASHTOTAL DOUBLE,CHECKOUTTIME
TIMESTAMP)
SET TABLE ENDOFDAY SOURCE "endofday.csv;ignore_first=true"

// INVOICES Table Definition

CREATE TEXT TABLE INVOICES(INVOICEID INTEGER,CUSTOMERID
INTEGER,SALESREP VARCHAR,INVOICEDATE DATE,SHIPDATE DATE,SHIPBY
VARCHAR,SHIPCOST DOUBLE,NOTES VARCHAR)
SET TABLE INVOICES SOURCE "invoices.csv;ignore_first=true"

// INVOICEITEMS Table Definition

CREATE TEXT TABLE INVOICEITEMS(INVOICEID INTEGER,ITEMID
INTEGER,QUANTITY INTEGER)
SET TABLE INVOICEITEMS SOURCE "invoiceitems.csv;ignore_first=true"

// CUSTOMERS Table Definition

CREATE TEXT TABLE CUSTOMERS(CUSTOMERID INTEGER,NAME VARCHAR,CONTACT
VARCHAR,ADDR1 VARCHAR,ADDR2 VARCHAR,CITY VARCHAR,STATE VARCHAR,ZIPCODE
VARCHAR)
SET TABLE CUSTOMERS SOURCE "customers.csv;ignore_first=true"

CREATE USER SA PASSWORD ""
GRANT DBA TO SA
SET WRITE_DELAY 10
```

Note that each table definition must be defined on a single line. This example uses
HSQLDB's **TEXT TABLE** to allow the CSV files to act as SQL tables. Each CSV
file contains a row heading, hence the `ignore_first=true` configuration in
setting the table sources. The CSV files must be in the same directory as the
`electrobarn.script` file. The seven CSV files, along with the `electrobarn.script`
file, are provided as a part of this book. You can also download them at
`http://www.packtpub.com/files/code/3193_Code.zip`.

ElectroBarn inventory report

The first example that you'll work with is of a standard inventory report. The report will include information about which products are on hand and on order, along with a summary pie chart to give an idea of which categories are mostly filling the inventory. This example will also include a static image in the report header, along with a page count to round up the report.

Configuring the data source

As with the report definition in the previous chapter, you'll start off using the Pentaho Report Designer and will define your report. Create a new report and start off by configuring a data source. Click on the **Data** tab, and right-click the **Data Sets** tree item, selecting JDBC as the data source.

Within the **JDBC Data Source** dialog, click the **Add Connection** button. You'll see a dialog for entering JDBC information. Set the **Connection Name** property to **ElectroBarn**, and select **Hypersonic** as the **Connection Type**. Now, set the **Host Name** to **file:** and the **Database Name** to the full path to your **chapter3\data\ electrobarn.script** file, minus the `.script` file extension. Set the **Port Number** to blank. Finally, set the **User Name** to **sa** and **Password** to blank. Click on the **Test** button to verify that you can connect to the database. Now click **OK** to save the connection information.

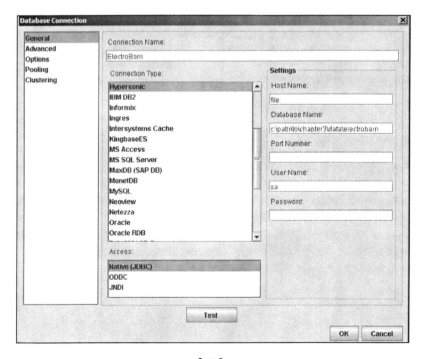

When configuring your **Database Connection** using the file-based **Hypersonic** database, a few common mistakes may occur. These include forgetting to remove the port number, typing an invalid path, or selecting the wrong **Connection Type**. If you are having problems, make sure your screen is as close to the screenshot previous as possible.

Creating a query

Once connected to the ElectroBarn JDBC SQL Database, you need to define a SQL query to populate the dataset, which the report will display. This example keeps it simple by selecting the entire contents of the **INVENTORY** table. First, click the add image button next to the **Available Queries**. This adds a new SQL query named **Query 1**, which will be referenced by your report. A report may contain multiple data sources, and each data source may define multiple queries. Click the edit image button at the top right of the **Query** text area, which launches a SQL Editor. You will first be prompted to select a database schema, from where you will derive your query. Select the **Public** option from the drop-down menu and click **OK**. This will bring up the SQLeonardo Query Builder.

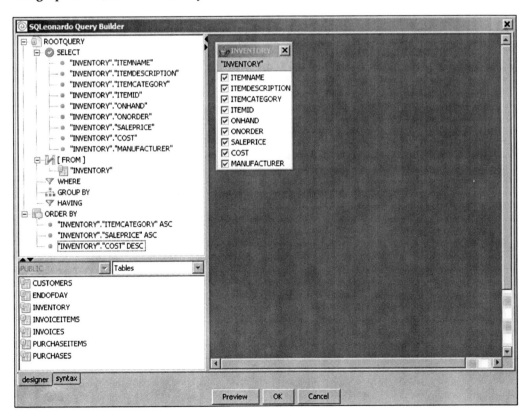

Simply double-click on the **INVENTORY** table in the bottom left panel. The **INVENTORY** database table will appear in the right window, with all columns of the table selected, and you will see a query tree in the top left panel. Now, in the SQL tree view on the left, drag the **ITEMCATEGORY** down to the **ORDER BY** section of the query. This sorts the items by category in the result set, which will allow for grouping inventory by categories within the report. At this time, you may click the **Preview** button to view the data in this table. Finally, click **OK**. You will see the following SQL query appear in the **Query** details section of the **JDBC Data Source** dialog:

```
SELECT
      "INVENTORY"."ITEMNAME",
      "INVENTORY"."ITEMDESCRIPTION",
      "INVENTORY"."ITEMCATEGORY",
      "INVENTORY"."ITEMID",
      "INVENTORY"."ONHAND",
      "INVENTORY"."ONORDER",
      "INVENTORY"."SALEPRICE",
      "INVENTORY"."COST",
      "INVENTORY"."MANUFACTURER"
FROM
      "INVENTORY"
ORDER BY
      "INVENTORY"."ITEMCATEGORY" ASC
```

You've now completed configuring your data source and query. Click **OK** to return to the main report editor view.

Creating the Report Header and Page Footer

Now that you have a defined dataset, it's time to start creating the inventory report. First add a report title, along with ElectroBarn's logo in the **Report Header**. Also, leave room for a pie chart in the report header.

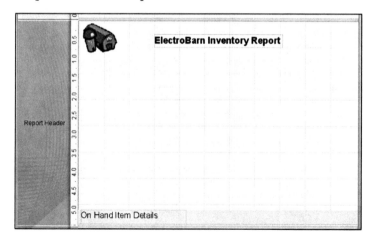

In addition to adding the labels and the background rectangle, drag-and-drop an image report element 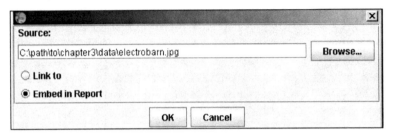 into the Report Header. This allows you to include an image in the report. Edit the **value** attribute of the content element by clicking the **...** button within the **Value** column. This will bring up a dialog where you can select the image.

The dialog allows you to embed the image in the report's prpt file or reference it externally. Leave the **Embed in Report** option checked. This way, if you move the report file in the future, the image will go along with it. Once you've selected the image, you may adjust its size. First, set the **scale** style attribute to true, and then drag the bottom right corner of the image for resizing. You may also want to set the **aspect-ratio** style attribute to true.

Now that you've configured the **Report Header**, add a page count to the **Page Footer**. This is a two step process. First, you must define a **Page Of Pages** report function. You may do this by right-clicking on the **Functions** tree item within the **Data** tab and selecting the **Add Function...** menu option. From there, select the **Page of Pages** function from within the **Common** category

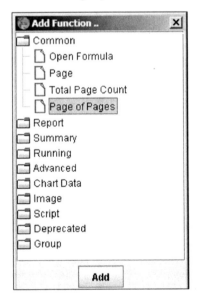

To display the **Page of Pages** function in your report, drag the function from the **Data** tab into the **Page Footer**.

Defining the Group Header

Now that you've defined the report header and page footer, it's time to start adding report content. First, configure a group with a visible header and footer. This group will organize the dataset into individual item categories. Right-click on the **Groups** tree item in the report **Structure** tab, and select **Edit Group....** Groups in a report are nested. There is only a single root group in a report. From the group fields dialog, add **ITEMCATEGORY** as your grouping field. This informs the report to group all the inventory items by category.

 The SQL result set and defined report groups must match each other in the ordering of their results, or groups rendered in the report may repeat themselves and return unexpected summary results.

Beneath the **Groups** tree item, you will see two child nodes—**Group Header** and **Group Footer**. Select each node and uncheck the **hide-on-canvas** attribute. This will render the group bands in the canvas, allowing you to add report elements to the bands as required.

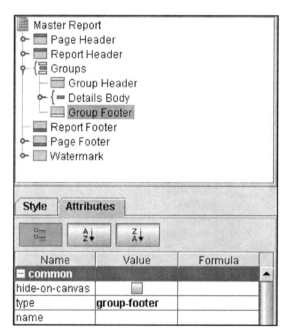

Now that the **Group Header** and **Group Footer** bands are visible, start adding some content to the report. First, drag-and-drop a `Category:` label into the **Group Header**, along with dragging the `ITEMCATEGORY` field into the header. Behind the text, place a shaded rectangle to highlight the category header. You can control the Z ordering or Layering of items in the canvas. After selecting the item to adjust, click **Alt-Up** or **Alt-Down**, in order to move the item either forward or backward, or in or out of the view.

Now, add column headings for all the items you'd like to display in the **Details** band, which appears right below the **Group Header**. Add the following labels: **ID, Name, Cost, On Hand, Total Cost,** and **On Order**.

> To help align the column headings vertically and horizontally, you can add line guides to the report. In the ruler area of the report, click your mouse and a blue line guide will appear. Labels, text fields, and other report elements dropped into the report will snap to these line guides, making it easier to get the report to look just right.

Finally, add a line that horizontally crosses the entire report to add a visual separation between the group's column headings and the data that follows after it.

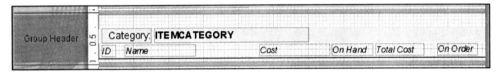

Defining the Details band

Now, place the necessary text and number fields in the **Details** band, in order to display the details of the report. Drag-and-drop all the corresponding fields below their headers in the Details band.

Cost, On Hand, and **On Order** are all directly available from the SQL query dataset. **Total Cost** is a derived value. Therefore, you will need to define a reporting function to represent this value in the report. Create a new function of type **Common | Open Formula**. Click within the value cell of the **Formula** property, and then click on the … within the cell. This will bring the formula editor. Enter the following formula in order to represent **Total Cost**:

```
= [COST] * [ONHAND]
```

Name the function `costonhand`. Drag-and-drop it into position within the **Details** band.

Finally, you may adjust the number formatting of the various fields as necessary. For financial fields, you can specify `$#,##0.00` to render the dollar amount in a standard form, and for integer-based numbers such as **On Hand**, you can specify `#,##0` without the decimal places. These format strings use Java's DecimalFormat patterns, discussed in more depth later in the book. You've now configured the **Details** band of your report.

Defining the Group Footer and the Report Footer band

To provide summaries of the inventory data, add some roll ups of your detailed information in the report. Start off by adding **On Hand** and **Total Cost** group totals. First, you need to define two functions of type **Running | Sum (Running)**, for both the **ONHAND** field and the previously defined **Open Formula** function `costonhand`. Once you've added these functions, you then need to drag-and-drop them into the **Group Footer** band of the report, formatting the fields accordingly.

Now that the **Group Footer** is complete, add two report summary values — the entire summation of all items in the inventory and the total cost of inventory. Use the **Running | Sum (Running)** function to represent these values. The first function should use the SQL query value **ONHAND** to populate the function, and the second function should use the already defined function **costonhand** as its input.

Place labels along with each of these functions within the **Report Footer**. The following is a screenshot of the progress so far in the report, including the **Group Header**, **Details**, **Group Footer**, and **Report Footer** bands:

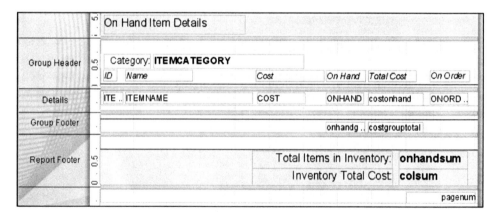

Adding a pie chart

To complete the inventory report, fill the blank space created in the report header with a pie chart that gives a visual idea of how each item category compares to the others in regards to overall inventory cost. First, drag-and-drop a chart report element 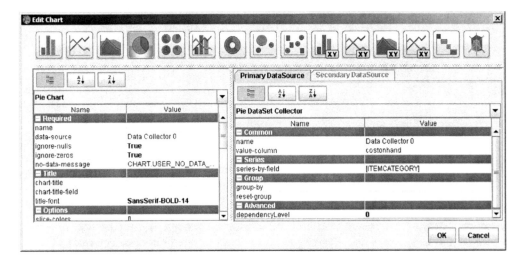 into the **Report Header**. Adjust the size of the chart to fill the area provided. Now, select the chart and right-click. Select the **Chart...** menu item. This brings up the **Edit Chart** dialog, which has many options for configuring your chart.

Select the **Pie** toggle button in the dialog. The only parameters that need to be modified in a pie chart are the **value-column** and **value-by-series**, which appear in the **Primary DataSource** list of parameters. For the **value-column**, select the previously defined **costonhand** function. For the **value-by-series** property, select the **ITEMCATEGORY** field.

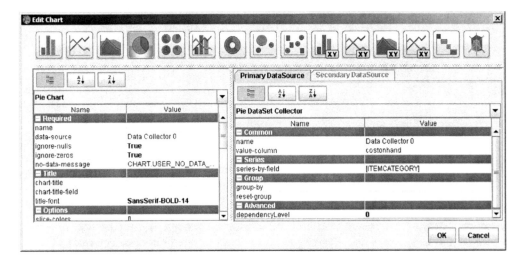

Click **OK** to save your changes. Congratulations! You've now completed building the report, and can save it for display in your J2EE environment. Select **File | Save** and save the report to chapter3\data\inventory.prpt.

Incorporating the inventory report into your J2EE environment

You'll now incorporate this report into your J2EE environment. Starting off with the servlet implementation from Chapter 2, you'll make the necessary changes to render this report, along with some other reports which you will build in this chapter. Copy the servlet file `chapter2\src\Chapter2Servlet.java` to `chapter3\src\Chapter3Servlet.java`, and rename the class to `Chapter3Servlet`.

Adding report selection as an input to the servlet

The first change necessary to the earlier Chapter 2 example is to add an HTTP request parameter `reportName`, which allows you to specify the report to be rendered. At the beginning of the `doGet` method, add the following lines of code:

```
String reportName = request.getParameter("reportName");
if (reportName == null) {
    response.getWriter().println("No report parameter specified");
    return;
}
```

Map the `reportName` parameter to the filename of the report, by modifying the `reportPath` variable declaration to the following:

```
String reportPath = "file:" + this.getServletContext().
getRealPath("data\" + reportName + ".prpt");
```

Now, you'll need to modify the Chapter 3 home page in order to link to your new report. Copy the contents of the `war` directory of Chapter 2 into the `chapter3\war` directory. Modify the `war/index.html` file report link to include the report parameter:

```
<a href="report?outputFormat=pdf&reportName=inventory">Generate
Inventory PDF Report</a>
```

Compiling and deploying the report servlet

You've now completed the changes necessary to display the inventory report in your J2EE environment. It's now time to compile, deploy, and test your new servlet. Start off by copying the JAR files, located in the `lib` directory of Chapter 2, into the `chapter3\lib` directory. Finally, copy the `build.xml` file, located in the `chapter2` directory, into the `chapter3` directory.

You'll need to make a few minor changes to the build environment to complete the job. First, you'll need to rename your servlet reference in your `web.xml` to `Chapter3Servlet`. Second, you'll need to place the `hsqldb.jar` file, included in the `lib\jdbc` directory of Pentaho Report Designer, in your `chapter3\lib` directory. Finally, you'll need to add the following charting JARs to your `lib` directory as well, all of which are located in Pentaho Report Designer's `lib` directory:

- `jfreechart.jar`
- `jcommon.jar`
- `pentaho-reporting-engine-legacy-charts.jar`

The `jfreechart` and `jcommon` JAR files are needed for basic JFreeChart capabilities, and the `pentaho-reporting-engine-legacy-charts` JAR contains the necessary Pentaho Reporting API code that allows rendering of JFreeChart within a report.

Finally, you'll need to update the Ant `build.xml` file's `war` target to deploy a `chapter3.war` file instead of the `chapter2.war` file. Once those changes have been made, execute `ant start_tomcat`, which will compile and deploy the new `chapter3.war` file to your tomcat server, along with restarting the server. Visit `http://localhost:8080/chapter3/`. After clicking on the **Inventory Report** link, you should see a PDF similar to the following:

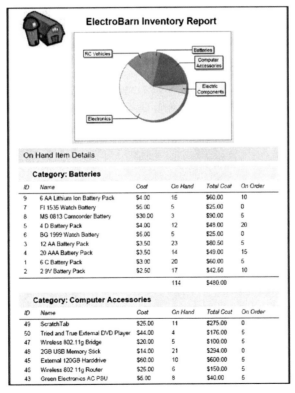

The ElectroBarn Inventory example highlights a lot of the basic functionality available to report builders, including simple formulas and functions, as well as static images and charts based on report data. This report also demonstrates connecting to a JDBC data source. In future chapters, you'll learn about the APIs necessary to manage JDBC connections within the servlet environment. In this example, the reporting engine managed the creation and closing of the HSQLDB file-based connection.

 There is a common issue associated when using HSQLDB file-based connections. It occurs when multiple processes attempt to connect to the file. If your report fails to render in your J2EE environment, make sure no other process is actively accessing the HSQLDB data source.

End of the day cashier balances

To continue with the ElectroBarn example, you'll now create an "End of the Day Cashier Balance" report. This report highlights additional functionality of the Pentaho Reporting Engine, including report parameters, commonly used functions, traffic lighting, sub-groups, as well as more advanced formula usage.

This report will display a brief summary of the day's activities for a cashier, along with a detailed list of all the cashier's sales on a given day. A cash register variance will be calculated. If it is less than a certain minimum amount, it will change color to alert managers that there may be an issue.

As in previous examples, you'll first build the report using Report Designer, and then update the `Chapter3Servlet` class with the necessary changes to render your report in your J2EE environment. Begin by creating a new report in the Pentaho Report Designer.

Configuring an input parameter

For this example, you'll define a Session ID input parameter, which will limit the results of the report to a specific end of day session. To start off the example, create a new report and right-click on the **Parameters** tree item in the **Data** tab, selecting the **Add Parameter...** menu option. This brings up the **Add Parameter** dialog. Click the add image button next to **DataSources** and select **JDBC**. This brings up the **JDBC Data Source** dialog demonstrated earlier. Select the already defined **ElectroBarn** connection and define a SQL query named **Sessions** that selects distinct **SESSIONID** column results from the ENDOFDAY table.

```
SELECT DISTINCT
      "ENDOFDAY"."SESSIONID"
FROM
      "ENDOFDAY"
ORDER BY
      "ENDOFDAY"."SESSIONID" ASC
```

This query will be used to populate a parameter drop down when rendering the report. Once you've defined the query, set the parameter **Name** to **SessionInput**, the **Label** to **Select Session:**, and the **Type** to **Drop Down**. Also, set the **Value Type** to `java.lang.Integer`. The dialog should look something like the following screenshot:

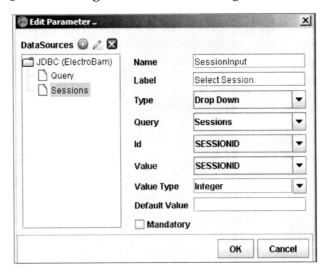

Now, click the preview button of the empty report. You'll see a parameter section appear above the rendered report, with a drop down to select the current session:

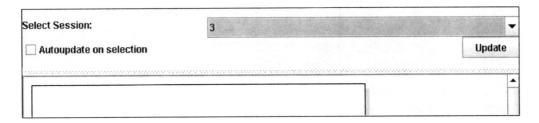

Selecting a session and clicking **Update** will refresh the report with the parameter value. The **Autoupdate on selection** checkbox may be selected to force an update every time you change the parameter value.

Configuring the data source query

Now that you've defined an input parameter, it is time to define the SQL query that populates the report. Launch the **JDBC Data Source** dialog from the **Data** tab. You've already configured the ElectroBarn JDBC connection, so simply select that option in the **Connections** list. Add a query and launch the query designer, making sure to select the **Public** schema.

The SQL query that will drive the balance report will involve multiple tables. First, double-click on the ENDOFDAY table, in order to add it to your SQL Query. The ENDOFDAY table contains summary information such as Actual Cash and Actual Check Total. Next, double-click on the PURCHASES and PURCHASEITEMS tables. These tables together define individual purchases made throughout the day, and will be used to calculate total sales, along with displaying the individual sales. Finally, double-click on the INVENTORY table, which contains details about an item, including its name and price.

Now that you've added all the necessary tables, you'll need to reduce the number of selections because you won't be using all of the columns in all of the selected tables in the report. For instance, you need only the ITEMNAME and SALEPRICE columns in your INVENTORY table.

You also need to define the relationships between these tables. Within the visual table views, drag-and-drop the ENDOFDAY.EMPLOYEEID column over to the PURCHASES.EMPLOYEEID column, along with the ENDOFDAY.SESSIONID column over to the PURCHASES.SESSIONID column. This sets up an inner join one-to-many relationship between the ENDOFDAY and PURCHASES tables. Now, drag-and-drop the PURCHASES.PURCHASEID column over to the PURCHASEITEMS.PURCHASEID column. This sets up a one-to-many relationship between a purchase and its items. Again, drag-and-drop the PURCHASEITEMS.ITEMID column over to the INVENTORY.ITEMID column. You've now set up the relationships between these tables.

As the next step, right-click on the WHERE clause and click **add condition....** Enter "ENDOFDAY"."SESSIONID" in the first text area, and ${SessionInput} in the second text area, leaving the = operator selected. This embeds the SessionInput parameter, which was defined earlier, into the SQL query.

Finally, you need to specify the correct ORDER BY columns, so the report groups correctly. First, right-click on the ENDOFDAY.SESSIONID column in the tree view and add it to the ORDER BY clause. Now, right-click on the PURCHASEID and add it also to the ORDER BY clause.

You should now have the following query defined for the report:

```
SELECT
     "PURCHASES"."SESSIONID",
     "PURCHASES"."PAYMENTTYPE",
     "PURCHASES"."PURCHASEID",
     "PURCHASEITEMS"."QUANTITY",
     "ENDOFDAY"."EMPLOYEEID",
     "ENDOFDAY"."ACTUALCHECKTOTAL",
     "ENDOFDAY"."ACTUALCASHTOTAL",
     "ENDOFDAY"."CHECKOUTTIME",
     "INVENTORY"."SALEPRICE",
     "PURCHASEITEMS"."ITEMID",
     "INVENTORY"."ITEMNAME",
     "PURCHASES"."PURCHASETIME"
FROM
     "PURCHASES" INNER JOIN "ENDOFDAY" ON "PURCHASES"."EMPLOYEEID" =
                                       "ENDOFDAY"."EMPLOYEEID"
     AND "ENDOFDAY"."SESSIONID" = "PURCHASES"."SESSIONID"
     INNER JOIN "PURCHASEITEMS" ON "PURCHASES"."PURCHASEID" =
                                       "PURCHASEITEMS"."PURCHASEID"
     INNER JOIN "INVENTORY" ON "PURCHASEITEMS"."ITEMID" =
                                       "INVENTORY"."ITEMID"
WHERE
     "ENDOFDAY"."SESSIONID" = ${SessionInput}
ORDER BY
     "PURCHASES"."SESSIONID" ASC,
     "PURCHASES"."PURCHASEID" ASC
```

Due to the `SessionInput` parameter, you will not be able to preview the data within the Data Source or Query Builder dialog.

Creating the Report Header and Page Footer

In this example, you'll create a very simple report header and page footer, with the same **Page of Pages** function that was used in the Inventory example. Include a title and the ElectroBarn's logo for good measure.

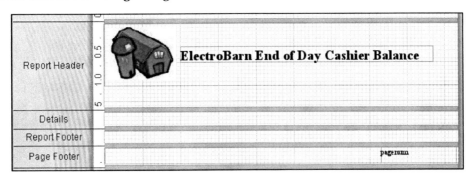

Defining the Details band

The **Details** band in this report will include the Item Purchase details, including Sales Price, Quantity, and Total. You'll start by defining an Open Formula function titled `TotalItemPrice`. First, right-click on the **Functions** tree item within the **Data** tab and select the **Add Function...** menu option. Select **Common | Open Formula** and click the **Add** button. In the formula editor, enter the following formula:

```
=[QUANTITY] * [SALEPRICE]
```

Now drag-and-drop the **ITEMNAME, QUANTITY, SALEPRICE,** and **TotalItemPrice** into the **Details** band as pictured below:

For the **SALEPRICE** and **TotalItemPrice** fields, select the menu item **Format | Morph | number-field**, and adjust their format attributes to match `$#,##0.00`.

Defining the Group bands

In this example, there are two levels of groupings. The top level group should use **SESSIONID** as its only group field. Right-click on the **Groups** tree item, click **Edit...**, and add **SESSIONID** to the selected items list. Give the name `sessionid` to the first group. To add the second level sub-group, right-click on the first group and click the **Add Group** menu option. This second group should use **PURCHASEID** as its only group field. You'll be placing group detail in both group headers and the sub-group footer. Therefore, enable visibility for those three tree items by de-selecting the **hide-on-canvas** attribute for each band.

You'll start off by defining the sub-group header of the report. This sub-group contains Individual Sales information such as payment type. Create labels for the **Purchase ID, Employee ID, Payment Type,** and **Purchase Time** fields, along with dragging and dropping those fields on the report layout. Morph the **PURCHASETIME** field into a date-field, and set the date format to `MM-dd-yyyy hh:mm a`. Note that Pentaho Reporting uses Java's SimpleDateFormat (`http://java.sun.com/javase/6/docs/api/java/text/SimpleDateFormat.html`).

Below the summary section, display column headers for the already defined Details band, including italicized labels for **Purchased Items, Quantity, Sale Price,** and **Total.** Also, add a line below the header columns to clearly separate them from the Details band. Your sub-group header band should look something like the following when complete:

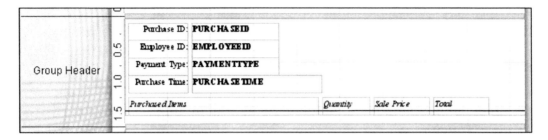

Now, it's time to begin work on the sub-group footer band. In this section, you're going to display a **Purchase Total:** label, along with the Purchase Total. You'll need to define a **Summary | Sum** function with `TotalItemPrice` as its field and `purchaseid` as its group. Name this function `PurchaseTotal`. To complete the sub-group footer band, drag-and-drop the `PurchaseTotal`, morphing the report element to a number-field and applying the appropriate format string. Also, add a line to separate the sub-group footer from the Details band.

Defining the main Group Header

Now that you've defined the low level reporting details, you are ready to present a summary of the day's activities in the form of the main **Group Header**. Before you begin the layout of this band, first define the necessary functions, which you need for populating your summary results. You'll want to display separate summaries of each payment type. In order to do so, you'll need to define formulas and functions to calculate these values.

To calculate Total Check Sales, you'll need to define an **Open Formula** function titled `CheckTotalItemPrice`. This **Open Formula** function will need to determine if the item is part of a check purchase. And if it is indeed a part of a check purchase, display its value, otherwise display zero. Here is the formula necessary:

```
=IF([PAYMENTTYPE]="check";[TotalItemPrice];0)
```

Notice the use of the `IF()` function as part of the formula. The first parameter of the `IF` function evaluates to either true or false. The second parameter, `TotalItemPrice`, is returned if `PAYMENTTYPE` is a check. Finally, the third parameter, `0`, is returned if `PAYMENTTYPE` is anything but a check.

Now that you've defined a row level expression, you also need to sum these values to get a global group sum for Total Checks. To accomplish this, define a **Summary | Sum** function titled ExpectedCheckTotal, with the group set to the sessionid group and the field set to the recently created CheckTotalItemPrice.

You must do this for the other payment options as well, including Cash, Credit, and Debit. The following table shows the **Open Formula** and **Sum** functions, which should be defined:

Function type	Function name	Function parameters (formula)
Open Formula	CashTotalItemPrice	=IF([PAYMENTTYPE] = "cash"; [TotalItemPrice]; 0)
Sum	ExpectedCashTotal	Group: sessionid, Field: CashTotalItemPrice
Open Formula	CreditTotalItemPrice	=IF([PAYMENTTYPE] = "credit"; [TotalItemPrice]; 0)
Sum	ExpectedCreditTotal	Group: sessionid, Field: CreditTotalItemPrice
Open Formula	DebitTotalItemPrice	=IF([PAYMENTTYPE] = "debit"; [TotalItemPrice]; 0)
Sum	ExpectedDebitTotal	Group: sessionid, Field: DebitTotalItemPrice

You also need to define a **Sum** for the entire total, by using TotalItemPrice as the field and **sessionid** as the group. Name this function ExpectedTotalItemPrice.

For the last function, you must define an additional **Open Formula** function that calculates the ActualTotal.

```
=[ExpectedCreditTotal] + [ExpectedDebitTotal] + [ACTUALCHECKTOTAL] +
[ACTUALCASHTOTAL]
```

The cashier is accountable for checks and cash. However, the credit card transactions are automated, so there is no need to calculate a potential variance with those purchases. You're now ready to lay out the **Group Header** band.

To begin, add a heading label titled **End of Day Summary:** with a colored rectangle in the background, in order to highlight its importance. Below that, add an **Employee ID** label, along with the **EMPLOYEEID** field. Also, add a **Date:** label and the **CHECKOUTTIME** field, morphing the time to a formatted date-field. You may want to also include the **SESSIONID** field.

Below that section, add a column of labels for expected totals, including **Credit Sales:**, **Debit Sales:**, **Check Sales:**, **Cash Sales:**, and **Expected Total:**. Next to each of those labels, add the appropriate data fields, using the functions defined above.

Now, add another label column for actual values, including labels for **Credit Actual:**, **Debit Actual:**, **Check Actual:**, **Cash Actual:**, and **Actual Total:**. Next to each of those labels, add the appropriate fields. For the Credit, Debit, and Actual Total fields, reuse the expected values. For Check and Cash, use the database fields **ACTUALCHECKTOTAL** and **ACTUALCASHTOTAL**.

You're almost done! To spice things up a bit, you may traffic light the **ActualTotal** report element based on variance. The term **traffic lighting** refers to dynamically changing the background color of a report element to highlight a range of values such as the color green to highlight a value within a certain variance, and red for values outside a variance. Select the **ActualTotal** report element in the report, and set the **bg-color** style formula to the following:

```
=IF(ABS([ActualTotal]-[ExpectedTotal]) < 5.00;"#00FF00";
IF(ABS([ActualTotal]-[ExpectedTotal]) < 10;"#FFFF00";"#FF0000"))
```

This formula sets the background color of the report element to either green, yellow, or red, depending on the variance calculation of ABS([ActualTotal]-[ExpectedTotal]). If the value is within $5, everything is well and good. If it is within $10, change the background to yellow. And for the value of variance above $10, the cashier is in a world of hurt, so display red as the background color.

As a final step, add the variance value. First, add a label titled **Variance**, beneath the **Expected Total**. Now, add a number field report element $3 next to it. Instead of relying on an existing function or data field, use the **value** formula property of the number field to calculate the variance. All styles and attributes may use inline formulas to determine their values by clicking in the formula cell of the property. Enter the following formula:

```
=[ActualTotal]-[ExpectedTotal]
```

You've now completed the main **Group Header** band. The band should look something like the following screenshot:

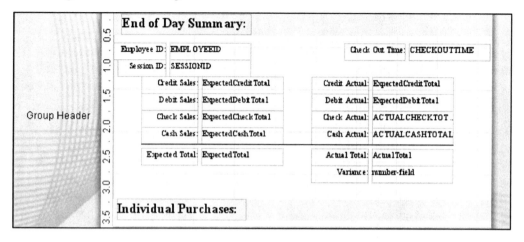

Congratulations! You're now ready to view this report in your J2EE environment. Save the report as `endofday.prpt` in the `chapter3\data` directory.

Incorporating the End of Day report into your J2EE environment

You've already set up the framework for incorporating the Chapter 3 examples into your J2EE environment. Now, all you need to do is make a minor update to the servlet, passing in the `sessionId` parameter to the report. First, get the `sessionId` from the HTTP request. Add the following code right after retrieving the `reportName` in the `doGet()` method:

```
String sessionId = request.getParameter("sessionId");
```

Now you need to provide the `MasterReport` object with the input parameter. Add the following code right after creating the `MasterReport` object:

```
if (sessionId != null) {
    report.getParameterValues().put("SessionInput",
                            new Integer(sessionId));
}
```

By placing the `sessionId` in the `MasterReport` object's parameter value map, the report has access to the parameter for execution of the SQL query. Under the covers, the report engine will use a `java.sql.PreparedStatement` to populate the SQL parameter and execute the query.

You will also need to add some additional HTML to the Chapter 3 home page, `index.html`, allowing the user to select which session the report should render.

```
<p>
<form action="report">
    <b>End Of Day Report</b><br>
    <input type="hidden" name="outputFormat" value="pdf">
    <input type="hidden" name="reportName" value="endofday">
    Session ID:
    <select name="sessionId">
        <option>1</option>
        <option>2</option>
        <option>3</option>
        <option>4</option>
        <option>5</option>
    </select>
    <br>
    <input type="submit" value="Run Report">
</form>
</p>
```

It would also be possible to use a JSP or servlet to render the home page, allowing the dynamic population of the HTML select list, similar to the Report Designer parameter dialog.

You're now ready to run the Ant script and deploy your modified web application. Type the `ant restart_tomcat` command to build the new web application archive. Visit `http://localhost:8080/chapter3`:

Select a **Session ID** from the list and run the report. The final result should look something like this:

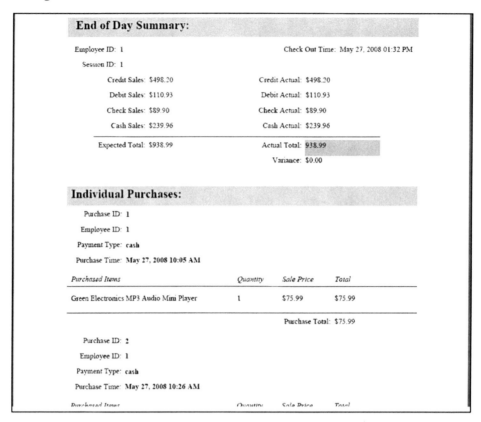

In this example, you learned how to incorporate reporting formulas and functions, along with using style expressions and multilevel groupings, in order to organize your data. You also learned how to define and use report parameters.

ElectroBarn invoice example

It's often the case that a small-or medium-sized business will want to customize their invoices and use a reporting engine to generate standard templates for use. In this example, you'll learn how to build a bursting invoice report, along with learning about additional capabilities of Pentaho Reporting, including sub-reports and external URL linking.

As in previous examples, you'll first build the report using the Pentaho Report Designer, and then update your J2EE environment with the necessary changes to render the invoice report.

Configuring the data source query

To start, launch the **JDBC Data Source** dialog. You've already configured the ElectroBarn JDBC data source, so simply select that option in the **Connection** list. Now, define a query and launch the query designer, making sure to select the **Public** schema.

This query will involve multiple tables. First, double-click the INVOICES table, in order to add it to your SQL Query. The INVOICES table contains general invoice information, such as the customer ID and shipping information. Next, double-click the INVOICEITEMS and INVENTORY tables. These tables define the individual invoice items purchased, and will be used to calculate the total invoice price, along with displaying the individual purchased items.

You now need to define the relationships between the tables. Within the visual table views, drag-and-drop the INVOICES.INVOICEID column over to the INVOICEITEMS.INVOICEID column. This sets up an inner join one-to-many relationship between the INVOICES and INVOICEITEMS tables. Now, drag-and-drop the INVOICEITEMS.ITEMID column over to the INVENTORY.ITEMID column. You've now set up the relationships between these tables.

Finally, you need to specify the correct ORDER BY columns. First, right-click on the INVOICE.INVOICEID column in the tree view and add it to the ORDER BY clause, followed by the INVOICEITEMS.ITEMID column being added to the **ORDER BY** clause.

You should now have the following query defined for the report:

```
SELECT
        "INVOICES"."INVOICEID",
        "INVOICES"."CUSTOMERID",
        "INVOICES"."SALESREP",
        "INVOICES"."INVOICEDATE",
        "INVOICES"."SHIPDATE",
        "INVOICES"."SHIPBY",
        "INVOICES"."SHIPCOST",
        "INVOICES"."NOTES",
        "INVOICEITEMS"."ITEMID",
        "INVOICEITEMS"."QUANTITY",
        "INVENTORY"."ITEMNAME",
        "INVENTORY"."ITEMDESCRIPTION",
        "INVENTORY"."ITEMCATEGORY",
        "INVENTORY"."ITEMID",
        "INVENTORY"."ONHAND",
        "INVENTORY"."ONORDER",
        "INVENTORY"."SALEPRICE",
```

```
        "INVENTORY"."COST",
        "INVENTORY"."MANUFACTURER"
FROM
        "INVENTORY" INNER JOIN "INVOICEITEMS" ON "INVENTORY"."ITEMID"
        = "INVOICEITEMS"."ITEMID"
        INNER JOIN "INVOICES" ON "INVOICEITEMS"."INVOICEID"
        = "INVOICES"."INVOICEID"
ORDER BY
        "INVOICES"."INVOICEID" ASC,
        "INVOICEITEMS"."ITEMID" ASC
```

Defining the Group Header

In this report, you'll define a single group. The root group should include the grouping field **INVOICEID**. For the group header and footer, uncheck the **hide-on-canvas** attributes.

Now, you're ready to begin populating the group header. Note that because you'll want the ability to burst multiple invoice reports, you'll place no header information in the report header. Instead, you'll place this information in the group header. Include the company's logo as in previous examples, along with displaying company details such as the address, by including labels.

Below the company details, add a label that will render as a hyperlink in the PDF. First, define a basic label with the URL `http://www.ElectroBarn.com`. Then edit the **url** style attribute of the label with the same URL. Defining the **url** style attribute lets the reporting engine's report layout renderer know to create a hyperlink over the defined report element.

On the right side of the invoice, include labels and fields to display the **INVOICEID**, **INVOICEDATE**, and **SALESREP** of the invoice, along with a large label clearly marking this report as an invoice.

Now, add a sub-report element to the group header, selecting the **Inline** option. An inline sub-report allows side-by-side sub-reporting, whereas a banded sub-report acts as an additional report band and can have a dynamic height. Size the sub-report to fill half the screen.

At the bottom of the group header, you'll add the column headings including **Invoice Items**, **Quantity**, **Sale Price**, and **Total**. Also, add a colorful rectangular background to the header row, in order to distinguish it from the invoice data.

When you've completed these steps, your group headers should look something like the following:

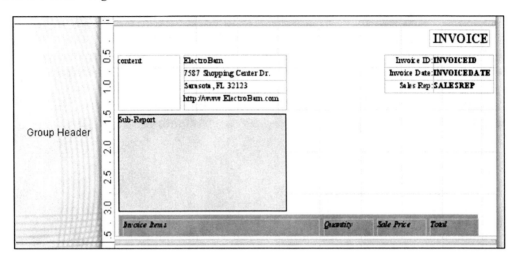

Defining the sub-report

In the sub-report, display the customer details of the invoice. Right-click on the sub-report element in the canvas and select **Edit SubReport**. This opens a new canvas tab, where you can edit the sub-report. Bring up the **Sub-report Parameters** dialog by right-clicking and editing the **Parameters** tree item in the **Data** tab of the sub-report.

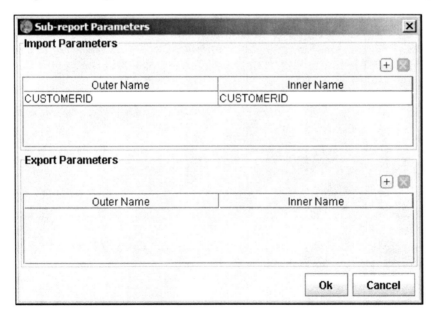

Add **CUSTOMERID** as an import parameter, using the same value for the **Outer Name** and **Inner Name**.

Once you've configured the CUSTOMERID as an input, configure the sub-report's SQL query. Right-click on the **Data Sets** tree item in the **Data** tab, and select the **JDBC** menu option. Add a data source query with the name customerdetails. This query should include all the columns of the CUSTOMERS table. In addition to adding the table, right-click on the WHERE clause and add a condition where "CUSTOMERS"."CUSTOMERID" = ${CUSTOMERID}. This limits the results of the sub-query to the current customer. Your query result should look like this:

```
SELECT
        "CUSTOMERS"."CUSTOMERID",
        "CUSTOMERS"."NAME",
        "CUSTOMERS"."CONTACT",
        "CUSTOMERS"."ADDR1",
        "CUSTOMERS"."ADDR2",
        "CUSTOMERS"."CITY",
        "CUSTOMERS"."STATE",
        "CUSTOMERS"."ZIPCODE"
FROM
        "CUSTOMERS"
WHERE
        "CUSTOMERS"."CUSTOMERID"=${CUSTOMERID}
```

You're now ready to populate the sub-report. In this example, place a rectangle with a black border in the sub-report **Details** band, along with a **Customer:** label and the appropriate fields to display the customer details. To add the Attn: in front of the CONTACT field, morph the field into a **message-field**, and edit the value to equal **Attn: $(CONTACT)**. For the CITY, STATE and ZIPCODE fields, morph the CITY field and edit the value to equal **$(CITY), $(STATE) $(ZIPCODE).**

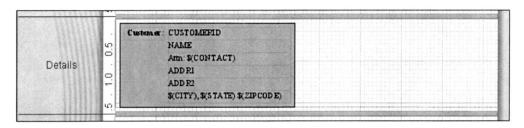

You've now created your first sub-report! This sub-report will be bundled as part of the .prpt file when saving the main report.

Defining the Details band

The Details band of the invoice report should contain the columns **ITEMNAME**, **QUANTITY**, and **SALEPRICE**. It should also contain a report function of the type `Open Formula` titled **TotalItemPrice**, with the formula:

```
=[QUANTITY] * [SALEPRICE]
```

In addition to the data fields, you'll also include a rectangular background that fills the entire height of the **Details** band. You'll do some row banding with this rectangle, so make sure to give it a name such as `detailsRect`.

Now, set the visible style formula of the rectangle to the following:

```
=IF(ISEVEN(ROWCOUNT()); TRUE(); FALSE())
```

For every other row, the rectangle will hide itself, allowing the rows of your invoice items to be clearly banded together.

Defining the Group Footer and Page Footer

To complete the invoice report, you'll need to populate the Group Footer with the necessary summary values, along with a notes section for the invoice. Define a new report function of type **Sum** that sums the **TotalItemPrice** expression, in order to calculate the `PurchaseTotal`. Also, define a formula-based number field called `TaxTotal` with the following formula:

```
=[PurchaseTotal]*0.06
```

Use a 6% sales tax in the example. For a grand total number field, define the following formula that sums all of the costs:

```
=[PurchaseTotal] * 1.06 + [SHIPCOST]
```

In addition to displaying the summarized invoice costs, also add the **NOTES** field to your report. Text fields have the ability to wrap multiple lines, if necessary. Resize the field to fill in the left portion of the Group Footer as shown in the following screenshot:

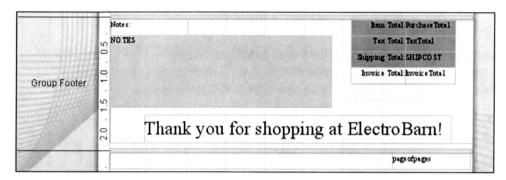

As a final touch to the Group Footer, add a friendly message such as **Thank you for shopping at ElectroBarn!**, which will encourage your customers to continue shopping at ElectroBarn. The very last step in completing the report is to add a page count in the **Page Footer** band, as well as to force page breaks after each **Group Footer**. To make this report burstable, you'll want to reset the page counter at the end of every invoice and begin each invoice at the top of a page. You can do this by selecting the **pagebreak-after** style property in the group footer, which forces a new page below the group footer. Also, you need to set the group property of the Page Of Pages Function to the invoice group. You've now completed the design of the report. Save the report as chapter3\data\invoices.prpt.

Incorporating the invoice report into your J2EE environment

You're now ready to update your J2EE environment, in order to render the invoices report. There are no changes required to the servlet, but you will need to update the home page of the web application. Add a link to the report, in the HTML of your chapter3 home page, index.html.

```
<a href="report?outputFormat=pdf&reportName=invoices">Invoice Burst
Report</a>
```

You're now ready to run the Ant script and deploy the modified web application. Type the `ant restart_tomcat` command to build the new war. Visit `http://localhost:8080/chapter3` and click the **Burst Report** link. The final result should look something like this:

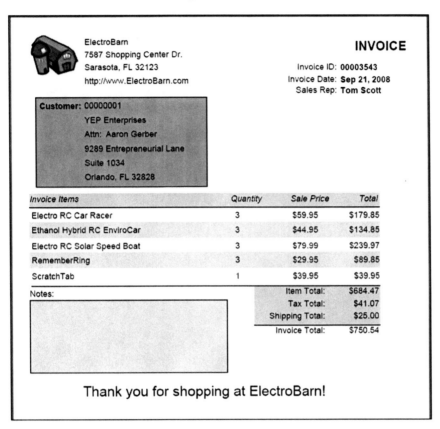

This report could be sent directly to a printer to generate all the invoices for a day. Or you could parameterize the report down to an individual invoice, allowing customers to access their invoices online. Another option for bursting might include generating individual PDFs per invoice, and either mailing them out or sending them to another system to process.

In this example, you learned how to add a sub-report to a main report, along with learning additional functions and styles, including row banding, URL display, and page breaking.

Summary

In this chapter, you built three real world reports, learning the breadth of functionality provided by Pentaho Reporting. In the first example, you learned how to work with SQL data sources, define charts, and how to use formulas and functions in an inventory report. In the second example, you defined a parameterized cashier balance report with dynamically driven styles, including adding traffic lighting to the report. In the third example, you incorporated inline sub-reports into an invoice report, along with adding hyperlinks and row banding to the report. You embedded these reports in a J2EE environment, which involved adding JAR dependencies for charting and updating your servlet to support parameterization.

Now that you've experienced Pentaho Reporting in the real world, it's time to dive deeper into each subject area, allowing you to gain the expertise to build advanced reports with Pentaho Reporting.

4
Design and Layout in Pentaho's Report Designer

In this chapter, you'll dive deep into the concepts and functionality of Pentaho's Report Designer, related to the design and layout of a report. The Report Designer is designed for business users who want to design reports in a what-you-see-is-what-you-get (WYSIWYG) drag-and-drop client environment.

You'll first learn about the Report Designer's user interface, highlighting the different components that work together to build a report. You'll then learn more about the core layout bands presented in the Report Designer, including detail and group bands. From there, you'll explore in detail the various elements available to designers, how they are used, and what they might be used for.

You'll also learn the ins and outs of visual layout within the reporting canvas, including advanced concepts such as grids and guides. You'll close the chapter with more details when working with fonts, along with considerations for dealing with the various output formats supported by Pentaho Reporting.

Report Designer user interface components

After launching the Report Designer, you'll notice the following six main user interface components that work together to create a report, from the top left to the bottom right of the main Report Designer window:

- The menu and toolbar
- The report element palette, where you can select report elements for your report
- The report canvas tab panel, which displays your reports

- The **Report Explorer** panel with **Structure** and **Data** tabs, which displays the entire report in object tree form

- The **Element Properties** panel, which displays all the **Styles** and **Attributes** associated with the currently selected report element

- The **Messages** panel, which displays warnings and errors related to the currently opened report

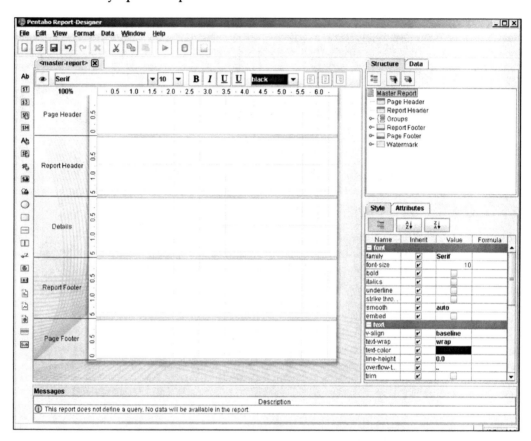

Menu and toolbar

The menu and toolbar contain useful functionality to make building a report easier, along with basic functionality such as saving, opening, and publishing of reports. Many of the options in the menu and toolbar are available as shortcut keys.

Report element palette

The report element palette panel is located on the left side of the Report Designer and contains an icon list of the types of elements that can be placed on the report, including labels, shapes, fields, charts, and more. To add an element to your report, drag-and-drop an element from the palette into the report canvas.

Report canvas tab panel

The report canvas tab panel is located in the center of the Report Designer. Once you've created a new report or opened an existing one, this is where you drag-and-drop report elements to build your report. In design mode, the canvas displays the currently visible report bands. The canvas offers many visual features that allow you to manage the alignment and sizing of your report elements.

In addition to the design canvas, you can also preview the current report. You can quickly toggle between live data and the report template in this fashion.

Report Explorer

The **Report Explorer**, located on the right side of the Report Designer, includes a **Structure** tab panel. The **Structure** tab panel contains the tree structure of a report, including all the report bands. The **Data** tab panel contains all the data sources, functions, and parameters of a report. Right-clicking on various portions of the structure and data trees presents options such as adding new data sources and sub-groups. The **Report Explorer** may be hidden through the **Window** application menu.

Element Properties

The **Element Properties** panel is located below the report explorer panel, on the right side of the Report Designer, and displays the details of the currently selected item in the report explorer or canvas. All styles and attributes, which are editable, appear in this panel. Many editable properties provide additional dialogs for advanced editing capabilities. The **Element Properties** panel may be hidden through the **Window** application menu.

Messages

The **Messages** panel is located at the bottom of the Report Designer and displays any active warnings or errors that are present in the report. Selecting a message will automatically select the element and property in question, making it easy to track down issues in your report. The **Message** panel is hidden by default, and can be made viewable through the **Window** application menu.

Report bands

When first creating a report in your canvas and report explorer structure tree, you will see a **Page Header**, **Report Header**, **Details** band, **Report Footer**, and a **Page Footer** band appear as part of the report. These bands, along with other bands, including **Group**, **Watermark**, and **No Data** bands that you may define, make up the entire visual report. All bands may contain elements from the palette, and act as containers for rendering these elements. Each band has a different life cycle, and is rendered based on their context. In this section, you'll go over each band's properties, along with the context in which each band renders itself.

Common properties

All bands share a common set of properties, which are explained using tables in the forthcoming sub-sections. Certain properties may offer a dialog for editing, which is displayed in the list as well.

Size and position properties

These properties define the size and position for the band. These properties may be edited together by selecting the band in the structure tree and then clicking on the **Format | Size & Border...** menu item, or individually within the **Report Element Styles** tab.

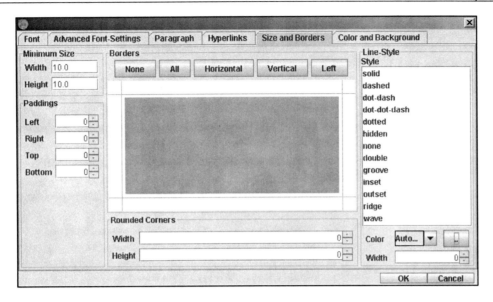

The following table lists the size and position properties:

Property name	Description
layout	Defines how elements within the band are rendered. <ul><li>The default layout is **canvas**, which allows you to specify exactly where each report element in the band should render.</li><li>The **block** layout stacks all the items in a band from top to bottom.</li><li>The **inline** layout stacks all the items left to right, with wrapping.</li><li>The **row** layout displays all the report elements in a single row.</li></ul>
height	The height of this element. A number between -100 and 0 represents a percentage of the parent container's height.
width	The width of this element. A number between -100 and 0 represents a percentage of the parent container's width.
x	The x location of this element within its parent container.
y	The y location of this element within its parent container.
visible	If set to false, the element is not rendered.
invisible-cosumes-space	If set to true, children of this band that are invisible will still consume space in the report.
dynamic-height	If set to true, informs the reporting engine that this element has a dynamic height.

Property name	Description
preferred-height	The preferred height of this element.
preferred -width	The preferred width of this element.
max-height	The maximum height of this element.
max-width	The maximum width of this element.
x-overflow	If set to true, text may overflow horizontally outside of the element.
y-overflow	If set to true, text may overflow vertically outside of this element.
fixed-position	If specified, sets the fixed vertical position of this band within a report.
box-sizing	This is either set to **content-box** or **border-box**. If set to **content-box**, the sizing styles do not include the border, and if set to **border-box**, the sizing styles do include the border box. The default value of this style is **content-box**.

Padding and border properties

These properties define the padding and border definition for the band. Border information includes thickness, line type, and color. These properties may be edited together by selecting the band and then clicking on the **Format | Size & Border...** menu item, or individually within the **Report Element Styles** tab.

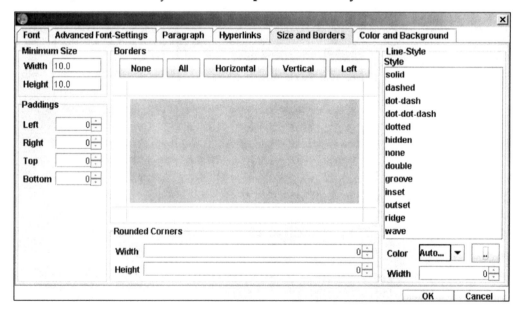

Padding Styles

Property name	Description
top	The height of the padding on the top of an element.
bottom	The height of the padding on the bottom of an element.
left	The width of the padding on the left of an element.
right	The width of the padding on the right of an element.

Border Styles

Property name	Description
top-style	The style of the top border.
top-size	The width of the top border.
top-color	The color of the top border
top-left-height	The height of the top left corner's radius.
top-left-width	The width of the top left corner's radius.
top-right-height	The height of the top right corner's radius.
top-right-width	The width of the top right corner's radius.
bottom-size	The width of the bottom border.
bottom-style	The style of the bottom border. Style values include **none, hidden, dotted, dashed, solid, double dot-dash, dot-dot-dash, wave, groove, ridge, inset,** and **outset.**
bottom-color	The color of the bottom border. Colors can be represented as strings using the same syntax as HTML colors, #RRGGBB hex values.
bottom-left-height	The height of the bottom left corner's radius.
bottom-left-width	The width of the bottom left corner's radius.
bottom-right-height	The height of the bottom right corner's radius.
bottom-right-width	The width of the bottom right corner's radius.
left-color	The color of the left border.
left-size	The width of the left border.
right-size	The width of the right border.
right-style	The style of the right border.
break-color	If the element is split, this is the color of the border where the break occurred.
break-size	If the element is split, this is the width of the border where the break occurred.
break-style	If the element is split, this is the style of the border where the break occurred.

Page behavior properties

Page behavior properties impact how bands are rendered relative to individual pages.

Property name	Description
pagebreak-before	Places a page break before rendering the band.
pagebreak-after	Places a page break after rendering the band.
avoid-page-break	Forces the band to skip to the next page instead of a split rendering.
orphans	The number of contiguous bands to group before a page break occurs.
widows	The number of contiguous bands to group after a page break occurs.

Foreground and background color properties

Bands have default foreground and background colors. These colors appear within the **Styles** tab as **text-color** and **bg-color**.

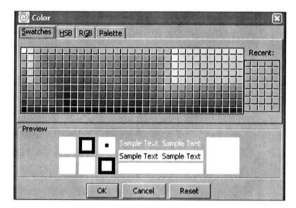

Excel properties

Report bands define specific properties related to Excel.

Property name	Description
sheet name	The name of the sheet to render the band.
format-override	The Excel cell data format string.
formula-override	The Excel cell data formula string.
wrap-text-override	If true, wraps a text-based report element text within an Excel Cell. This value is inherited by text-based report elements within the band.

Attribute properties

The following common attribute property is shared by all bands:

Property name	Description
hide-on-canvas	If checked, the band will not appear in the canvas, otherwise it will appear. This property does not impact whether a band is rendered or not during report generation. It is strictly a design time property.

Style inheritance

Additional styles are available for each band, which are inherited by the report elements within the band. Report elements inherit the style properties of their parent band.

Page Header and Page Footer

The **Page Header** and **Page Footer** bands appear at the beginning and end of each page, determined by the specific output format.

These bands differ slightly from the common properties defined earlier. The **pagebreak-before** and **pagebreak-after** properties do not apply to these bands. Also, the following properties are available in addition to the defaults:

Property name	Description
display-on-firstpage	The default value is true for this property. If set to false, the first page will not contain this band.
display-on-lastpage	The default value is true for this property. If set to false, the last page will not contain this band.
sticky	If the Page Header or Footer is defined as sticky, they will be printed on each page as if they were part of a sub-report definition being rendered.

Report Header and Report Footer

The **Report Header** and **Report Footer** appear at the beginning and end of a report, and are often used to display the title and summary information. The Report Header and Footer do not define any additional properties beyond the common set of properties.

Group Header and Group Footer

The **Group Header** and **Group Footer** bands may appear for each defined group configured as part of the report. A grouping defined in a report is a set of identical values in one or more selected data columns. A new group is triggered when the values change in the defined group column(s). It's critical that columns defined as groupings are sorted appropriately before being passed into Pentaho Reporting, otherwise, duplicate groups may appear in the rendered report.

The Group Header and Footer differ slightly from the common properties defined earlier.

Property name	Description
sticky	If the group header or footer is defined as sticky, they will be printed on each page as if they were part of a sub-report definition being rendered.
repeat-header	The band will be displayed at the beginning of new pages, in addition to its default rendering.

Details Body

The **Details Body** consists of four distinct bands. The **Details Header** and **Details Footer** band are rendered before and after a grouping of detail rows. A **Details** band is rendered for every row of data, and a **No Data** band is rendered when no data is available for the report. The **Details Header**, **Details Footer**, and **No Data** bands are hidden in the Report Designer by default. The Detail Header and Footer bands share the same additional properties, **sticky** and **repeat-header**, as the group bands. The rest of the detail bands define no additional properties beyond the common set of properties.

Watermark

The **Watermark** band appears behind all the other bands, and is used for background images and styling of the report. The Watermark band defines no additional properties beyond the common set of properties.

Report elements

All available report elements appear in the palette, and may be dragged and dropped into the report canvas. Report elements make up the content of your report. They range from the label and text elements to graphic, chart, and sub-report elements.

Common properties

Most report elements inherit from a common set of properties, which are listed in the following table:

Property name	Description
name	The unique name of the element within the report. This property is not commonly edited.
Size and Position Properties	The X and Y location of the element, in relation to its parent band. These properties appear in the style attributes list as **x** and **y**.
Padding and Border Properties	The padding and border definition of an element. Border information includes thickness, line type, and color. These properties may be edited together by selecting the band and then clicking on the **Format	Size & Border...** menu item, or individually within the **Report Element Styles** tab. Report Elements share the same individual padding and border properties as report bands defined above.

Additional properties shared by report elements, including HTML and Event properties, are defined in Chapter 9.

Common text properties

These are the list of common text properties shared by text elements, including the label, text-field, message, number-field, date-field, resource-field, and resource-message. One special consideration is that it is possible to morph one type of text field into another by using the menu option **Format | Morph**. For example, you could convert a text-field into a number-field by simply morphing the field.

Font style properties

Font properties of a report element may be edited as a group by selecting **Format | Font...**, or edited individually within the **Element Properties Style** tab. They may also be edited using the canvas toolbar.

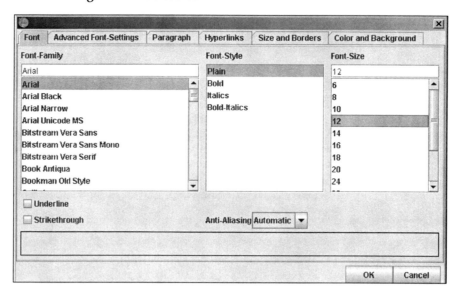

Individual font styles are defined later in the *Working with fonts* section.

Text style properties

The following properties impact the appearance of text within report elements:

Property name	Description
h-align	The horizontal alignment of the text within the element. This property is also editable in the main toolbar.
v-align	The vertical alignment of the text within the element. This property is also editable in the main toolbar.
v-align-in-band	Specifies the vertical alignment of text. Appropriate values include **use-script, baseline, sub, super, top, text-top, central, middle, bottom,** and **text-bottom**.
text-wrap	Specifies if the text should wrap. Appropriate values include **none** and **wrap**.
text-color	The foreground font color. This property is also editable in the main toolbar.
bg-color	The background color of the text element.
line-height	The value of the font's line height within the text element.

Property name	Description
overflow-text	This is normally set to "..", and is the text that is appended to the string if it appears longer than the available space to render. This appears as overflow-text in the styles list.
trim	If **trim** is set to true, any leading or trailing whitespace is removed.
trim-whitespace	**trim-whitespace** defines the following different trim modes: • The **preserve** option makes no changes to whitespace. • The **preserve-breaks** option trims all whitespace between words, and at the beginning and ending of new lines, but does not remove any new lines. • The **collapse** option trims all whitespaces down to single spaces, including new lines. • The **discard** option removes all whitespaces from the text element.
encoding	If set, this overrides the default PDF Font character encoding.
rich-text-type	The type of text to render in the report. This attribute defaults to text/plain, but also may be set to text/html and text/rtf. If text/html is specified, html formatting elements are rendered within the text report element, the same concept applies for the text/rtf format. This attribute is located in the common group within the **Attributes** tab.

Text spacing properties

Text spacing properties define how characters are rendered in text elements.

Property name	Description
character	Specifies the minimum character spacing when rendering justified text.
word	Specifies additional padding between words when rendering.
preferred-character	Specifies the preferred character spacing when rendering justified text.
character-spacing	Specifies the maximum character spacing when rendering justified text.

Link properties

Report elements may specify link properties, allowing links to appear in a report.

Property name	Description
html-anchor	The name of the anchor tag in HTML.
url	The url of the link.
url-tooltip	The tooltip of the link.
url-window-title	The window title of the link.

Excel properties

Report elements may customize specific style properties related to Excel. Report elements share the properties format-override, formula-override, and wrap-text-override, defined earlier in the common properties section of report bands.

label

The **label** element **Ab** allows you to specify static text within your report. Label utilizes the following property:

Property name	Description
value	The text to render the report.

text-field

The **text-field** element $T allows you to render a field as text within your report. The text-field utilizes the following properties.

Property name	Description
field	The source field to render within the text field.
if-null	The string to display if the source field value is null.

message

The **message** element $M enables field values to be included in larger messages, along with combining multiple fields into a single text element. The message element references the data source within the format string, by specifying "$(Field Name)" for the fields to render. The message element utilizes the following properties:

Property name	Description
value	The value attribute represents the format of the string. An example might be "Field: $(Field)".
if-null	The string to display if the message field value is null.

number-field

The **number-field** element $3 is similar to the text-field, with an additional ability to format a number based on a format string. The number-field utilizes the following properties:

Property name	Description
format	This field represents the format of the number, using Java's `DecimalFormat` definition. An example might be "#,##0.###".
field	The source field to render within the number field.
if-null	The string to display if the source field value is null.

date-field

The **date-field** element $⊟ is similar to the text-field, with the additional ability to format a date based on a format string. The date-field utilizes the following properties:

Property name	Description
format	This field represents the format of the date. An example might be mm-dd-yyyy.
field	The source field to render within the date field.
if-null	The string to display if the source field value is null.

resource-label

The **resource-label** element A*b* is similar to the label element, except that it loads its text from an internationalized resource file. The resource-label utilizes the following properties:

Property name	Description
resource-identifier	The primary name of the resource file. For example, if the default localized resource file is named `myreport`. `properties`, this value should be set to `myreport`. Also note, the report's resources path must be configured to point to the directory where the localized resource files exist.
value	The key name (located in the resource file) of the resource to render.

resource-message

The **resource-message** element $*b* is similar to the message field, except that it loads its format key from a resource file. The resource-message element utilizes the following properties:

Property name	Description
resource-identifier	The primary name of the resource file.
resource-value	The key name of the resource message to render.
if-null	The string to display if the resource format key message field's value is null.

resource-field

The **resource-field** element [S*b*] is similar to the resource-label, except that it determines the resource key using the field name provided by the data source. The resource-field utilizes the following properties:

Property name	Description
resource-identifier	The primary name of the resource file.
field	The name of the field to render as text within the resource file.
if-null	The string to display if the resource field value is null.

The following elements do not include the common text properties, and are not considered text elements.

chart

The **chart** element ▦ allows you to place a chart within your report. The chart element, in its various forms, contains a large number of properties that are covered in Chapter 6.

content (static image)

The **content** element ▨ allows you to place a static image in your report. You may edit the location of the content element by right-clicking on the element and selecting **Edit Content...**. When selecting an image, you may choose to embed it into the report definition, or link to it externally. The content element utilizes the following properties:

Property name	Description
value	The URL of the image to render. This displays a file dialog for selecting an image. HTTP and other virtual file system URLS may be used as well.
aspect-ratio	It should be set to true for the image to keep its aspect ratio when rendering. This is a style attribute within the object category.
scale	It should be set to true for the image to adjust its width and height, based on the report element's width and height. This is a style attribute within the object category.

content-field (dynamic image)

The **content-field** element ▨ is similar to the content element. However, it allows you to dynamically determine the content of the image, based on a report field. The content-field utilizes the following properties:

Property name	Description
field	The name of the data source field that populates the image. The content-field element is often used in conjunction with report functions that generate `Drawable` objects.
If-null	The content to display if the field is null.
aspect-ratio	It should be set to true for the image to keep its aspect ratio when rendering.
scale	It should be set to true for the image to adjust its width and height, based on the report element's width and height. This is a style attribute within the object category.

rectangle

The **rectangle** element ☐ allows you to render a rectangle within a report. The rectangle utilizes the following properties:

Property name	Description
fill	If set to true, it fills the rectangle with the selected value of **fill-color**.
fill-color	The color of the rectangle.
aspect-ratio	If true, maintains an equal width and height of the rectangle.
draw-outline	Draws the border of the rectangle if set to true.
arc-width	It defines the width of curved edges. The default value is 0.0.
arc-height	It defines the height of curved edges. The default value is 0.0.

ellipse

The **ellipse** element ◯ allows you to render an ellipse within a report. The ellipse element utilizes the following properties:

Property name	Description
fill	If set to true, it fills the rectangle with the selected value of **fill-color**.
fill-color	The color of the ellipse.
aspect-ratio	If true, maintains an equal width and height of the ellipse.
draw-outline	If set to true, it draws the border of the ellipse.

horizontal-line and vertical-line

The **horizontal-line** and **vertical-line** elements ⊟ ⊞ allow you to draw a line within a report. These elements utilize the following properties:

Property name	Description
stroke	The width and pattern in which to draw the line.
text-color	The color in which to render the line.

band

The **band** element ▦ allows the grouping of other elements into a single group, making it easier to control the group's location and size as a single unit. The band element utilizes the following properties:

Property name	Description
layout	The layout method of rendering the grouped components. This is identical to the layout attribute, which is defined above as a common property of bands.
hide-on-canvas	If true, the element will not appear in the canvas, otherwise it will appear. This property does not impact whether the element is rendered or not during report generation.

sub-report

The **sub-report** element ⸬Sub⸬ allows you to embed a sub-report within a band of your main report. The sub-report element utilizes the following properties:

Property name	Description
query	The query name to use as the data source for the sub-report.
limit	If specified, limits the rows of data rendered in a sub-report.
timeout	If specified, limits the maximum time a sub-report query may execute.

survey-scale

The **survey-scale** element ⸬ renders a simple scale within a report. The survey-scale element utilizes the following properties:

Property name	Description
field	If specified, the name of the data field which contains either a single value that renders a point in the scale, or a three value array that renders a point, along with a low and high marker within the survey scale.
value	If specified as a single number, this value is rendered as a point in the scale. If specified as a three number array, it will render as a point, along with a low and high marker. This value may also be a single string, with numbers separated by commas — for example, "3,1,5".
highest	The highest number to render in the scale.

Property name	Description
lowest	The lowest number to render in the scale.
upper-bound	The range-upper-bound value defines the upper bound of a background rectangle rendered as part of the survey-scale.
lower-bound	The range-lower-bound value defines the lower bound of a background rectangle rendered as part of the survey-scale.

line-sparkline

The **line-sparkline** element 🗠 renders a sparkline in a report. The line-sparkline element utilizes the following properties:

Property name	Description
field	If specified, the field represents an array of numbers, which get rendered as a sparkline. This array may be represented as a comma separated string as well.
value	If specified, the array of numbers is rendered as a sparkline.
spacing	It helps specify the pixel spacing between each point in the sparkline. Unless specified, it defaults to 2 pixels.

bar-sparkline

The **bar-sparkline** element 📄 renders a simple bar chart in a report. The bar-sparkline element has the same properties as the line-sparkline element.

pie-sparkline

The **pie-sparkline** element 📄 renders a simple pie chart, based on a single value between 0 and 1. The pie-sparkline element utilizes the following properties:

Property name	Description
field	If specified, it is the field containing the pie slice value.
value	If specified, it is the value of the pie slice.
low-slice	The maximum percentage value to be considered as a low slice. This value defaults to 0.30.
medium-slice	The maximum percentage value to be considered as a medium slice. This value defaults to 0.70.
high-slice	The maximum percentage value to be considered as a high slice. This value defaults to 1.0

Property name	Description
low-color	The color in which to render the pie slice if it's in the low-slice range. This value defaults to green.
medium-color	The color in which to render the pie slice if it's in the medium-slice range. This value defaults to yellow.
high-color	The color in which to render the pie slice if it's in the high-slice range. This value defaults to red.

simple-barcodes

The **simple-barcodes** element ▥ renders a barcode image in a report. The simple-barcodes element utilizes the following properties:

Property name	Description
type	Found under the **barcode-settings** category in the **Attributes** tab. This is the name of the type of barcode to render. To get a full list of supported types and supported values for each type, see the report engine extensions Javadoc for the following class: `org.pentaho.reporting.engine.classic.extensions.` `modules.sbarcodes.SimpleBarcodesUtility`
field	If specified, it is the field containing the barcode value.
value	If specified, the value of the barcode.
show-text	If set to true, the value of the barcode is displayed below the barcode.
checksum	If set to true, includes a checksum in certain types of barcodes.
bar-width	The width in pixels of the barcode lines. If not specified, defaults to one pixel.
bar-height	The height in pixels of the entire barcode. If not specified, defaults to 10 pixels.

Visual layout in Report Designer

With Pentaho Report Designer, you have pixel level control of your individual elements within a report. Grid and guide lines may appear within each report canvas band, which make it simple to align and configure locations of the elements.

The Grid

By default, the report grid is hidden from view. To enable the grid, enable the menu item **View | Grids | Show**. The grid presents itself in point units (also known as pixel units), with a light gray grid line displayed every five pixels, along with a darker shade guide line presented every 25 pixels.

Grid lines are useful for visual feedback of alignment, as well as providing a method to snap elements to the grid. This makes aligning of elements a simple exercise.

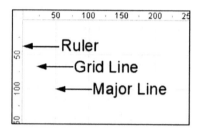

To adjust the ruler unit to centimeters, millimeters, inches, or picas, go to the **View | Units** sub-menu. The default grid size may be adjusted from five pixels to another number by launching the grid size dialog. Select the **View | Grids | Settings** menu item and adjust your grid sizing. Note that the darker shade major guide line appears between every five regular grid lines.

You may show or hide the grid by selecting the menu item **View | Grids | Show**, or by pressing *Ctrl+Quote*.

Guide lines

Guide lines allow you to specify a custom grid line. To add a new horizontal or vertical guide line, click within the ruler section of the report canvas. A new blue guide line should appear. Guide lines are useful for visual feedback of layout, as well as snap to grid features that simplify element placement.

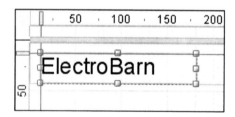

Guide lines may be moved by dragging their location within the ruler. They may also be moved by right-clicking on the line within the ruler and selecting **Properties...**, and then typing in the new value for the guide line.

It is possible to deactivate a single guide line by right-clicking and selecting **Deactivate**. This causes the guide line to be removed from the report canvas content, and appear as a greyed out mark within the ruler section of the canvas. Also, guide lines may be completely removed from the report by right-clicking and selecting **Delete**.

All guide lines may be activated and deactivated together by selecting **View | Guides | Show Rulers**, or by clicking *Ctrl+Semicolon*. This is useful if you use many guidelines and want to quickly see the report without all the blue lines running through it.

Additional visual indicators

In addition to grid lines and grid guides, a couple of other handy shortcuts exist to make it easier to lay out your report. By default, when selecting a report element, the style of the selection is considered an **Outline Selection**. An alternative selection style is **Clamp Selection**. You may toggle between these two types of selections by selecting **View | Outline Selection** or **View | Clamp Selection**.

Also, it is possible to show and hide all element frames by selecting **View | Guides | Toggle Element Frames**, or by clicking *Ctrl+H*. This is another tool to make it easy to visualize how the elements will be laid out next to each other, and to see potential overlaps that might cause problems when rendering the report.

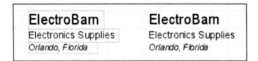

Another visual indicator within Report Designer is the **View | Show Overlapping Elements** menu option. With this option selected, any overlapping elements are highlighted, warning that there may be problems when rendering the report.

Finally, another useful capability within the Report Designer is the ability to zoom in and out of the grid. By default, the Report Designer displays the grid rendered at 100%. Within the **View | Zoom** menu, you may view the report as 50%, 100%, 200%, or 400% of its actual size.

By default, the Report Designer displays the grid rendered at 100%. Within the **View | Zoom** menu, you may view the report as 50%, 100%, 200%, or 400% of its actual size. You may also zoom in by holding your mouse down in the left corner of the report canvas over the current zoom level and dragging left and right to adjust the zoom.

Moving and aligning single elements

In addition to dragging and dropping elements around the report canvas, it is also possible to use shortcut keys and menu items to more easily align and move report elements.

To move an element, first select the element and then drag-and-drop it to the new location within a band. You may also use the arrow keys to move the selected element by individual pixels.

To control the visibility of an element in context of other elements that may overlap, select the element, and then select the **Format | Arrange | Bring Forward** or **Format | Arrange | Bring Backward** option to adjust the order in which elements appear within a band. This is also known as **Z ordering**.

Aligning groups of elements

To really sharpen a report, there are two easy-to-use shortcuts available for aligning groups of elements. First, select the elements as a group by holding the *Shift* key and dragging a selection area around the elements, or by holding the *Shift* key down while selecting individual elements.

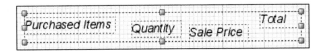

Once you've selected a group of elements, you can easily align all the elements in a group both horizontally or vertically. If you want to align all the labels in the example to the top, select the menu item **Format | Align | Top**. This will align all the selected elements to the topmost selection in the group. Additionally, you may align these elements in the **Middle** or **Bottom**. For elements grouped vertically, you can align them **Left**, **Center**, or **Right**.

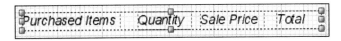

Now, assume that you want to evenly distribute all the elements that are selected. This is possible by selecting the menu item **Edit | Distribute | Equal Horizontal Space**. You can do the same vertically by selecting **Equal Vertical Space**.

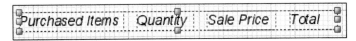

Miscellaneous layout capabilities

There are also some additional layout features that make your life easier when working within the Report Designer. The first feature is the ability to **Paste Formatting** of an element into another element. Select and copy the element you would like to use to share formatting with. Now, select the additional elements you would like to apply the formatting to and select the menu item **Edit | Paste Formatting**. All the formatting-related attributes are copied into the selected elements, preserving their data-related properties.

Pentaho Report Designer shortcut keys

The following table shows the list of all the shortcut keys available in Pentaho Report Designer:

Shortcut Key	Description	Shortcut Key	Description
Ctrl+Shift+N	Launches the Report Wizard to build a new report	Ctrl+Alt+L	Resize the Report Designer view of the bands
Ctrl+N	Creates a new report tab	Ctrl+Quote	Show or hide the grid
Ctrl+O	Brings up the Open Report dialog	Ctrl+H	Toggle element frames
Ctrl+S	Saves the current Report	Ctrl+Semicolon	Toggle guide lines
Ctrl+Z	Undo	Ctrl+P	Show preview
Ctrl+Y	Redo	Ctrl+Alt+Shift+P	Show PDF preview
Ctrl+X	Cut	Ctrl+Alt+Shift+H	Show HTML preview
Ctrl+C	Copy	Ctrl+Alt+Shift+X	Show Excel preview
Ctrl+V	Paste	Ctrl+Alt+Shift+R	Show RTF preview
Ctrl+Shift+V	Paste formatting	Ctrl+Alt+Shift+C	Show CSV preview
Delete Key	Delete the currently selected element	Alt+1	Select the Messages panel
Ctrl+Arrow Key	Move element one grid line in direction of the arrow key	Alt+2	Select the Properties panel
Arrow Key	Move element one pixel in the direction of the arrow key	Alt+3	Select the Structure panel
Alt+Up, Alt+Down	Move element in front of or behind other elements	Ctrl+U	Underline element font
Alt+Home, Alt+End	Move element to the front or behind all elements	Ctrl+Shift+O, Ctrl+Shift+P	Open from and publish to the BI Platform
Ctrl+A	Select all elements within a band	Ctrl+B	Bold element font
Escape	Deselect all elements	Ctrl+I	Italicize element font

Working with fonts

Pentaho Reporting uses Java's built-in font support for most of its font operations. Some additional functionality exists in `libfonts`, providing the report engine with additional information that is not available through Java's standard `Font` and `FontMetrics` API.

In Pentaho Report Designer, fonts may be modified in multiple ways. First, all text-based elements contain font properties. These properties allow the selection of the **Font-Family**, **Font-Size**, and **Font-Style**. When editing these properties through the menu **Format | Font...**, the following screen is presented:

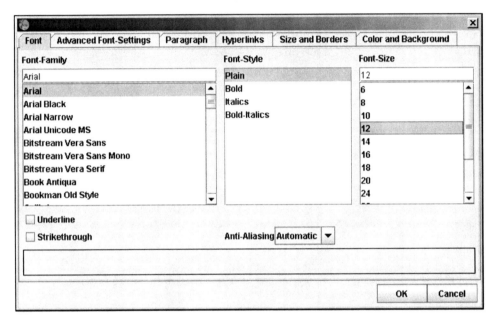

In addition to modifying the property, Pentaho Report Designer also provides a toolbar (shown in the following screen), where you can quickly modify the font name, size, and style.

Another way to configure fonts is using the property **Styles**. The following styles are available in relation to fonts:

Property name	Description
family	A string that represents the font type, for instance "Arial".
bold	If set to true, display the font in bold. For example, if the formula is set to "=TRUE()", the font will appear as bold.
embed	If this style equals true, embed the fonts included in the report, while rendering PDF.
encoding	A string that represents the character encoding of the font used in PDF output.
italics	If set to true, display the font in italic.
font-size	A number that represents the point size of the font.
smooth	If set to auto, fonts above 8 pts have anti-aliasing enabled. If set to always, all fonts have anti-aliasing enabled. Finally, if set to never, no fonts have anti-aliasing enabled.
strike through	If set to true, display the font with a strikethrough.

Additional font-related issues may arise if a report is designed in one operating system environment and published in other. For instance, Windows XP and Windows Vista come with a different standard set of fonts than Solaris, Mac, and Linux systems. Pentaho Reporting does its best to match the correct font, but you should verify after publishing that font sizes and styles are still working as expected.

Considerations for different output formats

Depending on your output format, there may be differences in rendering your designed report. You'll cover some of the more common issues faced when rendering to various output formats. When developing your report, make sure to preview the report in the formats you plan to render, in order to avoid any surprises after publishing your report.

Cell output

When rendering to CSV, Excel, RTF, and in some respects to HTML, cell layout becomes an important issue. The Pentaho Reporting Engine does its best to determine the most appropriate cell layout for your report, but certain best practices are necessary to ensure a nice looking report.

Alignment of elements is critical when dealing with cell output. Make sure all horizontal and vertical alignments are accurate. Even with subtle differences in horizontal or vertical locations, the report-to-cell-rendering algorithm can experience difficulties.

The following screenshot shows an illustrative example. The elements in the report aren't properly aligned.

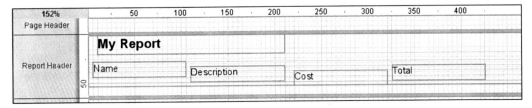

This is how the report will look in Excel:

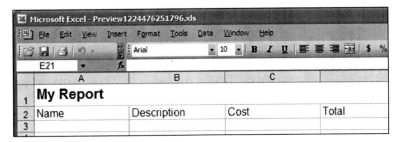

Notice how additional cells appear before the labels. The following screenshot shows a report where the elements are properly aligned.

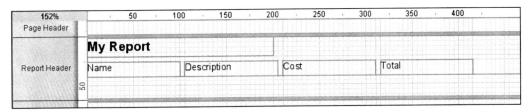

This is how the Excel output will look:

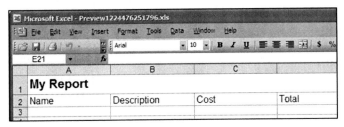

Another consideration when working with cell-based report generators is element overlap. Elements that overlap with one another will not render correctly, so it is important to avoid overlaps.

Paging

Certain output formats such as HTML, CSV, RTF, and Excel Output, treat the report (no matter how long the report is) as a single page. Use the page header and footer with the knowledge that many output types will not render identically.

In relation to paging, Excel output offers the ability to treat sheets as pages, as long as explicit page breaks are specified in the report bands using the **page-break-before** and **page-break-after** style attributes.

Limits to rich graphics and charts

While certain formats such as Excel, HTML, and PDF support images and charts, others such as CSV, Text, and RTF do not have the capability of embedding these rich elements. Keep that in mind when designing your reports.

Certain graphical elements such as ellipses do not render in most formats. Always verify how a report looks by previewing in the expected format!

Summary

In this chapter, you explored in-depth the ins and outs of design and layout of reports using the Pentaho Report Designer. You first learned about the various user interface components that make up the Report Designer. From there, you dove deep into each reporting band and its properties. You learned that each band may be accessed via the tree structure, and each band may display in the canvas as well as offering properties in the property editor.

You then received an exhaustive look at all the report elements. The chapter introduced you to the common properties seen throughout all the elements, along with displaying the dialogs that the various attributes present when editing. You also walked through utilizing the Menu, Toolbar, Canvas, and Shortcut keys to quickly arrange and layout your report. This included introducing shortcuts that make it easy to align and distribute groups of elements.

Finally, the chapter touched on additional details when dealing with fonts, along with common issues when dealing with the various output formats that Pentaho Reporting supports.

5
Working with Data Sources

In this chapter, you'll work with various methods for loading data into the Pentaho Reporting Engine, and dig deep into how the Pentaho Reporting Engine interacts with these data sources to render a report.

In the second chapter, you learned how to create a static data source right within Pentaho Report Designer. In the third chapter, you created a SQL data source using Hypersonic.

Additional data sources are available within Pentaho Report Designer, including XML XPath, Pentaho Metadata, Multi-Dimensional Expression queries, Pentaho Data Integration transformations, as well as scriptable data sources. At present, for all other data sources, including Hibernate, code is required to set up and configure the data source.

With the flexibility of Pentaho Reporting, you'll learn with the help of examples how to embed the included `DataFactory` implementations in your environment. You will also learn the details of the Pentaho Reporting Engine Data API specification, allowing you to implement your own `DataFactory`, if necessary.

Pentaho Reporting Engine Data API

The Pentaho Reporting Engine data API is a simple API that describes how Pentaho Reporting accesses data to populate reports. In this section, you'll learn about the core interfaces of the API. All the individual implementations discussed later in this chapter implement this API.

There are two main Java interfaces related to the Pentaho Reporting Engine Data API. The first interface you'll learn about is `org.pentaho.reporting.engine.classic.core.DataFactory`. The primary purpose of the `DataFactory` interface is to generate an object that implements the `javax.swing.table.TableModel` interface. The `TableModel` interface is a very simple API for accessing two-dimensional cell data. These two simple APIs are combined to manage all data input into Pentaho Reporting.

The DataFactory interface

The DataFactory interface defines seven methods, discussed in this section. The first method is queryData:

```
TableModel queryData(final String query, final DataRow parameters)
        throws ReportDataFactoryException;
```

The queryData method is called by the reporting engine to load a TableModel object. This is the main factory method. Both a query name and a set of parameters are passed to the DataFactory.

On a master report, the following built-in parameters are provided:

::org.pentaho. reporting::query-limit	The maximum number of resulting rows to be returned. If set to zero, returns all rows.
::org.pentaho. reporting::query-timeout	The maximum time to wait for a query to return. If set to zero, no timeout should be used.

Also, any parameters specified in the report definition file are available as part of the DataRow parameters object. If the query is used as part of a sub-report, parameters passed into the sub-report from the master report are made available as well.

If there is a problem executing the query, the implementer may throw a ReportDataFactoryException, which will be properly handled by the reporting engine.

The second method is derive:

```
DataFactory derive()
        throws ReportDataFactoryException;
```

The derive method creates a new DataFactory that should be independent of the parent DataFactory. Often times, this is simply making a call to the clone() method of the DataFactory implementation.

The third method is open:

```
void open() throws ReportDataFactoryException;
```

The open method is called during the initialization process, allowing the DataFactory to initialize if necessary.

The fourth method is close:

```
void close();
```

The `close` method is called once processing of all the `TableModel` interfaces generated by this `DataFactory` is complete.

The fifth method of the DataFactory API is `canExecuteQuery`:

```
Boolean canExecuteQuery(String query, DataRow parameters);
```

The `canExecuteQuery` method returns true if the `DataFactory` contains the named query.

The sixth method of the DataFactory API is `getQueryNames`:

```
String[] getQueryNames();
```

The `getQueryNames` method returns a list of available query names the `DataFactory` interface is currently aware of.

The seventh and final method of the DataFactory API is `cancelRunningQuery`:

```
void cancelRunningQuery();
```

If supported by the implementing `DataFactory`, the `cancelRunningQuery` method call will cancel the currently executing query of the `DataFactory`.

The ContextAwareDataFactory interface

The `org.pentaho.reporting.engine.classic.core ContextAwareDataFactory` is an extension of `DataFactory`, which also adds the following method for initialization:

```
public void initialize(Configuration configuration,
               ResourceManager resourceManager,
               ResourceKey contextKey,
               ResourceBundleFactory resourceBundleFactory);
```

The `initialize` method provides the `DataFactory` with access to the reporting engine's `ResourceManager`, allowing the `DataFactory` to access resources it may need to load properly. The `ResourceManager` class is the same class that is used to load a report from the file system.

The TableModel interface

The `javax.swing.table.TableModel` interface is part of the Java Platform API. Pentaho Reporting uses the `TableModel` interface to access the two-dimensional data necessary to render a report. Portions of the `TableModel` interface are not used within the Pentaho Reporting Engine. Specifically, the following four methods are not used:

```
public boolean isCellEditable(int rowIndex, int columnIndex);
public void setValueAt(Object aValue, int rowIndex, int columnIndex);
public void addTableModelListener(TableModelListener l);
public void removeTableModelListener(TableModelListener l);
```

All of the unused methods are related to updating a `TableModel`. The Pentaho
Reporting Engine uses the `TableModel` interface in a read-only fashion, so these
methods are not applicable. The following four methods are utilized by the
reporting engine:

```
public int getRowCount();
```

The `getRowCount` method returns the number of rows the `TableModel` contains.

```
public int getColumnCount();
```

The `getColumnCount` method returns the number of columns the
`TableModel` contains.

```
public String getColumnName(int columnIndex);
```

The `getColumnName` method returns the column name of the specified
column index.

```
public Object getValueAt(int rowIndex, int columnIndex);
```

The `getValueAt` method returns a particular cell of data based on the
specified row and column index. This is the main method for retrieving
information from the `TableModel` instance.

To implement your own Java data source for the Pentaho Reporting Engine, all you
need to do is implement the `DataFactory` and `TableModel` interfaces. But most
likely, you will be able to take advantage of one of the many existing `DataFactory`
implementations to load your data.

DataFactory serialization

In addition to these core interfaces, the Data API also defines interfaces and base
implementations for serializing and de-serializing `DataFactory` implementations.
This makes it possible for a user to define a data source in a client tool, and
have that information available to the reporting engine during execution of the
report on the server. The related interfaces for this portion of the API are the
`DataFactoryReadHandler` and `DataFactoryWriteHandler`.

Additional data source metadata

As an extension to the `TableModel`, the Pentaho Reporting Engine provides the `MetaTableModel` interface. `MetaTableModel` defines an API to access additional metadata that might be available as part of the data source. Examples of additional metadata might be font or style information. One example of this in use is the `BandedMDXDataFactory` implementation. Chapter 12 includes a tutorial on writing your own `MetaTableModel` implementation.

Existing DataFactory implementations

The following `DataFactory` implementations are made available as part of the Pentaho Reporting Engine. In this section, you'll learn about the nine commonly used `DataFactory` implementations, including a working example of each `DataFactory`. Before you begin the examples, create a new folder called `chapter5`, and copy over JAR files in the `lib` folder from Chapter 2 into `chapter5/lib`. Also, copy the `chapter2_report.prpt` into the `chapter5/data` folder.

TableDataFactory

The `org.pentaho.reporting.engine.classic.core.TableDataFactory` class is the simplest form of a `DataFactory` for loading data into the Pentaho Reporting Engine. The `TableDataFactory` manages a set of existing `TableModel` instances and makes them available to the reporting engine. Behind the scenes, the `TableDataFactory` was used in Chapter 2. If you were to implement the same capability in code, you would need to define the `TableDataFactory` explicitly. To construct a `TableDataFactory`, you can either use the default constructor or the following convenience constructor:

```
public TableDataFactory(final String name,
                        final TableModel tableModel);
```

This convenience constructor adds a `TableModel` instance with a particular name to the list of `TableModel` instances that the `TableDataFactory` is aware of. The other method for adding `TableModel` instances to the `TableDataFactory` is via the following API call:

```
public void addTable(final String name, final TableModel tableModel);
```

The `addTable` method adds an additional table to the list of named `TableModel` instances, which are maintained by the `TableDataFactory`.

While there is no CSV `DataFactory` defined, a helper class named `CSVTableModelProducer` is available, which is located in the `org.pentaho.reporting.engine.classic.core.modules.misc.tablemodel` package. This `CSVTableModelProducer` class will generate another class `CSVTableModel`, which you could then add to a `TableDataFactory`.

NamedStaticDataFactory

The `org.pentaho.reporting.engine.classic.core.modules.misc.datafactory.NamedStaticDataFactory` class allows you to use your own method of loading a `TableModel` to populate your report. There are various ways to configure the factory. First, you must implement the `TableModel` interface, and then either tell the factory to instantiate the `TableModel` implementation directly or through a specified factory class. You may want to use this over the `TableDataFactory` to avoid writing any directly linking code to the Pentaho Reporting Engine API, or if you already have a `TableModel` defined that you want to reuse for reporting.

`NamedStaticDataFactory` is often used when you would like to specify the construction of a `TableModel` or its factory within the report configuration. `NamedStaticDataFactory` is available in the Pentaho Report Designer as the **Named Java Method Invocation** data source. You must add your classes to Report Designer's classpath to enable previewing. You can do this by placing your JAR file in Report Designer's `lib` folder. Report Designer will automatically add the JAR file to the classpath.

Query syntax

The `NamedStaticDataFactory` accepts a specific syntax for its query. The syntax includes a fully-qualified class name, constructor parameters if necessary, followed by an optional method name and method parameters. The fully-qualified class name provided may either implement `TableModel`, or return a table model with the provided method call. Here is the exactly expected syntax:

```
<full-qualified-class-name>
<constructor-parameters>?('#'<method-name><method-parameters>?)?
```

Method parameters are passed in as `DataRow` parameters. All specified parameters in the query definition must be available in the `DataRow` object, which is provided during the `queryData` API call.

NamedStaticDataFactory example

In this example, you'll define a simple TableModel called ExampleTableModel, along with a factory class called ExampleFactory, in order to demonstrate the use of NamedStaticDataFactory. The ExampleTableModel class uses the data from Chapter 2, and can be constructed to return either a list of all the example JAR files or just the example library JAR files. Create the following ExampleTableModel.java file in the chapter5/src folder:

```java
import java.util.Vector;
import javax.swing.table.DefaultTableModel;
public class ExampleTableModel extends DefaultTableModel {
    Object data[][] = new Object[][] {
            {"LibBase","Library containing common functions",121745},
            {"LibLoader","Loading and caching library",122900},
            {"LibSerializer","Java serialization utility library",
                25689},
            {"LibRepository","Hierarchical storage library",63655},
            {"LibXml","Xml utility library",72896},
            {"LibFormula","Implementation of OpenFormula",368263},
            {"LibFonts","Font utility library",248320},
            {"LibDocBundle","Zip bundle library",71186},
            {"LibFormat","String formatting library",69464},
            {"Report Engine Core","Base report engine",3375047},
            {"Report Engine Extensions",
                "Group of common extensions",92335}
    };
    Object columnNames[] = new Object[] {"Library Name",
                        "Library Description", "Library Size"};
    public Vector<Vector<Object>> generateData() {
            Vector<Vector<Object>> v = new Vector<Vector<Object>>();
            for (int i = 0; i < data.length; i++) {
                    Vector<Object> r = new Vector<Object>();
                    for (int j = 0; j < data[i].length; j++) {
                            r.add(data[i][j]);
                    }
                    v.add(r);
            }
            return v;
    }
    public Vector<Object> getColumnNames() {
            Vector<Object> names = new Vector<Object>();
            for (int i = 0; i < columnNames.length; i++) {
                    names.add(columnNames[i]);
            }
            return names;
```

```
        }
        public ExampleTableModel() {
                super();
                setDataVector(data, columnNames);
        }
        public ExampleTableModel(boolean libsOnly) {
                super();
                if (libsOnly) {
                        Vector<Vector<Object>> vData = generateData();
                        vData.remove(vData.size() - 1);
                        vData.remove(vData.size() - 1);
                        setDataVector(vData, getColumnNames());
                } else {
                        setDataVector(data, columnNames);
                }
        }
}
```

You can now use the following two strings to instantiate this `TableModel` for your report, instantiating the two constructors you defined in earlier sections:

```
ExampleTableModel
ExampleTableModel(true)
```

In addition to constructing a `TableModel` directly, you can also use a factory class to instantiate the `TableModel`. Here is the example `ExampleFactory`, which simply generates either a fully populated `ExampleTableModel` or one limited to just the example libraries. Create the `ExampleFactory.java` file in the `chapter5/src` folder, as shown next:

```
public class ExampleFactory {
    public ExampleTableModel getAllData() {
            return new ExampleTableModel();
    }

    public ExampleTableModel getLibData(boolean libOnly) {
            return new ExampleTableModel(libOnly);
    }
}
```

You can now load the `TableModel` using the following syntax:

```
ExampleFactory#getAllData
ExampleFactory#getLibData(true)
```

Now that you've defined your example `TableModel` and factory class, you can use `NamedStaticDataFactory` to instantiate these objects. First, copy `Chapter2SwingApp.java` from Chapter 2 and rename it to `chapter5/src/NamedStaticDataFactoryApp.java`, also renaming the class definition in the file to `NamedStaticDataFactoryApp`. Using the example code you created in Chapter 2, add the following load data section to the `onPreview` method within the `NamedStaticDataFactoryApp` class, right below loading the report object and before instantiating the `PreviewDialog`:

```
// load data
NamedStaticDataFactory factory = new NamedStaticDataFactory();
factory.setQuery("default", "ExampleFactory#getAllData");
report.setDataFactory(factory);
```

This code overrides the report's data source with the `NamedStaticDataFactory`. Note that you named the master report's data source `default` earlier in Chapter 2. Also, make sure to add the following import at the beginning of the file:

```
import org.pentaho.reporting.engine.classic.core.modules.misc.
datafactory.NamedStaticDataFactory;
```

Finally, you'll need to copy the `build.xml` file from Chapter 2 into the `chapter5` folder. Add the following Ant target to the build file:

```
<target name="runstatic" depends="compile">
    <java fork="true" classpathref="runtime_classpath"
                            classname="NamedStaticDataFactoryApp"/>
</target>
```

Now, type `ant runstatic` on the command line to view the results.

SQLReportDataFactory

The `org.pentaho.reporting.engine.classic.core.modules.misc.datafactory.sql.SQLReportDataFactory` class allows you to easily use JDBC and SQL to populate your reports. In Chapter 3, the `SQLReportDataFactory` was used behind the scenes.

To set up the `SQLReportDataFactory` correctly in your environment, you first need to create an instance of `ConnectionProvider`. Three `ConnectionProvider` implementations are available for use. The `ConnectionProvider` interface and three implementations are available in the same package as `SQLReportDataFactory`. The `ConnectionProvider` interface defines a single `getConnection` method, which should return a JDBC connection for `SQLReportDataFactory` to use when generating a result set to populate a report.

StaticConnectionProvider

The first implementation of `ConnectionProvider` is the `StaticConnectionProvider` class, which takes in an existing `java.sql.Connection` object as part of its constructor:

```
ConnectionProvider connectionProvider = new StaticConnectionProvider
                                        (existingConnection);
```

DriverConnectionProvider

The second implementation of `ConnectionProvider` is the `DriverConnectionProvider` class, which allows you to easily configure a connection. It is recommended to avoid using `DriverConnectionProvider`, as it will create a new connection to the underlying database every time the `getConnection` method is called on the API. The `DriverConnectionProvider` has a default constructor, and must be configured via setter methods that are provided below:

```
void setDriver(String driver);
```

The `setDriver` method's driver value should be set to the fully qualified name of the driver class used in JDBC.

```
void setUrl(String url);
```

The `setUrl` method's URL value should be set to the JDBC URL for connecting to a database.

```
void setProperty(String name, String value);
```

The `setProperty` method adds an additional property to the JDBC configuration properties. Properties such as username and password are often passed in through the properties list for a new connection to be generated via `java.sql.DriverManager`. Make sure to include the JDBC driver JAR file in your Java classpath when using `DriverConnectionProvider`.

JndiConnectionProvider

The third available `ConnectionProvider` is the `JndiConnectionProvider`. The `JndiConnectionProvider` uses **Java's Naming and Directory Interface (JNDI)** to obtain a connection to a database. The `JndiConnectionProvider` has a default constructor, along with the following setter methods that may be configured to connect to a JNDI data source. Only the connection path property is mandatory:

```
void setConnectionPath(String connectionPath);
```

The `setConnectionPath` method should be set to the full JNDI path of your JDBC data source. Examples of JNDI paths are provided later in this section.

```
void setUsername(String username);
```

The `setUsername` method is an optional field, which may be required when connecting to your data source.

```
void setPassword(String password);
```

The `setPassword` method is an optional field, which may be required when connecting to your data source.

JNDI is available in many application servers. It may also be used in a regular Java application with the help of Simple JNDI, available at `http://www.osjava.org/simple-jndi`. The following table shows the examples of JNDI connection strings in different environments, assuming that you've already configured the JNDI data sources in that environment:

Tomcat	`java:comp/env/jdbc/<DataSourceName>`
JBoss	`java:<DataSourceName>`
Simple JNDI	`No Standard, configurable to match other containers`

Once a `ConnectionProvider` has been created, it's now time to set up a `SQLReportDataFactory` instance. The `SQLReportDataFactory` contains two constructors. The first constructor takes a `ConnectionProvider`. The second constructor takes an existing `Connection`, which uses the `StaticConnectionProvider` under the hood to provide the connection.

In addition to configuring the `ConnectionProvider`, you also must provide `SQLReportDataFactory` with queries to execute. Use the `setQuery` method to configure named queries:

```
void setQuery(final String name, final String queryString)
```

The `setQuery` method takes in the name of the query and the SQL query itself. As mentioned earlier, the master report in the examples in this chapter use the name "default" to reference the main query.

To incorporate report parameters into the query, you may specify variables with the following format in your SQL:

```
${<PARAMETER NAME>}
```

A `PreparedStatement` is generated, and these variables are parameterized appropriately via the JDBC specification, in order to avoid potential SQL injection attacks. In addition to traditional SQL statements, you may also make a call to a SQL stored procedure. These calls begin with the string "call", and are recognized by the `SQLReportDataFactory` so that the correct JDBC API method is executed.

As mentioned earlier, the Query Limit and Query Timeout parameters made available to all `DataFactory` instances also apply to the `SQLReportDataFactory`. These values are passed on to the `Connection` object. Therefore, the underlying JDBC driver must also support these properties to have an effect.

SQLReportDataFactory example

In this example, you'll define a `SQLReportDataFactory` to populate your report. First, you'll need to define a file-based HSQLDB data source, similar to the data source defined in Chapter 3. Place the library data in a tab delimited file, or use the provided `libraries.txt` tab delimited file. Copy this file into the `chapter5/data` folder. Now, create the `data/libraryinfo.script` file with a simple HSQLDB text table:

```
CREATE SCHEMA PUBLIC AUTHORIZATION DBA
CREATE TEXT TABLE LIBRARYINFO(NAME VARCHAR,DESCRIPTION VARCHAR,
                             SIZE INTEGER)
SET TABLE LIBRARYINFO SOURCE "libraries.txt;fs=\t;ignore_first=true"
CREATE USER SA PASSWORD ""
GRANT DBA TO SA
```

Now that you've defined the data source, make sure to place the `hsqldb.jar` file, located in Pentaho Report Designer's `lib` folder, in the `chapter5/lib` folder. You're now ready to add the embedded data source code. As in the earlier example, add the following load data section to the `onPreview` method, within a freshly copied `Chapter2SwingApp`, which would be renamed to `SQLReportDataFactoryApp`:

```
// load report sql data
DriverConnectionProvider provider = new DriverConnectionProvider();
provider.setDriver("org.hsqldb.jdbcDriver");
provider.setProperty("user", "sa");
provider.setProperty("pass", "");
provider.setUrl("jdbc:hsqldb:file:data/libraryinfo");
SQLReportDataFactory dataFactory = new SQLReportDataFactory(provider);
String sqlQuery = "SELECT * FROM LIBRARYINFO";
dataFactory.setQuery("default", sqlQuery);
report.setDataFactory(dataFactory);
```

Also, make sure to add the following imports at the beginning of the file:

```
import org.pentaho.reporting.engine.classic.core.modules.misc.
datafactory.sql.DriverConnectionProvider;
import org.pentaho.reporting.engine.classic.core.modules.misc.
datafactory.sql.SQLReportDataFactory;
```

Due to the naming of column headers in the HSQLDB database, you must also modify the sample report. Copy `chapter2_report.prpt` to `chapter5/data/sql_report.prpt`, and change the following referenced field names in Pentaho Report Designer:

- `Library Name` to `NAME`
- `Library Description` to `DESCRIPTION`
- `Library Size` to `SIZE`

Also change the Total Library Size function's **Field Name** to `SIZE`. Once you've saved your changes, update the `SQLReportDataFactoryApp` class with the new location of the report PRPT file.

Finally, you'll need to add the following Ant target to your `build.xml` file:

```
<target name="runsql" depends="compile">
    <java fork="true" classpathref="runtime_classpath"
                          classname="SQLReportDataFactoryApp"/>
</target>
```

Type `ant runsql` on the command line to verify the results.

XPathDataFactory

The `org.pentaho.reporting.engine.classic.extensions.datasources.xpath.XPathDataFactory` class allows you to populate your report based on XML data, provided that it is formatted in a specific way. This `DataFactory` accepts XML formatted as rows and columns, where the XPath expression returns a list of row elements that contain column elements. Each column element's node name represents the column name, and each column's text data represents the column's value. An example of a row supported by `XPathDataFactory` might be:

```
<Row>
    <Column1>Row 1 Data In Column 1</Column1>
    <Column2>Row 1 Data In Column 2</Column2>
</Row>
```

By default, column values are typed as Java Strings. The `XPathDataFactory` provides a mechanism to specify certain Java data types, including the following:

- `java.lang.String`
- `java.sql.Date`

- `java.math.BigDecimal`
- `java.sql.Timestamp`
- `java.lang.Integer`
- `java.lang.Double`
- `java.lang.Long`

These types can be specified in the XML as either a preprocessor step or a comment:

Preprocessor step	`<?pentaho-dataset java.lang.Integer, java.lang.String?>`
Root document comment	`<!-- java.lang.Integer, java.lang.String -->`
Root <result-set> comment	`<!-- java.lang.Integer, java.lang.String -->`

The column types should appear in the same order as the elements in the first row. Beyond the first row, the order of columns is not relevant. The names of the columns will be used to place them in the correct position of the generated `TableModel`. The `java.sql.Date` and `java.sql.Timestamp` classes both require a long numeric value corresponding to milliseconds since January 1, 1970, 00:00:00 GMT.

To create an `XPathDataFactory`, use the default constructor. To configure the `XPathDataFactory`, you must specify an XML file, along with a set of XPath queries. For a good introduction to XPath, please see `http://www.w3.org/TR/xpath`.

The `XPathDataFactory` uses Pentaho Reporting Engine's `ResourceManager` for loading the XPath file. To set the location of the XML file, use the `setXQueryDataFile` method:

```
void setXqueryDataFile(String filename);
```

Named queries may be added with the `setQuery` method:

```
Void setQuery(String name, String xpath);
```

One additional note, there is no standard way to easily sort row data via XPath, so be sure to have your data in the correct order before loading it with the `XPathDataFactory`. The inability to sort limits the capabilities of this `DataFactory`.

XPathDataFactory example

In this example, you'll create a compatible data source XML file, along with the necessary code to load the XML into your report. Save the following simple XML file as `chapter5/data/xpathexample.xml`:

```
<?xml version="1.0" encoding="UTF-8"?>
<?pentaho-dataset java.lang.String,java.lang.String,java.lang.Integer?>
<ExampleResultSet>
    <Row>
            <NAME>LibBase</NAME>
            <DESCRIPTION>Base library containing common functions
            </DESCRIPTION>
            <SIZE>113210</SIZE>
    </Row>
    <Row>
            <NAME>LibLoader</NAME>
            <DESCRIPTION>Loading and caching library</DESCRIPTION>
            <SIZE>53552</SIZE>
    </Row>
</ExampleResultSet>
```

Due to the verbosity of XML, this example is limited to a couple of rows. Once you've created the XML file, you need to deploy the correct extension JAR files to the `chapter5/lib` directory. Copy the `pentaho-reporting-engine-classic-extensions-xpath.jar` file, located in the Report Designer's `lib` folder, into the `chapter5/lib` folder.

Now, you're ready to write some code. As in the earlier examples, add the following load data section to the `onPreview` method within a freshly copied `Chapter2SwingApp`, renamed to `XPathDataFactoryApp`:

```
// load report xpath data
XPathDataFactory factory = new XPathDataFactory();
factory.setXqueryDataFile("file:data/xpathexample.xml");
factory.setQuery("default", "/ExampleResultSet/Row");
report.setDataFactory(factory);
```

Also, make sure to add the following import at the beginning of the file:

```
import org.pentaho.reporting.engine.classic.extensions.datasources.
xpath.XPathDataFactory;
```

Due to the naming of column headers in `XPathDataFactory` being mapped to the element node names in the XML file, you must also modify the sample report. Copy `chapter2_report.prpt` to `chapter5/data/xpath_report.prpt`, and change the referenced field names in Pentaho Report Designer, as shown in the following bullet list:

- `Library Name` to `NAME`
- `Library Description` to `DESCRIPTION`
- `Library Size` to `SIZE`

Also change the Total Library Size function's **Field Name** to `SIZE`. Once you've saved your changes, update the `XPathDataFactoryApp` class with the new location of the report PRPT file.

Finally, you'll need to add the following Ant target to your `build.xml` file:

```
<target name="runxpath" depends="compile">
    <java fork="true" classpathref="runtime_classpath"
                             classname="XPathDataFactoryApp"/>
</target>
```

Type `ant runxpath` on the command line to verify the results.

HQLDataFactory

The `org.pentaho.reporting.engine.classic.extensions.datasources.hibernate.HQLDataFactory` class allows you to populate your report based on a Hibernate query. Hibernate is an open source relational persistence engine. Hibernate allows you to easily persist your Java objects to a database.

Much like many of the other `DataFactory` implementations, the `HQLDataFactory` is configured with information to connect to Hibernate, along with the ability to specify named queries. The `HQLDataFactory` API defines an interface called `SessionProvider`, which it uses to gain access to the current Hibernate `Session` object. The `SessionProvider` contains a single API method, `getSession()`, which returns an instance of `org.hibernate.Session`. There are two implemented versions of this session provider.

At this time, `HQLDataFactory` is not available as a data source within Pentaho Report Designer, so code is required to utilize Hibernate as a data source.

StaticSessionProvider

The StaticSessionProvider simply takes in an org.hibernate.Session object as a constructor parameter, making available the already existing Session object to the HQLDataFactory. This would be used if your system already has an initialized Hibernate session.

DefaultSessionProvider

The DefaultSessionProvider requires no constructor parameters, and uses the following API call to generate a SessionFactory from Hibernate:

```
sessionFactory = new Configuration().configure().
buildSessionFactory();
```

The created sessionFactory instance is used to create new sessions, which the HQLDataFactory uses to query Hibernate.

The HQLDataFactory provides two constructors. The first constructor takes in a SessionProvider, as described above. The second constructor simply takes in a Hibernate Session instance, which it uses to query Hibernate. This constructor uses a StaticSessionProvider, under the covers, to pass in the Session to HQLDataFactory.

Once you've instantiated your factory, you may add named queries to the factory by making the following API call:

```
void setQuery(String name, String queryString);
```

The setQuery method takes in the name of the query, and the Hibernate query, in order to execute.

HQLDataFactory uses Hibernate's query language, which is well-documented at http://www.hibernate.org/hib_docs/reference/en/html/queryhql. html You may include report parameters in your query by using the HQL syntax ":ParameterName" The max results and query timeout parameters are supported by HQLDataFactory.

HQLDataFactory Example

To demonstrate using `HQLDataFactory`, you must first set up a simple Hibernate application. To begin, download the latest version of Hibernate from `http://www.hibernate.org`. This example uses version 3.2.6.ga. Place the `hibernate.jar` file and all the JAR files from the Hibernate distribution's `lib` folder into the `chapter5/lib` folder. You must also deploy the `pentaho-reporting-engine-classic-extensions-hibernate.jar` file, located in Pentaho Report Designer's `lib` folder, into the `chapter5/lib` folder.

In the `SQLReportDataFactory` example given earlier, you defined an HSQLDB data source. You'll reuse that data source in this example. Once you've moved the appropriate JAR files into Chapter 5, you'll need to define a simple Java class, `chapter5/src/LibraryInfo.java`, which maps to your HSQLDB data source:

```java
public class LibraryInfo {
    private String name;
    private String description;
    private long size;
    public LibraryInfo() {}
    public void setName(String name) {
        this.name = name;
    }
    public String getName() {
        return name;
    }
    public void setDescription(String description) {
        this.description = description;
    }
    public String getDescription() {
        return description;
    }
    public void setSize(long size) {
        this.size = size;
    }
    public long getSize() {
        return size;
    }
}
```

Define the Hibernate mapping between the HSQLDB database and the `LibraryInfo`
class, saved as `chapter5/src/LibraryInfo.hbm.xml`:

```
<?xml version="1.0"?>
<!DOCTYPE hibernate-mapping PUBLIC
        "-//Hibernate/Hibernate Mapping DTD 3.0//EN"
        "http://hibernate.sourceforge.net/hibernate-mapping-3.0.dtd">
<hibernate-mapping>
<class name="LibraryInfo" table="LIBRARYINFO">
    <id name="name" column="name" type="string"/>
    <property name="description" type="string"/>
    <property name="size" type="long"/>
</class>
</hibernate-mapping>
```

Now, you're ready to configure the Hibernate settings file with the appropriate
JDBC information and mapping input. Save the following as `chapter5/src/`
`hibernate.cfg.xml`:

```
<?xml version='1.0' encoding='utf-8'?>
<!DOCTYPE hibernate-configuration PUBLIC
        "-//Hibernate/Hibernate Configuration DTD 3.0//EN"
        "http://hibernate.sourceforge.net/hibernate-configuration-
3.0.dtd">
<hibernate-configuration>
    <session-factory>
        <property name="connection.driver_class">
                        org.hsqldb.jdbcDriver</property>
        <property name="connection.url">
                        jdbc:hsqldb:file:data/libraryinfo </property>
        <!-- SQL dialect -->
        <property name="dialect">org.hibernate.dialect.HSQLDialect
                        </property>

        <!-- Enable Hibernate's automatic session context management
-->
        <property name="current_session_context_class">
                        thread</property>

        <!-- Disable the second-level cache  -->
        <property name="cache.provider_class">
                        org.hibernate.cache.NoCacheProvider</property>

        <mapping resource="LibraryInfo.hbm.xml"/>
    </session-factory>
</hibernate-configuration>
```

At this point, you're ready to add a load data section to the `onPreview` method within a freshly copied `Chapter2SwingApp`, renamed to `HQLDataFactoryApp`:

```
// load hql data source

DefaultSessionProvider sessionProvider = new DefaultSessionProvider();
HQLDataFactory factory = new HQLDataFactory(sessionProvider);
factory.setQuery("default", "select name as NAME, description as
DESCRIPTION, size as SIZE from LibraryInfo");
report.setDataFactory(factory);
```

Be sure to add the following import statements at the beginning of the file:

```
import org.pentaho.reporting.engine.classic.extensions.datasources.
hibernate.DefaultSessionProvider;
import org.pentaho.reporting.engine.classic.extensions.datasources.
hibernate.HQLDataFactory;
```

Due to the naming of column headers in `HQLDataFactory` being mapped to the attributes of queried objects, you must also modify the sample report. Copy `chapter2_report.prpt` to `chapter5/data/hql_report.prpt`, and change the column names, as shown in the following list:

- `Library Name` to `NAME`
- `Library Description` to `DESCRIPTION`
- `Library Size` to `SIZE`

Also change the Total Library Size function's **Field Name** to `SIZE`. Once you've saved your changes, update the `HQLDataFactoryApp` class with the new location of the report XML file.

As the last step, you'll need to add the following Ant target to your `build.xml` file:

```
<target name="runhql" depends="compile">
    <java fork="true" classpathref="runtime_classpath"
                                    classname="HQLDataFactoryApp"/>
</target>
```

Type `ant runhql` on the command line to view the results!

PmdDataFactory

The `org.pentaho.reporting.engine.classic.extensions.datasources.pmd.`
`PmdDataFactory` class allows you to populate your report, using a Pentaho Metadata
Query. Pentaho Metadata allows a database administrator to define a business layer
of their relational data for end users, simplifying the ability to query the data, as
well as protecting users from the complexities that may exist in a database schema.
Pentaho's **Metadata Query Language (MQL)** is an XML-based query model that
simplifies querying databases, and is currently used within the Pentaho Report
Designer and Pentaho Web Ad Hoc Report client tools.

In order for `PmdDataFactory` to initialize properly, it must have access to certain
Pentaho Metadata configuration properties that can be configured at runtime, or
be passed in by a configuration file.

XMI file

The XMI file contains a serialized version of the defined metadata model, and
is required in order to execute MQL queries. The XMI file contains information
including how to connect to the relational data source, as well as the business
model mapping of the relational data. This file is loaded at runtime into the
configured repository of Pentaho Metadata. The XMI file may be configured by
calling the setXmiFile method. This file is loaded with Pentaho Reporting Engine's
`ResourceManager`.

Domain Id

The metadata domain id is used to map a name to the XMI file within the metadata
repository. This name is also referenced in the MQL query file. Therefore, it is
important to use the same name in the MQL query, as well as the `PmdDataFactory`.
The domain may be set by the setDomainId method.

IPmdConnectionProvider

`PmdDataFactory` uses the `IPmdConnectionProvider` interface to obtain the
metadata domain objects as well as the database connection for the query. The
`IPmdConnectionProvider` must be specified via the setConnectionProvider
method. A default implementation, `PmdConnectionProvider`, manages loading
the XMI file as well as determining the database connection to be used based on
metadata information provided in the XMI file. The `IPmdConnectionProvider`
defines the following methods:

```
// returns a connection object based on the relational data source
Connection gu8etConnection(DatabaseMeta databaseMeta) throws
ReportDataFactoryException;

// returns a metadata repository based on the domain id and xmi file

IMetadataDomainRepository getMetadataDomainRepository(String domain,
ResourceManager resourceManager, ResourceKey contextKey, String
xmiFile) throws ReportDataFactoryException;
```

Registering MQL Queries

Once you've configured the `PmdDataFactory` correctly, you need to provide named MQL queries via the `setQuery(String name, String query)` method. Please see `http://wiki.pentaho.com/display/ServerDoc2x/03.+Pentaho+Metadata+MQL+Schema` to learn more about the MQL query format.

PmdDataFactory example

To begin, you'll need to build a very simple Pentaho Metadata model. First, download Pentaho Metadata Editor from SourceForge: `http://sourceforge.net/projects/pentaho`. Click on the **Download** link, and select the Pentaho Metadata package. Download the latest "pme-ce" zip or tar distribution, depending on your operating system environment. For Windows, unzip the download, and run `metadata-editor.bat`. For Linux and Mac, untar the download and run `metadata-editor.sh`. From the main window, select **File | new Domain File...** Now, it's time to define your physical model. Right-click on the **Connections** tree item and select **New Connection...** Name the Connection **Library Info** and select **Hypersonic** as the connection type. Set the **Host Name** to **file:** and the **Database Name** to the full path to your example `libraryinfo.script` file minus the `.script` file extension. Set the **Port Number** to blank, and finally set the **username** to **sa** and **password** to blank.

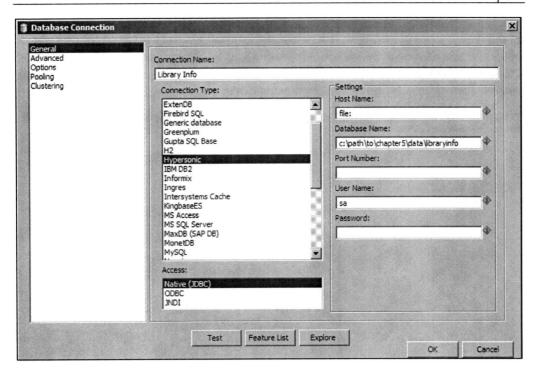

Click **Test** to make sure you are connected properly, and then click **OK**. This will
bring up an **Import Tables** dialog. Select **LIBRARYINFO** and click **OK**.

This will generate a default physical model. Now that you've defined the physical model, you'll need to build a business model. Right-click on **Business Models** and select the **New Business Model** menu item. Give this model the **ID** of **LIBRARYINFO_MODEL**, and select **Library Info** as the connection. Finally, under the **Settings** section, set the **Name** to **Library Info**.

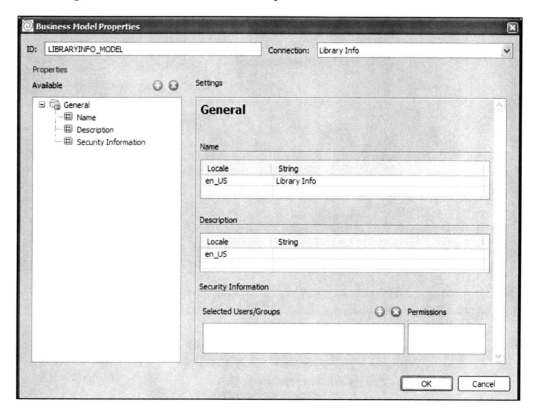

In the main window, drag-and-drop the **LIBRARYINFO** table from the **Library Info** connection into the **Business Tables** tree. This will bring up a new Business Table Properties dialog. Click **OK**. Double-click on the **Business View** tree element to bring up the **Manage Categories** dialog. Select the **LIBRARYINFO** business table and click the **Add** Arrow in between the two list boxes. This will create a new category with the same name as the business table.

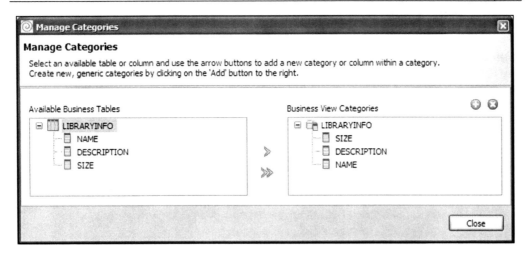

Once completed, the main Business Model Tree should look like this:

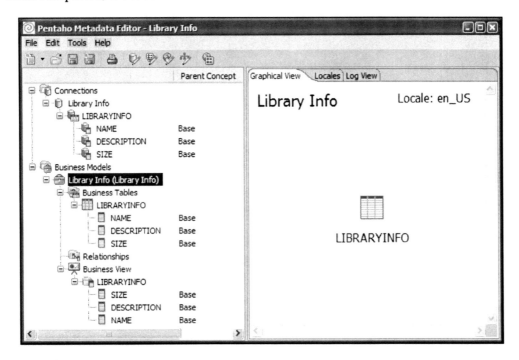

Now that you've defined your metadata model, export the model as an XMI file by selecting the **File | Export to XMI File...** menu item. First, you will be prompted to save the Domain file. Name the Domain **Library Info**. Finally, save your XMI file as `chapter5/data/libraryinfo.xmi`.

Once you've exported your metadata model, you must set up your environment with the necessary JAR files. Copy all the JAR files located in the `lib` and `lib-ext` folders from the Pentaho Metadata Editor distribution into the `chapter5/lib` folder. Also, copy the `pentaho-reporting-engine-classic-extensions-pmd.jar` file, located in the Pentaho Report Designer `lib` folder, into the `chapter5/lib` folder.

After copying the correct JAR files, go ahead and add a new load data section of the `onPreview` method within a freshly copied `Chapter2SwingApp`, renamed to `PmdDataFactoryApp`:

```
// load MQL data source

PmdDataFactory factory = new PmdDataFactory();
factory.setConnectionProvider(new PmdConnectionProvider());
factory.setXmiFile("data/libraryinfo.xmi");
factory.setDomainId("Library Info");
factory.setQuery("default",
    "<?xml version=\"1.0\" encoding=\"UTF-8\"?>" +
    "<mql>" +
    "       <domain_type>relational</domain_type>" +
    "       <domain_id>Library Info</domain_id>" +
    "       <model_id>LIBRARYINFO_MODEL</model_id>" +
    "       <model_name>Library Info</model_name>" +
    "       <selections>" +
    "            <selection>" +
    "                  <view>BC_LIBRARYINFO</view>" +
    "                  <column>BC_LIBRARYINFO_NAME</column>" +
    "            </selection>" +
    "            <selection>" +
    "                  <view>BC_LIBRARYINFO</view>" +
    "                  <column>BC_LIBRARYINFO_DESCRIPTION</column>" +
    "            </selection>" +
    "            <selection>" +
    "                  <view>BC_LIBRARYINFO</view>" +
    "                  <column>BC_LIBRARYINFO_SIZE</column>" +
    "            </selection>" +
    "       </selections>" +
    "</mql>");
```

Notice that MQL is in XML format. Much like your other queries, you've selected library name, description, and size from the data source.

Finally, make sure to add the following imports to the class:

```
import org.pentaho.reporting.engine.classic.extensions.datasources.
pmd.PmdDataFactory;
import org.pentaho.reporting.engine.classic.extensions.datasources.
pmd.PmdConnectionProvider;
```

Due to the built in naming of column headers in `PmdDataFactory`, you must also modify your sample report. Copy `chapter2_report.prpt` to `chapter5/data/pmd_report.prpt`, and change the column names as shown in the following list:

- `Library Name` to `BC_LIBRARYINFO_NAME`
- `Library Description` to `BC_LIBRARYINFO_DESCRIPTION`
- `Library Size` to `BC_LIBRARYINFO_SIZE`

Also change the Total Library Size function's **Field Name** to `BC_LIBRARYINFO_SIZE`. Once you've saved your changes, update the `PmdDataFactoryApp` class with the new location of the report PRPT file.

Finally, you'll need to add the following Ant target to the `build.xml` file:

```
<target name="runpmd" depends="compile">
   <java fork="true" classpathref="runtime_classpath"
                            classname="PmdDataFactoryApp"/>
</target>
```

Type `ant runpmd` on the command line to view the results!

You may also consider doing this example without the necessity of the load data section, by adding a **Metadata** data source to your report within Pentaho Report Designer.

KettleDataFactory

The `org.pentaho.reporting.engine.classic.extensions.datasources.kettle.KettleDataFactory` class allows you to populate your report from a Kettle transformation. **Kettle** is a data integration tool, also known as an ETL (Extract Transform and Load) tool. Kettle transformations support a multitude of data source inputs and transformation capabilities. Kettle, also known as Pentaho Data Integration, provides mechanisms to incorporate data from Excel, SQL, XML, Text, and many other data sources. It also provides the ability to combine the results into a single result set, which Pentaho Reporting can use to render a report.

To initialize `KettleDataFactory`, you must provide the location of the Kettle transformation to execute, along with the step within the transformation to use the data from. This is done via the `KettleTransformationProducer` interface. There are two provided implementations of `KettleTransformationProducer`. The first is `KettleTransFromFileProducer`, which loads a Kettle transformation from the file system. The `KettleTransFromFileProducer` class must be instantiated with the following parameters:

```
final String repositoryName, // the repository name
final String transformationFile, // the path of the tranformation file
to execute
final String stepName, // the step name to collect data from
final String username, // the repository user name
final String password, // the repository password
final String[] definedArgumentNames, // the names of reporting
properties to be passed into Kettle via Transformation Arguments
final ParameterMapping[] definedVariableNames // the names of
reporting properties to be passed into Kettle via Transformation
Parameters
```

The second implementation of `KettleTransformationProducer` is `KettleTransFromRepositoryProducer`. This loads the transformation from an existing Kettle Repository. The `kettleTransFromRepositoryProducer` class must be instantiated with the following parameters:

```
final String repositoryName, // the repository name
final String directoryName, // the repository directory
final String transformationName, // the transformation name in the
repository
final String stepName, // the step name to collect data from
final String username, // the repository user name
final String password, // the repository password
final String[] definedArgumentNames, // the names of reporting
properties to be passed into Kettle via Transformation Arguments
final ParameterMapping[] definedVariableNames // the names of
reporting properties to be passed into Kettle via Transformation
Parameters
```

The `KettleDataFactory` has a default constructor. To add Kettle transformation queries to the `KettleDataFactory`, call the `setQuery(String, KettleTransformationProducer)` method.

KettleDataFactory example

To start the example, you first need to build a Kettle transformation. Download Pentaho Data Integration 3.2 from SourceForge: http://sourceforge.net/projects/pentaho. Click on the **Download** link, and select the **Data Integration** package. Download the latest "pdi-ce" ZIP (compressed file), TAR, or DMG distribution, depending on your operating system environment. Install the distribution. To bring up the user interface, run Kettle.exe if you are a Windows user. For Linux and Mac users, run spoon.sh.

On Kettle's intro screen, select the button **No Repository**. Kettle allows you to store and manage your transformations in a central repository, but you won't be using that feature in this example.

In the main window, double-click on the **Transformations** folder to begin creating your first transformation. Drag-and-drop a **Table** input step from the step's **Input** folder into your transformation. Double-click on the new step to configure the Table input.

In the Table input dialog, first configure a new connection to your HSQLDB file-based database. Click the **New...** button next to the **Connection**.

In the **Database Connection** dialog, enter the **Connection Name** as **Library Info** and select **Hypersonic** as the **Connection Type**. Set the **Database Name** to the full path to your example, that is, libraryinfo.script file minus the .script file extension. Set the **Host Name** to **file:** and the **Port Number** to blank. Finally, set the **user name** to **sa** and **password** to blank.

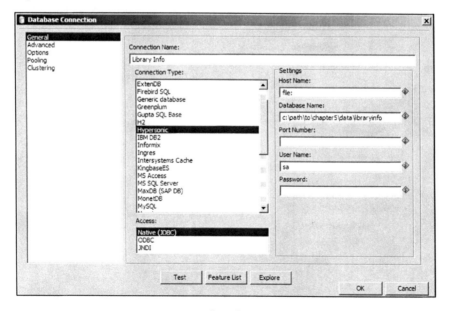

Once you've configured your connection, click the **Test** button to make sure it can connect successfully, and then click the **Explore** button and verify that the LIBRARYINFO table exists:

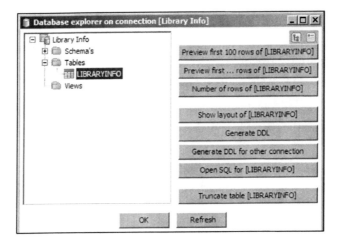

Now click the **OK** button to return to the **Table input** dialog.

Click the **Get SQL select statement...** button. This brings up the database explorer. Select the **LIBRARYINFO** table from the list of tables and click **OK**. An additional dialog should appear asking if you would like to include the field names in the SQL. Click the **Yes** button. Your **Table input** dialog should look like this:

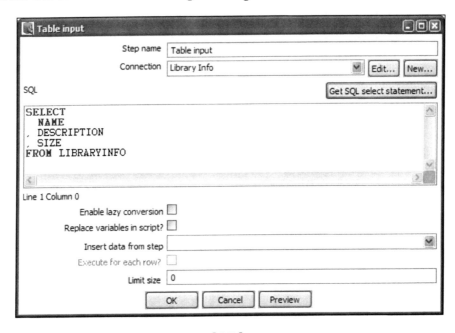

Click **OK** on the **Table input** dialog to update the transformation step. Finally, save your transformation as chapter5/data/libraryinfo.ktr.

Now that you've created your transformation file, it's time to set up the DataFactory. First, you must place the necessary JAR files into the chapter5/lib folder. You'll need to place all the JAR files located in Kettle's lib and libext folders into the chapter5/lib folder. Also, you'll need to place the pentaho-reporting-engine-classic-extensions-kettle.jar file, located in the Pentaho Report Designer lib folder, into the chapter5/lib folder as well.

This example also uses the libraryinfo.script and libraries.txt files you defined earlier, so make sure they are available in the chapter5/data folder. Now, you are ready to go ahead and add a new load data section to the onPreview method within a freshly copied Chapter2SwingApp, renamed to KettleDataFactoryApp:

```
// load Kettle data source

// Initialize Kettle
EnvUtil.environmentInit();
StepLoader.init();
JobEntryLoader.init();
// Build Data Factory
KettleTransFromFileProducer producer = new KettleTransFromFileProducer
("Embedded Repository", "data/libraryinfo.ktr", "Table input", "", "",
new String[0], new ParameterMapping[0]);
KettleDataFactory factory = new KettleDataFactory();
factory.setQuery("default", producer);
report.setDataFactory(factory);
```

StepLoader and JobLoader both may throw a KettleException, so you must also add the following catch block to the end of the onPreview method:

```
catch (KettleException e) {
    e.printStackTrace();
}
```

You must also add the following imports to complete the example:

```
import org.pentaho.di.core.exception.KettleException;
import org.pentaho.di.core.util.EnvUtil;
import org.pentaho.di.job.JobEntryLoader;
import org.pentaho.di.trans.StepLoader;
import org.pentaho.reporting.engine.classic.core.ParameterMapping;
import org.pentaho.reporting.engine.classic.extensions.datasources.
kettle.KettleTransFromFileProducer;
import org.pentaho.reporting.engine.classic.extensions.datasources.
kettle.KettleDataFactory;
```

Due to the names of column headers in this example, you must also modify your sample report. Copy `chapter2_report.prpt` to `chapter5/data/kettle_report.prpt`, and change the column names, as shown in the following bullet list:

- `Library Name` to `NAME`
- `Library Description` to `DESCRIPTION`
- `Library Size` to `SIZE`

Also change the Total Library Size function's **Field Name** to `SIZE`. Once you've saved your changes, update the `KettleDataFactoryApp` class with the new location of the report PRPT file.

Finally, you'll need to add the following Ant target to the `build.xml` file:

```
<target name="runkettle" depends="compile">
    <java fork="true" classpathref="runtime_classpath"
                              classname="KettleDataFactoryApp"/>
</target>
```

Type `ant runkettle` on the command line to view the results!

BandedMDXDataFactory

The `org.pentaho.reporting.engine.classic.extensions.datasources.olap4j.BandedMDXDataFactory` class allows you to populate your report from An `olap4j` data source. `olap4j` is a Java API for connecting to multi-dimensional **OLAP (Online Analytical Processing)** data sources. As of olap4j 0.9.7.145, there is a driver written for the Mondrian Relational OLAP Engine, as well as an **Extensible Markup Language for Analysis (XMLA)** driver implementation, which provides communication with Microsoft Analysis Services, along with other XMLA compatible OLAP services.

Natively, OLAP data sources support result sets with more than two axes. In a traditional result set used by Pentaho Reporting, there are column headers, along with rows of data. When using OLAP data, the data source needs to determine how to map the richer OLAP data into a standard `TableModel` data source.

With `BandedMDXDataFactory`, the factory maps the row and column axes of the OLAP result set to a `TableModel`. The column headers display the dimensions selected in the column axis. The rows show the row axis information selected. For instance, if a year was selected from the time dimension on the column axis, in the column header you would see the member name **[Time].[1997]**.

To learn more about olap4j and Mondrian's Relational OLAP engine, please visit `http://www.olap4j.org` and `http://mondrian.pentaho.org`.

To configure the `BandedMDXDataFactory`, you must first create an object that implements the `OlapConnectionProvider` interface. The `DriverConnectionProvider` provides an implementation. The `DriverConnectionProvider` contains a default constructor, and may be configured with the following methods:

```
void setDriver(String driver);
```

The `setDriver` method specifies the driver class to use.

```
void setURL(String url);
```

The `setURL` method specifies the URL the driver should connect to.

```
void setProperty(String name, String value);
```

The `setProperty` method specifies additional connection properties.

After creating a valid `OlapConnectionProvider`, pass that object into the `BandedMDXDataFactory` constructor. Once you've created the factory, you may add Multi-dimensional Expression (MDX) queries by calling the `setQuery (String name, String mdxQuery)` method.

BandedMDXDataFactory example

To begin this example, you first need to create a simple OLAP model that you can query. First, download Mondrian's Schema Workbench from the following SourceForge URL: `http://sourceforge.net/projects/mondrian`. Once you've unzipped the Schema Workbench, copy the `hsqldb.jar` into the `workbench/ drivers` folder. To bring up the main window, run `workbench.bat` in Windows, or run `workbench.sh` if you are a Mac or Linux user. Before you design an OLAP Model, first configure your relational data source. Select the menu item **Tools | Preferences**. Now, specify the necessary JDBC information. Set **org.hsqldb. jdbcDriver** for the **Driver Class Name** and **jdbc:hsqldb:file:c:\path\to\chapter5\ data\libraryinfo** for the **Connection URL**. Finally, set the **username** to **sa**, and the **password** to blank. Now, click the **Accept** button.

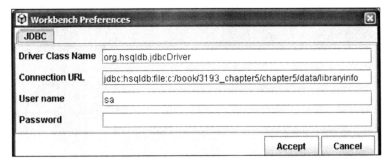

Select the menu item **File | New | Schema**. Right-click on the schema and select the **add Cube** menu item. Name the **Cube** as **Library Info**. Select the cube's Table tree node and set the **name** attribute of the Table to **Library Info**. This will act as your fact table. Now, right-click on the cube and select the **Add Dimension** menu item. Set the dimension name to **Library**. Because you're using the fact table for the dimension, also known as a degenerate dimension, there is no need for a foreign key. Right-click on the **Table** element within the **Hierarchy** and select the **Delete** menu item. This element is also not needed.

Right-click on the **Hierarchy** and select the **Add Level** menu item. Set the level's **name** attribute to Library Name, and the **column** attribute to NAME. Now, right-click on the level and select the **Add Property** menu item. Rename the property to LibDescription and set the **column** attribute to DESCRIPTION. Set the **type** attribute to **String**.

Finally, right-click on the **Library Info** cube again and select the **Add Measure** menu item. Set the measure's **name** to Size, and enter SIZE for the **column** attribute. Select **sum** for the **aggregator**.

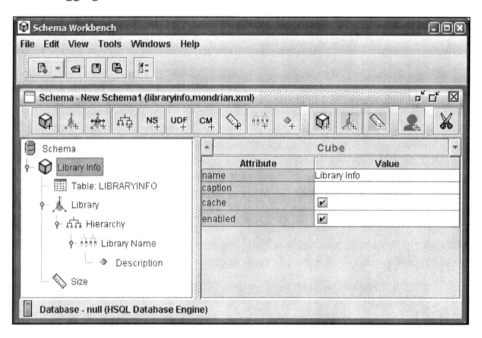

You're now done creating a very simple OLAP model. Go ahead and save this model to data/libraryinfo.mondrian.xml. Once saved, verify the model by selecting the menu item **File | New | MDX Query**, and typing in the following query:

```
WITH
MEMBER [Measures].[Name] AS '[Library].CurrentMember.Caption'
MEMBER [Measures].[Description] AS '[Library].CurrentMember.
Properties("LibDescription")'
select [Library].Children on rows, {[Measures].[Name], [Measures].[Des
cription], [Measures].[Size]} on columns from [Library Info]
```

Make sure results are returned.

Now that you have your OLAP schema file defined, you're ready to begin interfacing the OLAP data source with Pentaho Reporting. First, you must copy over the necessary JAR files. Place all the JAR files that exist in the workbench/lib folder in chapter5/lib folder. Also, place the pentaho-reporting-engine-classic-extensions-olap4j.jar and olap4j.jar files, found in Pentaho Reporting's lib folder, into the chapter5/lib folder.

Add the following load data section to the onPreview method within a freshly copied Chapter2SwingApp, renamed to BandedMDXDataFactoryApp:

```
// load olap data

DriverConnectionProvider provider = new  DriverConnectionProvider();
provider.setDriver("mondrian.olap4j.MondrianOlap4jDriver");
provider.setUrl("jdbc:mondrian: ");
provider.setProperty("Catalog", "data/libraryinfo.mondrian.xml");
provider.setProperty("JdbcUser", "sa");
provider.setProperty("JdbcPassword", "");
provider.setProperty("Jdbc", "jdbc:hsqldb:file:data/libraryinfo");
provider.setProperty("JdbcDrivers", "org.hsqldb.jdbcDriver");

// create the factory

BandedMDXDataFactory factory = new BandedMDXDataFactory(provider);

// add the MDX query

factory.setQuery("default", "WITH MEMBER [Measures].[Name] AS
'[Library].CurrentMember.Caption' MEMBER [Measures].[Description]
AS '[Library].CurrentMember.Properties(\"LibDescription\")'
select [Library].Children on rows, {[Measures].[Name], [Measures].
[Description], [Measures].[Size]} on columns from [Library Info]");

report.setDataFactory(factory);
```

You must also add the following imports to complete the example:

```
import  org.pentaho.reporting.engine.classic.extensions.datasources.
olap4j.DriverConnectionProvider;
import  org.pentaho.reporting.engine.classic.extensions.datasources.
olap4j.BandedMDXDataFactory;
```

Due to the built in naming of column headers in `BandedMDXDataFactory`, you must also modify your sample report. Copy the `chapter2_report.prpt` to `chapter5/data/banded_mdx_report.prpt`, and change the column names as shown in the following bullet list:

- `Library Name` to `[Measures].[Name]`
- `Library Description` to `[Measures].[Description]`
- `Size` to `[Measures].[Size]`

Also change the Total Library Size function's **Field Name** to `[Measures].[Size]`. Once you've saved your changes, update `BandedMDXDataFactoryApp` with the correct PRPT file to load. Finally, you'll need to add the following Ant target to the `build.xml` file:

```
<target name="runmdx" depends="compile">
    <java fork="true" classpathref="runtime_classpath"
                         classname="BandedMDXDataFactoryApp"/>
</target>
```

Type `ant runmdx` on the command line to view the results.

 You may also consider doing this example without the necessity of the load data section, by adding an **olap4j** data source to your report within Pentaho Report Designer.

DenormalizedMDXDataFactory

The `org.pentaho.reporting.engine.classic.extensions.datasources.olap4j.DenormalizedMDXDataFactory` class queries an `olap4j` data source in a similar fashion as the `BandedMDXDataFactory`. The only difference is the mapping from OLAP to a two-dimensional result set.

The `DenormalizedMDXDataFactory` maps all the axes of the OLAP result set to a `TableModel`, in a denormalized or flattened fashion. The column headers display the dimensional metadata selected in the axes, as well as the measure metadata selected. For instance, if a year was selected from the time dimension, in the column header you would see the level name **[Time].[Year]**. `DenormalizedMDXDataFactory` is often used with crosstabs, and will be used again in Chapter 8.

CompoundDataFactory

The `org.pentaho.reporting.engine.classic.core.CompoundDataFactory` class is a useful factory when working with sub-reports that contain different data sources than the primary report. For instance, with `CompoundDataFactory`, you may use a `SQLReportDataFactory` for your master report query, as well as an `XPathDataFactory` for a sub-report query. The `CompoundDataFactory` has a default constructor, and you may add child data factories by calling the `add(DataFactory)` or `add(index, DataFactory)` methods. `DataFactory` instances are queried in the order of their index.

All reports generated by the Report Designer use the `CompoundDataFactory`, making it possible for users to add different types of data sources to their report in the user interface.

Experimental data factories

Additionally, there are community contributed `DataFactory` implementations that are available. Two examples include the `XQJReportDataFactory`, which uses the `javax.xml.xquery` API to query XML database data sources, as well as the `ScriptableDataFactory`, which uses the Bean Scripting Framework to execute query scripts in different scripting languages that return a `TableModel` implementation.

Accessing data throughout a report

Once you've configured your `DataFactory` implementation, it is important to know how to access this data within a report. As mentioned in the previous chapter, elements that contain the field name property access row data via the column headers provided by the data source. In addition to accessing the fields directly, you may also access this data in functions and formulas.

Functions in Pentaho Reporting will contain a property named "Field" or "Fields" that allow you to select a list of fields from the defined data source. To reference a field in a formula, you will need to place brackets around the field name. An example reference to a field name in a formula might be "[Library Description]".

When using a `DataFactory` that isn't supported directly in the Report Designer such as the Hibernate `HQLDataFactory`, you will need to manually type in the name of the fields into the Report Designer. Another issue with using non-supported `DataFactory` classes in the Report Designer is that the report preview won't be available for use. One strategy to avoid these issues is to build a sample dataset, which contains the identical column headers in a Report Designer supported `DataFactory` implementation, in order to verify that reports look as expected.

Summary

In this chapter, you were introduced to the Pentaho Reporting Engine Data API. The Data API provides a rich, easy-to-implement mechanism for providing data to a report. The `DataFactory` interface, along with the `TableModel` interface, make up the backbone of this API. Additional capabilities of this API include the ability to serialize connection information, as well as provide a richer set of metadata for result sets by using `MetaTableModel`.

Out of the box, the Pentaho Reporting Engine comes with a rich set of `DataFactory` implementations that make it possible to connect to practically any type of backend data, including Java Objects, JDBC, XML XPath, HQL, Pentaho Metadata, Pentaho Integration, and OLAP data sources.

Once you've configured access to your underlying data, it's simple to reference that data within your report, via report elements, functions, and formulas.

6

Including Charts and Graphics in Reports

In this chapter, you'll learn how to incorporate charts and graphics into Pentaho Reports. You'll learn about the different types of charts supported, and how to configure them in Pentaho Report Designer. You'll also learn how to populate a chart with various types of data.

In addition to learning all about charts, this chapter also covers the various methods for including visual information in your report, including embedding images and Java graphics in your report.

Supported charts

Pentaho Reporting relies on JFreeChart, an open source Java chart library, for charting visualization within reports. From within Report Designer, many chart types are supported. In the chart editor, two areas of properties appear when editing a chart. The first area of properties is related to chart rendering, and the second tabbed area of properties is related to the data that populates a chart.

Following is the screenshot of the chart editor within Pentaho Report Designer:

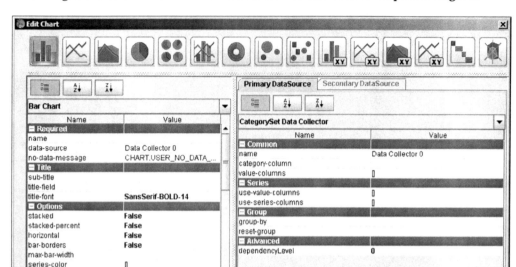

All chart types receive their data from three general types of datasets. The first type is known as a **Category Dataset**, where the dataset series and values are grouped by categories. A series is like a sub-group. If the exact category and series appear, the chart will sum the values into a single result. The following table is a simple example of a category dataset:

Category	Series	Sale Price
Store 1 Sales	Cash	$14
Store 1 Sales	Credit	$12
Store 2 Sales	Cash	$100
Store 2 Sales	Credit	$120

Pentaho Reporting builds a Category Dataset using the `CategorySetDataCollector`. Also available is the `PivotCategorySetCollector`, which pivots the category and series data. Collector classes implement Pentaho Reporting's Function API.

The second type of dataset is known as an **XY Series Dataset**, which is a two dimensional group of values that may be plotted in various forms. In this dataset, the series may be used to draw different lines, and so on. Here is a simple example of an XY series dataset:

Series	Cost of Goods (X)	Sale Price (Y)
Cash	10	14
Credit	11	12
Cash	92	100
Credit	105	120

Note that **X** is often referred to as the **domain**, and **Y** is referred to as the **range**. Pentaho Reporting builds an XY Series Dataset using the `XYSeriesCollector`. The `XYZSeriesCollector` also exists for three dimensional data.

The third type of dataset is known as a **Time Series Dataset**, which is a two dimensional group of values that are plotted based on a time and date. The Time Series Dataset is more like an XY Series than a Category Dataset, as the time scale is displayed in a linear fashion with appropriate distances between the different time references.

Time	Series	Sale Price
May 05, 2009 11:05pm	Cash	$14
June 07, 2009 12:42pm	Credit	$12
June 14, 2009 4:20pm	Cash	$100
June 01, 2009 1:22pm	Credit	$120

Pentaho Reporting builds a Time Series Dataset using the `TimeSeriesCollector`.

Common chart rendering properties

Most charts share a common set of properties. The following properties are common across most charts. Any exceptions are mentioned as part of the specific chart type.

Required Property Group	
Property name	**Description**
name	The name of the chart object within the report. This is not displayed during rendering, but must be unique in the report. A default name is generated for each chart added to the report.
data-source	The dataset name for the chart, which is automatically populated with the name of the dataset in the **Primary DataSource** panel of the chart editor.
no-data-message	The message to display if no data is available to render the chart.

Title Property Group

Property name	Description
chart-title	The title of the chart, which is rendered in the report.
chart-title-field	A field representing the chart title.
title-font	The chart title's font family, size, and style.

Options Property Group

Property name	Description
horizontal	If set to **True**, the chart's X and Y axis are rotated horizontally. The default value is set to **False**.
series-colors	The color in which to render each series. The default for the first three series colors are **red**, **blue**, and **green**.

General Property Group

Property name	Description
3-D	If set to **True**, renders the chart in a 3D perspective. The default value is set to **False**.
anti-alias	If set to **True**, renders chart fonts as anti-aliased. The default value is set to **True**.
bg-color	Sets the background around the chart to the specified color. If not set, defaults to gray.
bg-image	Sets the background of the chart area to the specified image. If not set, the background of the chart area defaults to white. The chart area is the area within the axes of the chart. Supported image types include PNG, JPG, and GIF file formats.
show-border	If set to **True**, displays a border around the chart. The default value is set to **True**.
border-color	Sets the border to the specified color. If not set, defaults to black.
plot-border	If set to **False**, clears the default rendering value of the chart border.
plot-bg-color	Sets the plot background color to the specified color. If not set, defaults to white.
plot-fg-alpha	Sets the alpha value of the plot foreground colors relative to the plot background. The default value is set to 1.0.
plot-bg-alpha	Sets the alpha value of the plot background color relative to the chart background color. The default value is set to 1.0.

Legend Property Group

Property name	Description
show-legend	If set to **True**, displays the legend for the chart. The default value is set to **False**.
location	The location of the legend in relation to the chart, which may be set to **top**, **bottom**, **left**, or **right**. The default location is **bottom**.
legend-border	If set to **True**, renders a border around the legend. The default value is set to **True**.
legend-font	The type of Java font to render the legend labels in.
legend-bg-color	Sets the legend background color. If not set, defaults to white.
legend-font-color	Sets the legend font color. If not set, defaults to black.

Advanced Property Group

Property name	Description
dependencyLevel	The dependency level field informs the reporting engine what order the chart should be executed in relation to other items in the report. This is useful if you are using special functions that may need to execute prior to generating the chart. The default value is set to **0**. Negative values execute before 0, and positive values execute after 0.

Common category series rendering properties

The following properties appear in charts that render category information:

Options Property Group

Property name	Description
stacked	If set to **True**, the series values will appear layered on top of one another instead of being displayed relative to one another.
stacked-percent	If set to True, determines the percentages of each series, and renders the bar height based on those percentages. The property stacked must be set to True for this property to have an effect.

General Property Group

Property name	Description
gridlines	If set to **True**, displays category grid lines. This value is set to **True** by default.

X-Axis Property Group

Property name	Description
label-rotation	If set, adjusts the inline item label rotation value. The value should be specified in degrees. If not specified, labels are rendered horizontally. You must have **show-labels** set to true for this value to be relevant.
date-format	If the item value is a date, a Java date format string may be provided to format the date appropriately. Please see Java's `SimpleDateFormat` JavaDoc for formatting details.
numeric-format	If the item value is a decimal number, a Java decimal format string may be provided to format the number appropriately. Please see Java's `DecimalFormat` JavaDoc for formatting details.
text-format	The label format used for displaying category items within the chart. This property is required if you would like to display the category item values. The following parameters may be defined in the format string to access details of the item: • {0}: To access the Series Name detail of an item • {1}: To access the Category detail of an item • {2}: To access the Item value details of an item To display just the item value, set the format string to "{2}".
x-axis-title	If set, displays a label describing the category axis.
show-labels	If set to true, displays x-axis labels in the chart.
x-axis-label-width	Sets the maximum category label width ratio, which determines the maximum length each category label should render in. This might be useful if you have really long category names.
x-axis-label-rotation	If set, adjusts the category item label rotation value. The value should be specified in degrees. If not specified, labels are rendered horizontally.
x-font	The font to render the category axis title and labels in.

Y-Axis Property Group

Property name	Description
y-axis-title	If set, displays a label along the value axis of the chart.
label-rotation	If set, determines the upward angle position of the label, where the value passed into JFreeChart is the mathematical pie over the value. Unfortunately, this property is not very flexible and you may find it difficult to use.
y-tick-interval	The numeric interval value to separate range ticks in the chart.
y-font	The font to render the range axis title in.

Y-Axis Property Group

Property name	Description
y-sticky-0	If the range includes zero in the axis, making it sticky will force truncation of the axis to zero if set to True. The default value of this property is True.
y-incl-0	If set to True, the range axis will force zero to be included in the axis.
y-min	The minimum value to render in the range axis.
y-max	The maximum value to render in the range axis.
y-tick-font	The font to render the range tick value in.
y-tick-fmt-str	The DecimalFormat string to render the numeric range tick value.
enable-log-axis	If set to true, displays the y-axis as a logarithmic scale.
log-format	If set to true, will present the logarithmic scale in a human readable view.

Common XY series rendering properties

The following properties appear in charts that render XY series information.

X-Axis Property Group

Property name	Description
x-incl-0	If set to **True**, the domain axis will force zero to be included in the axis. The default value of this property is **True**.
x-min	The maximum value to render in the domain axis.
x-max	The minimum value to render in the domain axis.
x-sticky-0	If the domain includes zero in the axis, making it sticky will force truncation of the axis to zero if set to **True**. The default value of this property is **True**.
x-tick-font	The font in which to render the domain tick value.
x-tick-fmt-str	The DecimalFormat string to render the numeric domain tick value.
x-title	The title to display on the domain axis.
x-font	The font in which to render the domain axis title.
x-vtick-label	If **True**, renders the domain tick labels vertically. This value defaults to **False**.
x-tick-interval	The numeric interval value to separate x-axis ticks in the chart.
x-tick-time-period	If rendering a time series dataset, this property is the time period to display in the x-axis.

Property name	Description
y-incl-0	If set to **True**, the range axis will force zero to be included in the axis.
y-max	The maximum value to render in the range axis.
y-min	The minimum value to render in the range axis.
y-sticky-0	If the range includes zero in the axis, making it sticky will force truncation of the axis to zero if set to **True**. The default value of this property is **True**.
y-tick-font	The font to render the range tick value in.
y-tick-fmt-str	The DecimalFormat string to render the numeric range tick value.
y-title	The title to display on the range axis.
y-font	The font to render the range axis title in.
y-tick-interval	The numeric interval value to separate y-axis ticks in the chart.
enable-log-axis	If set to true, displays the y-axis as a logarithmic scale
log-format	If set to true, will present the logarithmic scale in a human readable view.

Common dataset properties

The following properties are common across all chart datasets:

Common Property Group

Property name	Description
name	The name of the chart's dataset, also referenced in the chart rendering properties.

Series Property Group

Property name	Description
series-by-value	If set, values entered act as the series name for the value columns provided.
series-by-field	If set, fields entered act as the series name for the value column provided. Setting this property will slice the value column into series groups.

Group Property Group

Property name	Description
reset-group	This property defines the group level at which the data should be reset.
group-by	This property defines the group level at which the data should be collected.

Advanced Property Group

Property name	Description
dependencyLevel	The dependency level field informs the reporting engine about the order in which the chart data source should be executed in relation to other items in the report. This is useful if you are using special functions that may need to be executed` prior to generating the data for the chart. The default value is set to **0**.

Common category series dataset properties

The following properties are common across all charts that utilize category series dataset for populating the chart:

Common Property Group

Property name	Description
category-column	The data source column used to determine the category.
value-columns	The data source columns used to determine the chart values.

Common XY series dataset properties

The following properties are common across all charts that utilize the XY series dataset for populating a chart:

Common Property Group

Property name	Description
x-value-columns	The data source column that populates the X axis.
y-value-columns	The data source column that populates the Y axis.

Now that you've reviewed the common set of properties for all charts, you'll begin to explore the individual charts, including going through their configurable properties, as well as providing a quick example.

Area chart

The **area chart** displays a category dataset as a line, with the area underneath the line filled in. Multiple areas may appear depending on the number of series provided. The area chart is useful for visualizing the differences between two or more sets of data. It utilizes the common properties defined in the previous tables, including the category series common properties. The area chart defines no additional properties.

Area chart example

This example will demonstrate the area chart's capabilities. First, you'll need a rich enough dataset to demonstrate this and all the other charts in this chapter. You'll reuse the ElectroBarn HSQLDB data source configured in Chapter 3. To begin, launch Pentaho Report Designer and create a new report.

Now, select the **Data** tab. Right-click on the **Data Sets** tree element, and select the **JDBC** data source. If ElectroBarn is not already configured as a connection type, click the **Connections** add image button and fill in the following values, customizing the database location for your particular environment:

Connection Name	ElectroBarn
Connection Type	Hypersonic
Host Name	file:
Database Name	c:\path\to\chapter3\data\electrobarn
Port Number	\<BLANK\>
Username	sa
Password	\<BLANK\>

Click the **Test** button to verify your connection, and then click **OK** when you are done.

You need to define a SQL statement to populate your chart. You'll define a simple query that takes a look at the inventory data. Add a new query with the following SQL code:

```
SELECT
     "INVENTORY"."ITEMCATEGORY",
     "INVENTORY"."SALEPRICE",
     "INVENTORY"."COST"
FROM
     "INVENTORY"
ORDER BY
     "INVENTORY"."ITEMCATEGORY" ASC
```

Click **OK**. You're now ready to add a chart to your empty report. For this example, select the **Chart** report element ⊙ from the palette and drag it into the **Report Header**. Double-click on the chart, or right-click on the chart and select **Chart....** Once the **Edit Chart** dialog appears, select the **Area Chart** 🖿.

In the **Primary DataSource** tab, select the ITEMCATEGORY data field as your **category-column**. For your **value-columns**, select SALEPRICE and COST. Enter the strings Sale Price and Cost as the **series–by-value** values. When rendering an area chart, the order of value columns is important. If a larger value is rendered after a smaller value, the smaller value will not appear on the chart.

Once you configured the data for the chart, you can also make some customizations to the rendering. Set **horizontal** to True, as well as specifying the **bg-color** as yellow. Finally, set the **show-legend** property to True. Click the **OK** button and then preview your report to see the results!

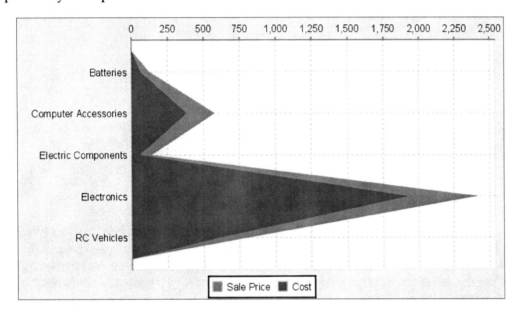

Bar chart

The **bar chart** displays individual bars broken out into individual categories and series. Bar charts are useful for comparing relative sizes of data across categories. The bar chart utilizes the common properties defined earlier, including the category series common properties.

The bar chart defines the following additional rendering properties:

Options Property Group	
Property name	**Description**
bar-borders	If set to **False**, clears the default rendering value of the chart border. Identical to the **plot-border** property.
max-bar-width	The maximum width of a bar in pixels. Unless set, bars will generally expand to the available space within the chart.

Bar chart example

You'll now build an example bar chart. Create a new report with the ElectroBarn data source, and use the following SQL query, which investigates purchase quantity and payment type:

```
SELECT
      "INVENTORY"."ITEMCATEGORY",
      "PURCHASES"."PAYMENTTYPE",
      "PURCHASEITEMS"."QUANTITY"
FROM
      "PURCHASES" INNER JOIN "PURCHASEITEMS" ON
"PURCHASES"."PURCHASEID" = "PURCHASEITEMS"."PURCHASEID"
      INNER JOIN "INVENTORY" ON "PURCHASEITEMS"."ITEMID" =
"INVENTORY"."ITEMID"
ORDER BY
      "INVENTORY"."ITEMCATEGORY" ASC,
      "PURCHASES"."PAYMENTTYPE" ASC
```

Place a **Chart** element in the **Report Header** of the report, selecting bar as its type. To begin, configure the dataset properties for your bar chart. Set **category-column** to ITEMCATEGORY, **value-columns** to QUANTITY, and **series-by-field** to PAYMENTTYPE. By setting the **series-by-field** property, the chart will create a series for each PAYMENTTYPE in the dataset.

Now, you'll customize the look of your chart. First, set the X-Axis **show-labels** property to True and **text-format** to {2}. This will display the value of each bar at the top of the bar. Then set **max-label-width** to 2.0, so that you can easily see all the category names in the chart. Finally, set the **show-legend** to True, in order to see what types of payments map to which bar color. You're now ready to preview your chart!

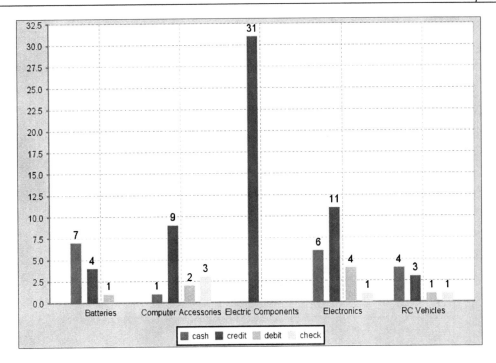

Line chart

The **line chart** displays connected lines between categories for each series provided. This chart is useful for visualizing trends. The line chart utilizes the common properties defined in the previous tables, including the category series common properties. The line chart defines the following additional rendering properties:

Options Property Group

Property name	Description
line-style	The style of line to draw. Appropriate values for this property are **solid, dash, dot, dashdot,** and **dashdotdot.**
line-size	The thickness of the line to draw in pixels. The default value is set to **1.**
show-markers	If set to **True**, displays markers at each category location within the line.

Note that the stacked and stacked-percent properties do not apply to the line chart type.

Line chart example

In this example, reuse the SQL query and dataset sections from your area chart example. Select the **Line** chart type ⬚, and customize the chart with **show-markers** set to **True** as well as **line-size** set to 4.0. The result should look like this:

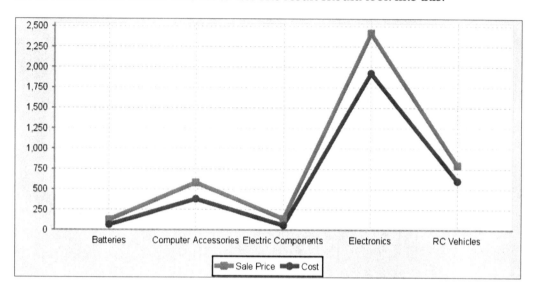

Pie chart

The **pie chart** displays a sliced, multi-colored pie with individual slices consisting of individual series information. The pie chart uses its own dataset type, versus using a category or XY series dataset. The pie chart utilizes the common properties defined above, but does not utilize the category or XY dataset properties. Instead, it defines its own properties for providing chart data using the `PieDataSetCollector`. The pie chart defines the following rendering properties:

Required Property Group

Property name	Description
ignore-nulls	If set to **False**, the pie chart will render series data containing null values as a point in the pie chart, otherwise it will ignore the series item and will not render it.
ignore-zeros	If set to **False**, the pie chart will render series data containing zero values as a point in the pie chart, otherwise it will ignore the series item and will not render it.

Options Property Group

Property name	Description
slice-colors	The color in which to render each slice of the pie. The default for the first three series colors are **red**, **blue**, and **green**.
explode-pct	The percentage value to extract the sliced segment out of the main pie chart. This is used only if **explode-slice** is set.
explode-slice	The slice to extract from the pie chart, starting with zero. The values **minValue** or **maxValue** may be used instead, which select the minimum or maximum slice from the pie.
label-format	The pie label format string has a default value of {0}, and can reference the following fields: • {0}: Series name • {1}: Series raw value • {2}: Percentage value • {3}: Total raw value
rotate-clockwise	If set to **True**, the pie's series are laid out in a clockwise fashion, otherwise the series are laid out counter clockwise. This property defaults to **True**.

Legend Properties

Property name	Description
legend-label-format	The pie legend label format string has a default value of {0}, and can reference the same fields as Pie Label Format.

Note that the pie chart does not share the common properties **horizontal**, **series-color**, **stacked**, or **series-names**. The pie chart defines the following dataset properties:

Required Property Group

Property name	Description
series-by-field	The data source column used to determine the pie slice series.
value-column	The data source column used to determine the pie slice percentages.

Pie chart example

For the pie chart example, you'll compare the various costs of inventory items to one another by category. First, you'll need to define an SQL query as shown next:

```
SELECT
      "INVENTORY"."ITEMCATEGORY",
      "INVENTORY"."ITEMNAME",
      "INVENTORY"."COST"
FROM
      "INVENTORY"
ORDER BY
      "INVENTORY"."ITEMCATEGORY" ASC,
      "INVENTORY"."ITEMNAME" ASC
```

You'll then need to define a **Group Header** for your report. Right-click on the **Groups** section within the report structure and edit the root group, naming the group Item Category. Select the ITEMCATEGORY field as the only field in the **Selected Items** list. Expand the **Group** node in the structure tree, and select the **Group Header**. Now, uncheck the **hide-on-canvas** property, so you can view the **Group Header** in the canvas.

Drag-and-drop the ITEMCATEGORY field at the top of the **Group Header**. Place a chart below the text field, and click **Edit Chart...**

Select the **Pie** chart type ●. You'll start configuring the chart by selecting the correct dataset. For the **value-column**, select the COST field. For the **series-by-field** property, select the ITEMNAME field.

You'll also need to tell the chart collector to reset the data after each group. Set the **reset-group** property to the already defined Item Category group.

Finally, you'll want to customize some of the rendering properties. Set the **explode-slice** to maxValue, and set the **explode-pct** to 0.5. This will highlight the most expensive item in each category. Also set **show-legend** to **False** to hide the legend and **show-labels** to **True** to display the individual pie slice labels.

Click the **OK** button and preview the report. You should see a group of charts as shown in the following figure:

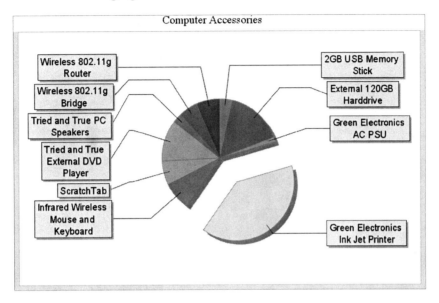

Ring chart

The **ring chart** is identical to the pie chart, except that it renders as a ring versus a complete pie. In addition to sharing all the properties similar to the pie chart, it also defines the following rendering property [icon]:

Options Property Group	
Property name	**Description**
section-depth	This property defines the percentage of the radius to render the section as. The default value is set to **0.5**.

Ring chart example

For this example, simply open the defined pie chart example and select the **Ring** chart type. Also, set the **section-depth** to 0.1, in order to generate the following effect:

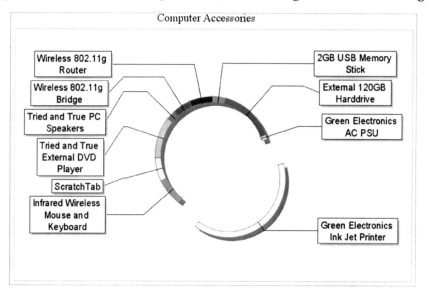

Multi pie chart

The **multi pie chart** renders a group of pie charts, based on a category dataset. This meta-chart renders individual series data as a pie chart, each broken into individual categories within the individual pie charts. The multi pie chart utilizes the common properties defined above, including the category dataset properties. In addition to the standard set of properties, it also defines the following two properties:

Options Property Group

Property name	Description
label-format	This label defines how each item within a chart is rendered. The default value is set to "{0}". The format string may also contain any of the following: • {0}: To render the item name • {1}: To render the item value • {2}: To render the item percentage in relation to the entire pie chart
by-row	This value defaults to **True**. If set to **False**, the series and category fields are reversed, and individual charts render series information.

Note that the **horizontal, series-color, stacked** and **stacked-percent** properties do not apply to this chart type.

Multi pie chart example

This example demonstrates the distribution of purchased item types, based on payment type. To begin, create a new report. You'll reuse the bar chart's SQL query. Now, place a new **Chart** element into the **Report Header**. Edit the chart, selecting **Multi Pie** as the chart type.

To configure the dataset for this chart, select ITEMCATEGORY as the **category-column**. Set the **value-columns** property to QUANTITY and the **series-by-field** to PAYMENTTYPE.

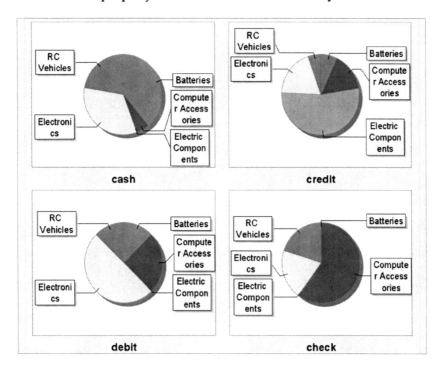

Waterfall chart

The **waterfall chart** displays a unique stacked bar chart that spans categories. This chart is useful when comparing categories to one another. The last category in a waterfall chart normally equals the total of all the other categories to render appropriately, but this is based on the dataset, not the chart rendering. The waterfall chart utilizes the common properties defined above, including the category dataset properties. The **stacked** property is not available for this chart. There are no additional properties defined for the waterfall chart.

Waterfall chart example

In this example, you'll compare by type, the quantity of items in your inventory. Normally, the last category would be used to display the total values. The chart will render the data provided with or without a summary series, so you'll just use the example SQL query from the bar chart example. Add a **Chart** element to the **Report Header** and select **Waterfall** as the chart type.

Set the **category-column** to ITEMCATEGORY, the **value-columns** to QUANTITY, and the **series-by-value** property to Quantity. Now, apply your changes and preview the results.

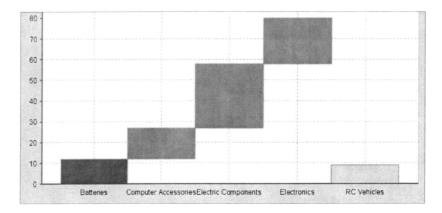

Bar line chart

The **bar line chart** combines the bar and line charts, allowing visualization of trends with categories, along with comparisons. The bar line chart is unique in that it requires two category datasets to populate the chart. The first dataset populates the bar chart, and the second dataset populates the line chart. The bar line chart utilizes the common properties defined above, including the category dataset properties. This chart also inherits the properties from both the bar chart, as well as the line chart. This chart also has certain additional properties, which are listed in the following table:

Required Property Group	
Property name	**Description**
bar-data-source	The name of the first dataset required by the bar line chart, which populates the bars in the chart. This value is automatically populated with the correct name.
line-data-source	The name of the second dataset required by the bar line chart, which populates the lines in the chart. This value is automatically populated with the correct name.

Bar Options Property Group	
Property name	**Description**
ctgry-tick-font	Defines the Java font that renders the Categories.

Line Options Property Group	
Property name	**Description**
line-series-color	Defines the color in which to render each line series.
line-tick-fmt	Specifies the Java `DecimalFormat` string for rendering the Line Axis Labels
lines-label-font	Defines the Java font to use when rendering line labels.
line-tick-font	Defines the Java font to use when rendering the Line Axis Labels.

As part of the bar line chart, a second y-axis is defined for the lines. The property group **Y2-Axis** is available with similar properties as the standard y-axis.

Bar line chart example

To demonstrate the bar line chart, you'll reuse the SQL query from the area chart example. Create a new report, and add a **Chart** element to the **Report Header**. Edit the chart, and select **Bar Line** as the chart type.

You'll begin by configuring the first dataset. Set the **category-column** to ITEMCATEGORY, the **value-columns** to COST, and the **series-by-value** property to Cost. To configure the second dataset, set the **category-column** to ITEMCATEGORY, the **value-columns** to SALEPRICE, and the **series-by-value** property to Sale Price. Set the **x-axis-label-width** to 2.0, and reduce the **x-font** size to 7. Also, set **show-legend** to True.

You're now ready to preview the bar line chart.

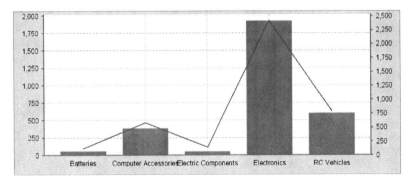

Bubble chart

The **bubble chart** allows you to view three dimensions of data. The first two dimensions are your traditional X and Y dimensions, also known as domain and range. The third dimension is expressed by the size of the individual bubbles rendered. The bubble chart utilizes the common properties defined above, including the XY series dataset properties. The bubble chart also defines the following properties:

Options Property Group

Property name	Description
max-bubble-size	This value defines the diameter of the largest bubble to render. All other bubble sizes are relative to the maximum bubble size. The default value is **0**, so this value must be set to a reasonable value for rendering of bubbles to take place. Note that this value is based on pixels, not the domain or range values.

The bubble chart defines the following additional dataset property:

Required Property Group

Property name	Description
z-value-columns	This is the data source column to use for Z value, which specifies the bubble diameter relative to the maximum bubble size.

Bubble chart example

In this example, you need to define a three dimensional SQL query to populate the chart. You'll use inventory information, and calculate Item Category Margin:

```
SELECT
     "INVENTORY"."ITEMCATEGORY",
     "INVENTORY"."ONHAND",
     "INVENTORY"."ONORDER",
     "INVENTORY"."COST",
     "INVENTORY"."SALEPRICE",
     "INVENTORY"."SALEPRICE" - "INVENTORY"."COST" MARGIN
FROM
     "INVENTORY"
ORDER BY
     "INVENTORY"."ITEMCATEGORY" ASC
```

Now that you have a SQL query to work with, add a **Chart** element to the **Report Header** and select **Bubble** 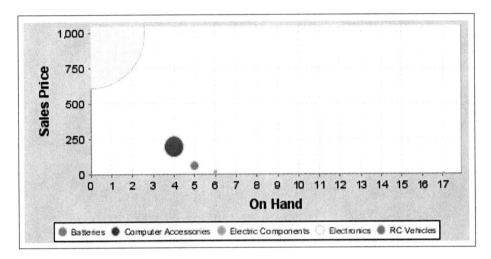 as the chart type. First, you'll populate the correct dataset fields. Set the **series-by-field** property to ITEMCATEGORY. Now, set the X, Y, and Z value columns to ONHAND, SALEPRICE, and MARGIN.

You're now ready to customize the chart rendering. Set the **x-title** to On Hand, the **y-title** to Sales Price, the **max-bubble-size** to 100, and the **show-legend** property to **True**. The final result should look like this:

Scatter chart

The **scatter chart** renders all items in a series as points within a chart. This chart type utilizes the common properties defined above, including the XY series dataset properties. The scatter chart also defines the following two properties:

Options Property Group	
Property name	**Description**
dot-height	The height to render the individual points in pixels. The default value is **5**.
dot-width	The width to render the individual points in pixels. The default value is **5**.

Scatter chart example

For this example, you'll reuse the SQL query defined in your bubble chart example, as well as the default rendering properties configured. Simply select the **Scatter** chart type in the chart editor ![icon]. The chart below shows Sales Price and On Hand values:

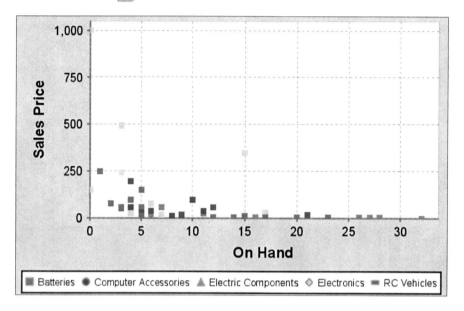

XY Area, XY Bar and XY Line charts

The **XY Area**, **XY Bar**, and **XY Line** charts graph an XY series dataset as an area, bar, or a simple line chart. These chart types utilize the common properties defined above, including the XY series dataset properties. The XY Bar chart also uses the property **show-bar-borders**, which is defined earlier in the bar chart. The XY Area and XY Line charts share the properties **line-style**, **line-size**, and **show-markers**, defined earlier in the line chart.

In addition to the standard XY Series Dataset, XY charts may use a Time Series Dataset to render data. To use the **TimeSeriesCollector**, you can select it in the **Primary DataSource** drop-down list. The Time Series Dataset is similar to the Category Dataset, but instead of a category it defines a **category-time-column**. The field selected for the **category-time-column** must be of the type `java.util.Date`. Also defined is the **time-period-type**, which defines at what interval of time should the results be grouped together. Valid values for this property include **Millisecond**, **Second**, **Minute**, **Hour**, **Day**, **Week**, **Month**, **Quarter**, and **Year**.

XY charts example

In this example, you'll reuse the SQL query defined in the bubble chart example, as well as the default rendering properties configured for each of the individual charts, **XY Area** 🖼️, **XY Bar** 📊, and **XY Line Chart** 📈. You'll also reuse the X and Y dataset configuration specified for the scatter chart.

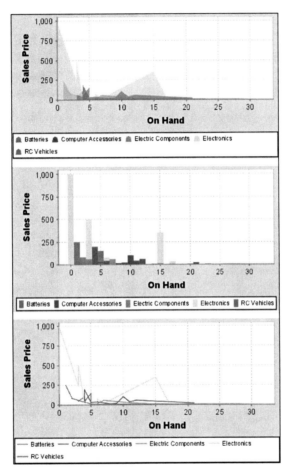

Extended XY Line chart

The **Extended XY Line chart** allows the rendering of three additional chart types—StepChart, StepAreaChart, and DifferenceChart. The Step chart types display an XY series dataset as a set of steps, and the Difference Chart renders two XY series and highlights the differences between the two. The Extended XY Line chart utilizes the common properties defined above, including the XY series dataset properties. The Extended XY Line chart also defines the following property:

Options Property Group	
Property name	**Description**
ext-chart-type	The type of chart to render. Valid values are **StepChart**, **StepAreaChart**, and **DifferenceChart**.

Extended XY Line chart example

In this example, you'll reuse the SQL query defined in the bubble chart example, as well as the default rendering properties configured for each of the individual charts. Select **Extended XY Line** as the chart type and specify **StepChart**, **StepAreaChart** and **DifferenceChart** as the **Chart Type** to see the different renderings:

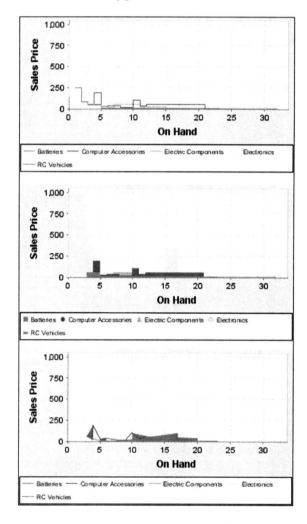

You've now worked with all the major chart types within Pentaho Reporting. Under the covers, charts are simply dynamic images that are generated and included in your reports. You'll now learn more about including images within reports.

Radar chart

The **Radar chart** renders a web-like chart that displays a categorical dataset. The Radar chart utilizes the common properties defined above, including the category series common properties. The Radar chart also defines the following properties:

Options Property Group	
Property name	**Description**
thickness-primary-series	This value determines the line thickness of the web.
head-size	This value determines the size rendered for each data point. The value is a percentage of the entire chart.
radar-web-filled	If true, fills the web with the series color. This also shades the grid.
gridline-interval	The interval between gridlines in the radar chart. This value may be a fixed value length or percent. To enter a percent value, use the "%" sign at the end of the number.

Radar chart example

In this example, reuse the SQL query and dataset sections from your area chart example. The result should look like this:

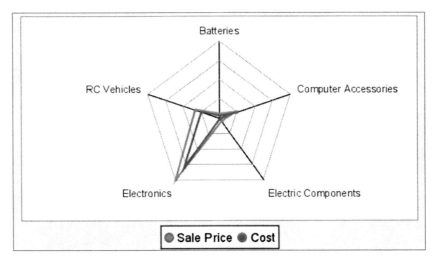

Including static images in your report

To include static images in your report, select the **image** report element ▲ from the report designer palette and place it in your report. Double-click on the element, or right-click on the element and select **Edit Content** to select the static image. This brings up a resource dialog, where you can browse to the specific file location. You may **Link to** or **Embed** the image in the PRPT file. An example of a static image, with the ElectroBarn logo, is provided in Chapter 3.

The **image** report element uses Pentaho Reporting's `ResourceManager` API to load the image. The `ResourceManager` interface is located in the `org.pentaho.reporting.libraries.resourceloader` package.

Including dynamic images in your report

To add dynamic images to your report, use the **content-field** report element 🖼. The content field accepts different types of image inputs for rendering. The first approach is dynamically changing the image location within your dataset. If you have a field that contains a URL or file system location to your image, the **content-field** element will render the specified image.

The second approach is to populate the **content-field** with an object of type `java.awt.Image` for rendering. This approach would require a custom-implemented `TableModel` (as described in Chapter 5), or a custom function that returns an `Image` object.

The third approach is to populate the content-field with an object that contains the following method, which is determined through Java introspection:

```
void draw(Graphics2D g2, Rectangle2D area);
```

In addition to this API, Pentaho Reporting also defines an extended `org.pentaho.reporting.engine.classic.core.util.ReportDrawable` API with the following methods, for more detailed access into the report rendering process:

- `void draw(Graphics2D g2, Rectangle2D area);`
- `void setConfiguration(Configuration config);`
- `void setStyleSheet(StyleSheet style);`

- `void setResourceBundleFactory(ResourceBundleFactory bundleFactory);`
- `ImageMap getImageMap(final Rectangle2D bounds);`

A custom `TableModel` implementation or custom function would also be required to make this object available to the Reporting engine.

Summary

In this chapter, you learned how to incorporate many chart types into your reports in many different ways. You learned how to configure a chart's dataset as well as customizing how each chart type looks in a report. You learned how to populate a category series dataset, as well as an XY series dataset, and make that data available to the various types of charts that render in your report. You also learned how to include static and dynamic images, as well as graphics, in your reports.

7
Parameterization, Functions, Formulas, and Internationalization in Reports

In this chapter, you'll start off by learning how to parameterize a report. You'll then learn about all the predefined functions and expressions available for use within a report. From there, you'll learn about Pentaho Reporting's formula capabilities, including the correct syntax and available formula methods. Finally, you'll learn about the details involved in internationalizing a report.

Report parameterization

Report parameterization allows end users to customize results of Pentaho reports, by entering values that limit report datasets or trigger rendering decisions. Using the `DataFactory` API, Pentaho Reporting provides a mechanism to provide parameters to data sources. As presented in Chapter 5, there are many different options for providing data to Pentaho Reporting. Each data source type uses its underlying method for parameterizing queries. For instance, the default syntax for XPATH, Kettle, MDX, and Hibernate Query Language are supported through their respective `DataFactory` implementations. Each data source query syntax defines how to specify parameters, and Pentaho Reporting provides those parameters via the `DataRow` API.

The two exceptions from the default management of parameters include SQL and static data. When specifying a SQL statement in JDBC, you would normally specify a question mark to denote which parameters should be specified. Pentaho Reporting requires that you specify the parameters by name, so some parsing is done on the SQL query before passing the query to JDBC. You may specify parameters as `${PARAM}`, and the `SQLReportDataFactory` will replace each named parameter with a question mark (?) before making the prepared JDBC call.

The NamedStaticDataFactory allows for Java class methods with parameters to be executed. The names provided when configuring the `DataFactory` are used when resolving the values from the `DataRow` provided.

Providing report parameters

In Chapter 3, you implemented two example reports that used report parameterization. The first report parameterization was done as part of the End of the Day Cashiers report example. You defined a `Sessions` dataset to populate a drop down within Pentaho Report Designer, which determined the results of the report.

The second parameterization example was in the definition of the sub-report in the Invoice report example. The sub-report defined the parameter `${CUSTOMERID}`, and the value was available to the sub-report, based on the current data row retrieved from the primary report. Both of these are examples of parameterization.

To provide a master report with parameters, you need to access the parameter values collection from the master report. To do this, call `MasterReport.getParameterValues()`. Then you may add parameters to the report by calling `ReportParameterValues.put(column, value)`. The `ReportParameterValues` class implements the `DataRow` API, which makes it possible to pass these parameters to the various `DataFactory` implementations.

Available report parameter types

Pentaho Reporting defines the following parameter types, which each render differently within Pentaho Report Designer and Pentaho's BI Server:

- **Drop Down**
- **Single Value List**
- **Multi Value List**
- **Radio Button**
- **Check Box**

- **Single Selection Button**
- **Multi Selection Button**
- **Text Box**

When embedding Pentaho Reporting into a custom application, it is the embedded program's responsibility to render parameters, as demonstrated in Chapter 3.

All parameter types may specify a data source for population of possible selections, as well as for validation. It is possible to nest parameters by parameterizing the data sources, which are used to populate selections. For example, a top level drop-down parameter such as Country could drive a secondary radio button parameter such as Region. Queries are executed in the order in which they appear in the data source list.

Multi Value List, Check Box, and Multi Selection Button parameter types allow the selection of multiple types. These parameter types return an array of values rather than a single value. Data sources, including SQL, have special logic that maps the array of values into the generated query.

Working with functions and expressions

Pentaho Reporting provides many functions and expressions that may be used during report creation. A function in Pentaho Reporting is used to calculate a computed value. An expression in Pentaho Reporting is a function whose scope is limited to the current dataset row. A function may maintain state, having access to many rows of data.

All functions share the following properties:

- **Name**: Used to reference the function or expression in elements, formulas, and other functions
- **Dependency Level**: Used to determine the order in which to execute the functions

Listed below are the available functions and expressions, and how they are used. Chart related functions were covered in depth within Chapter 6, so there is no need to restate them in this list.

Common functions

Common functions include the most commonly used functions within Pentaho Report Designer.

Function name	Description
Open Formula	This function evaluates a LibFormula formula defined later in this chapter. Following is the property of this function: • **Formula**: The **formula** to evaluate.
Page	This function returns the current page number. The following are properties of this function: • **Reset on Group Name**: If this value is set, the page total value is reset when the named group appears. • **Page Increment**: The amount by which to increase the count for each page. • **Start Page Number:** The page from which to start counting.
Total Page Count	This function calculates the total number of pages in a report. The following are properties of this function: • **Reset on Group Name**: If this value is set, the page total value is reset when the named group appears. • **Page Increment**: The amount by which to increase the count for each page. • **Start Page Number**: The page from which to start counting.

Page of Pages	This function returns a string that displays the current page and the total page count.
	
	The following are properties of this function:
	• **Format Pattern**: The format string to render the current page and total pages into. The default value is "{0} / {1}".
	   ◦ {0}: To the current page.
	   ◦ {1}: To render the total page count.
	• **Reset on Group Name**: If this value is set, the page total value is reset when the named group appears.
	• **Page Increment**: The amount by which to increase the count for each page.
	• **Start Page Number**: The page from which to start counting.

Report functions

Report functions are related to the rendering of a report.

Function name	Description
Is Export Type	This function returns **True** if the export type of the report string begins with the export type property provided.
	Following is the property of this function: • **Export Type ID**: The string to compare to the report export type string.
Row Banding	The row banding function manages changing background colors for rows in a report.
	The following are properties of this function: • **Active Banding Color**: The primary banding color • **Apply to Element(s) Named**: The name of the element to change the background color of. • **Inactive Banding Color**: The secondary banding color • **Number of Rows**: The number of rows to render before changing the banding color. • **State On New Groups**: If set to **True**, resets the banding color for each new group. • **State On New Pages**: If set to **True**, resets the banding color for each new page.
Hide Repeating	This function hides repeated elements of a specified field in the item band.
	The following are properties of this function: • **Apply to Element(s) Named**: The element to hide in the item band. • **Field Name**: The field to watch for changes. • **Ignore All Group Breaks**: If set to **False**, this function will reset itself on group breaks. • **Ignore All Page Breaks**: If set to **False**, this function will reset itself on page breaks.
Hide Page Header & Footer	This function will hide the page header and footer if the export type is not pageable.
	The following are properties of this function: • **Disable Repeating Headers**: Disables any repeating group headers and footers. • **Hide Page Bands**: If set to **True**, hides page bands. • **Export Descriptor**: This property is used to determine whether the current report export type should disable page headers and footers. Its default value is `table`.

Function name	Description
Show Page Footer	This function hides the page footer except for the last page. It has no additional properties.

Summary functions

Summary functions calculate values during the first phase of report processing and make those values available during report rendering.

Function name	Description
Sum	This function sums a field within a group during the prepare run stage of a report, making available the total group sum in later stages of report generation.
	The following are properties of this function:
	• **Field Name**: The field to sum.
	• **Reset on Group Name**: The name of the group that should be counted. If set to empty, counts all the groups within a parent group.
Count	This function counts the rows within a group during the prepare run stage of a report, making available the total group count in later stages of report generation.
	Following is the property of this function:
	• **Reset on Group Name**: The name of the group that should be counted. If set to empty, counts all the groups within a parent group.
Group Count	This function counts the occurrence of groups within a report during the prepare run stage of a report, making available the total group count in later stages of report generation.
	The following are properties of this function:
	• **Group Name to Count**: The name of the group that should be counted. If set to empty, counts all groups within a parent group.
	• **Reset on Parent Group Name**: The name of the group which resets the count. If set to empty, counts the sub-groups of the entire report.

Function name	Description
Minimum	Determines the global minimum value of a specified field in a report. The following are properties of this function: • **Field Name:** The field which should be assigned the minimum value. • **Reset on Group Name:** If this value is set, the minimum aggregation value is reset when the named group appears.
Maximum	Determines the global maximum value of a specified field in a report. The following are properties of this function: • **Field Name:** The field which should be assigned the maximum value. • **Reset on Group Name:** If this value is set, the maximum aggregation value is reset when the named group appears.
Sum Quotient	This function sums a dividend and a divisor, and then divides the two for the result value, using the **Sum** function to sum the values. The following are properties of this function: • **Field Name:** The field to sum. • **Reset on Group Name:** The name of the group that should be counted. If set to empty, counts all the groups within a parent group. • **Dividend Field:** The field that holds the dividend of this division calculation. • **Divisor Field:** The field that holds the divisor of this division calculation. • **Rounding Mode:** Java's BigDecimal Rounding mode. Please see Java's documentation for values. • **Scale:** The scale of the quotient returned. The default value is 14.
Sum Quotient Percent	This function is an extension of the **Sum Quotient** function, and simply multiples the final result by 100. It shares the same properties as the **Sum Quotient** function.

Function name	Description
Calculation	This function stores the result of a field calculated during the prepare run stage of report generation, allowing access later on in the report. The following are properties of this function: • **Field Name**: The field to store. • **Reset on Group Name**: If this value is set, the aggregation value is reset when the named group appears.
Count for Page	This function is identical to the **Count** function, but also resets at the beginning of each page. It has no additional properties.
Sum for Page	This function is identical to the **Sum** function, but also resets at the beginning of each page. It has no additional properties.

Running functions

Running functions calculate values during report rendering, allowing for incremental aggregation information throughout a report.

Function name	Description
Sum (Running)	Calculates the sum total value of a specified field over a number of rows in a report. The following are properties of this function: • **Field Name**: The field to sum. • **Reset on Group Name**: If this value is set, the sum total value is reset when the named group appears.
Count (Running)	Maintains the value of the current number of rows in a dataset. Following is the property of this function: • **Reset on Group Name**: If this value is set, the count is reset when the named group appears.
Group Count (Running)	This method counts the occurrence of groups within a report. The following are properties of this function: • **Reset on Group Name**: The name of the group that should be counted. If set to empty, counts all the groups within a parent group. • **Reset on Parent Group Name**: The name of the group which resets the count. If set to empty, counts the sub-groups of the entire report.

Function name	Description
Count Distinct (Running)	This method counts the distinct occurrences of a value within a specified field. The following are properties of this function: • **Field Name**: The field to count. • **Reset on Group Name**: If this value is set, the count value is reset to zero when the named group appears.
Average (Running)	Calculates the average value of a specified field over a number of rows within a report. The following are properties of this function: • **Field Name**: The field whose average to calculate. • **Reset on Group Name**: If this value is set, the average value is reset when the named group appears. • **Rounding Mode**: Java's `BigDecimal` Rounding mode. Please see Java's documentation for values. • **Scale** : The scale of the quotient returned, defaults to 14.
Minimum (Running)	Determines the minimum value of a specified field over a number of rows in a report. The following are properties of this function: • **Field Name**: The field to calculate a minimum value. • **Reset on Group Name**: If this value is set, the minimum value is reset when the named group appears.
Maximum (Running)	Determines the maximum value of a specified field over a number of rows in a report. The following are properties of this function: • **Field Name**: The field which should be assigned the maximum value. • **Reset on Group Name**: If this value is set, the maximum value is reset when the named group appears.
Percent of Total (Running)	Calculates the percentage value of a specified field, by summing all the data rows and dividing the current row by the total sum. The following are properties of this function: • **Field Name**: The field whose average to be calculated. • **Reset on Group Name**: If this value is set, the average value is reset when the named group appears. • **Rounding Mode**: Java's `BigDecimal` Rounding mode. Please see Java's documentation for values. • **Scale Result To 100**: Multiply the value by 100. • **Scale**: The scale of the quotient returned. The default value is **14**.

Advanced functions

Advanced functions include functions that are specialized, and are not generally used.

Function name	Description
Message Format	Formats a message, based on the current data row.
	The following are properties of this function:
	• **Encoding**: Use this encoding if URL Encode properties are set.
	• **Null-String**: What value to render if the field referenced is null.
	• **Message Pattern**: A string pattern to render, with row data referenced by ${FIELD}.
	• **URL-Encode the result**: To encode the final result.
	• **URL Encode all Values**: To encode the individual row data rendered within the message.
Resource Message Format	Returns a formatted message from a resource bundle.
	The following are properties of this function:
	• **Resource-Key of Pattern**: The format string to render, which may contain references to the current row fields, using the ${FIELD} syntax.
	• **ResourceBundle Identifier**: The name of the resource bundle.
	• **Null String**: The value to return if a field is null.
Lookup	This function allows you to choose between different strings, a value based on key matching.
	The following are properties of this function:
	• **Fall Back Value**: If no keys match the field value, return this value.
	• **Field Name**: The field to compare keys, to determine the mapping.
	• **Ignore Case When Matching**: If set to **True**, ignores the case when making key comparisons.
	• **Key Values**: Values to compare to the field. Each key should have a corresponding Texts value.
	• **Null Value**: If the field is null, return this value.
	• **Text Values**: It is a list of strings. A string is chosen from the list depending on which key matches the field value.

Function name	Description
Indirect Lookup	This function allows you to choose between different columns, a value based on key matching.
	The following are properties of this function: • **Fallback Forward-Field**: If no keys match the field value, return this field's value. • **Field Name**: The field to compare keys, to determine the mapping. • **Forwarding Field List**: It is a list of fields. A field is chosen from the list depending on which key matches the field value. • **Ignore Case when Matching**: If set to **True**, ignores the case when making key comparisons. • **Key Values**: Values to compare to the field. Each key should have a corresponding forwarding field. • **Null Value**: If the field is null, return this value.
Resource Bundle Lookup	Returns a value from a resource bundle, based on a key provided by a field.
	The following are properties of this function: • **Field Name**: The field which contains the resource bundle key. • **Resource-Bundle Identifier**: The name of the resource bundle.
Open Formula (Advanced)	This function is a stateful version of the Formula Expression.
	The following are properties of this function: • **Formula**: The formula to evaluate. • **Initialization Formula**: If specified, this formula will be evaluated when the Formula Function is called for the first time, instead of evaluating the default formula.

Image functions

Image functions render various graphical objects, which may be used in conjunction with a content field element.

Function name	Description
BarCode	This function generates a simple barcode `ReportDrawable` object, which may be rendered in a content field element. The following are properties of this function:<ul><li>**barHeight**: The height of the bar in pixels</li><li>**barWidth**: The width of the bar in pixels</li><li>**checksum**: If set to **True**, includes the checksum in the barcode</li><li>**rawDataField**: The field containing the barcode value</li><li>**rawTypeField**: If **type** is not specified, use this field name to resolve the barcode type</li><li>**showText**: If set to **True**, shows the barcode text below the barcode</li><li>**Type**: The type of the barcode</li></ul>
Sparkline	This function generates a sparkline `ReportDrawable` object, which may be rendered in a content field element. The following are properties of this function:<ul><li>**backgroundColor**: The background color of the sparkline</li><li>**color**: The foreground color of the sparkline</li><li>**counterclockwise**: If rendering a pie, render the slices counter clockwise</li><li>**Field**: An array of field names used to render the sparkline</li><li>**highColor**: The color of the largest bars or pie slices</li><li>**highSlice**: The threshold value of the largest slices</li><li>**lastColor**: The color of the last bar chart</li><li>**lowColor**: The color of the smallest bars or pie slices</li><li>**lowSlice**: The threshold value of the smallest slices</li><li>**mediumColor**: The color value of the medium bars or slices</li><li>**mediumSlice**: The threshold value of the medium slices</li><li>**rawDataField**: If specified, use this as the source field for the array of values, populating a sparkline graph</li><li>**spacing**: The spacing of pixels between each data input, having a default value of **2**</li><li>**startAngle**: The start angle of the pie sparkline</li><li>**Type**: The type of sparkline to render — **bar**, **line**, or **pie**</li></ul>

Function name	Description
Survey Scale	This function generates a survey scale `ReportDrawable` object, which may be rendered in a **content field** element.

The following are properties of this function:

- **Field Name**: The fields to render as tick marks on the scale
- **Highest Response Value**: The maximum number to render on the scale
- **Lowest Response Value**: The minimum number to render on the scale
- **Lower Range Bound Field**: If set along with the upper bound field, a box will render over a certain range, based on the field value provided
- **Range Paint**: The color to render the range in, which defaults to gray
- **Upper Range Bound Field**: If set along with lower bound field, a box will render over a certain range

Script functions

Scripting functions make it easy to customize your report through various scripting languages.

Function name	Description
Bean-Scripting Framework (BSF)	This function uses Apache's Bean Scripting Framework to generate a result. Please see `http://jakarta.apache.org/bsf` for more information on the Bean Scripting Framework. The following are properties of this function: - **Expression Programming Language**: The programming language used in the expression. - **Expression**: An expression defined in the programming language specified. - **Initialization Script**: A script defined in the programming language specified, which is executed during the initialization of the scripting language environment.

Function name	Description
Bean-Scripting-Host (BSH)	This function uses the BeanShell framework to generate a result. Please see `http://www.beanshell.org` for more information on BeanShell.
	Following is the property of this function:
	• **Expression**: A bean shell expression, which must be in the form of `getValue()` `{FUNCTION}`, returning the value. The `DataRow` object is accessible to the expression, allowing access to the current data row.
JavaScript	This function uses Javascript to generate a result. Please see `http://www.mozilla.org/rhino/` for more information on Rhino Javascript.
	Following is the property of this function:
	• **Expression**: A Javascript expression, which must be in the form of `getValue()` `{FUNCTION}`, returning the value. The `DataRow` object is accessible to the expression, allowing access to the current data row.
Single Value Query	This function executes an existing named query against a data source, and returns a result from the first row.
	The following are properties of this function:
	• **Field Name**: If the query is parameterized, you must specify the fields that it needs to execute.
	• **Result Column**: The named column within the first row to return. If the property is not set, the first column is returned.
	• **Query Name**: The query to execute.
	• **queryTimeout**: the amount of time allowed for query execution.

Working with formulas

In addition to providing functions within reports, formulas may also be used to generate dynamic content in a report. Formulas may be used to derive element property and style values. Also, the **Open Formula** and **Open Formula (Advanced)** functions defined earlier may be used to combine the formula and function mechanisms in a report.

Formulas in Pentaho Reporting are based on the OpenFormula standard. This standard is similar to Excel Formula support, and is used in Open Office, as well as other tools such as Pentaho Metadata. This formula system is often referred to as **LibFormula**, which is the library name for reporting's formula sub-project.

Formula syntax

A formula evaluates to a final value. Formulas support a standard set of data types, along with operators and functions that may be used to derive new values. Here is a simple example formula:

```
IF([COL1] > 10; "Big"; "Small");
```

This formula uses the IF function with parameters separated by semi-colons. The first parameter is a comparison, resulting in true or false. To reference an outside data column or named function, reference the column in brackets, as shown for COL1. If the comparison example evaluates to true, the second parameter in the IF function is returned. To specify a string, use double quotes, shown with "Big" and "Small". If the statement evaluates to false, the third parameter is returned.

Also, the term NULL may be used to denote a null reference.

Formula data types

Column data, as well as literal values, all get mapped to a formula data type. The following data types are supported. Different types may inherit from one another:

Data Type	Description
Numeric	A Numeric value, represented in Java as a BigDecimal object. Literal values of this type may take the following forms: • 123 • 123.456 • 123e10 or 456E-10 • -1.2
Text	A text value, represented in Java as a String object. Literal values of this type must be quoted with double quotes: "Text Here" To place a double quote within a string, reference it twice: " Here is a "" quote"
Logical	The Logical type inherits from the Numeric type. The values of this type are Boolean—either true or false. You may specify a logical value through the functions **TRUE()** and **FALSE()**.
Error	Various formula functions may fail. When this occurs, an error is created. Certain functions are available to determine if an error has occurred.

Data Type	Description
Date	The Date type inherits from the Numeric type. This type is represented as a `java.util.Date` object within Java, and represents the Date portion of a complete date.
Time	The Time type inherits from the Numeric type. This type is represented as a `java.util.Date` object within Java, and represents the Time portion of a complete date.
DateTime	The DateTime type inherits from the Numeric type, as well as the Date and Time types. This type is represented as a `java.util.Date` object within Java. Functions such as **DATEVALUE()** are available to generate a date object.

Array	Arrays may be declared in a formula, or generated by functions. You may specify one or two dimensional arrays with the following syntax:
	
	`{ROW1|ROW2|ROW3...}`
	
	And a row may be broken into multiple columns by semicolons. Here is an example:
	
	`{1;2;3|4;5;6|7;8;9}`

Formula operators

The following operators may be used within a formula expression. Note that all operators, except the percent operator, are infix operators, with the operator appearing between the values — for instance, Value1 OPERATOR Value2.

Operator	Description
+	Adds two numbers together.
-	Subtracts two numbers.
*	Multiples two numbers.
/	Divides two numbers.
=	Returns true if both values are equal.
!=	Returns true if values are not equal.
<=	Returns true if the first value is less than or equal to the second value.
>=	Returns true if the first value is larger than or equal to the second value.
<	Returns true if the first value is less than the second value.
>	Returns true if the first value is greater than the second value.
^	Returns the first value powered to the second value.

Operator	Description
&	Concatenates two strings.
%	Divides a number by 100, converting it to percent. For instance, 100% will return 1.

Formula functions

Pentaho Reporting defines many functions available for use within the formula system. Below is the exhaustive list, along with the detailed information about each function:

Date time functions

These functions allow for creation and manipulation of Date, Time, and DateTime objects.

Function name	Description
DATE(Year; Month; Day)	Creates a Date object based on the year, month, and day.
DATEDIF(StartDate; EndDate; Format)	Returns the difference between two dates, depending on the format code, which may be one of the following: • y: The difference in years. • m: The difference in months. • d: The difference in days. • yd: The difference in days, ignoring the years. • ym: The difference in months, ignoring the years. • md: The difference in days, ignoring the months and years.
DATEVALUE(Text)	Parses a string into a date. The string must match one of the supported formats. By default, the following formats are supported: • M/d/yy • yyyy-MM-dd
DAY(Date)	Returns the day of the month.
DAYS(Date1; Date2)	Calculates the number of days between two dates.
HOUR(Time)	Returns the hour of the time.
MINUTE(Time)	Returns the minute of the time.
MONTH(Date)	Returns the numeric month of the year, where January = 1, and so on.
NOW()	Creates a DateTime object with the current time.
SECOND(Time)	Returns the second of the time.

Function name	Description
TIME(Hour; Minute; Second)	Creates a Time object, based on the hour, minute, and second value.
TIMEVALUE(Text)	Returns a sequential number for a text shown in a possible time entry format.
TODAY()	Creates a Date object with the current date.
WEEKDAY(Date)	Returns the day of the week, where Sunday = 1, and so on.
YEAR(Date)	Returns the year.

Logical functions

These functions perform various Boolean logic operations.

Function name	Description
AND(Expression1; Expression2; ...)	If all expressions evaluate to true, returns true, otherwise returns false. Note that any number of expressions may be ANDed together.
FALSE()	Returns the Boolean value false.
IF(Expression; ReturnTrue; ReturnFalse)	If the first parameter evaluates to true, return the second parameter, otherwise return the third parameter.
NOT(Expression)	Return false if the expression is true, true if the expression is false.
OR(Expression1; Expression2; ...)	Return true if any of the expressions evaluates to true. Note that any number of expressions may be ORed together.
TRUE()	Returns the Boolean value true.
XOR(Expression1; Expression2; ...)	Returns true if an odd number of expressions evaluate to true.

Mathematical functions

These functions offer various forms of numeric calculations.

Function name	Description
ABS(Value)	Returns the absolute value.
ACOS(Value)	Returns the arccosine of a number.
ACOSH(Value)	Returns the inverse hyperbolic cosine of a number.
ASIN(Value)	Returns the arcsine of a number.
ATAN(Value)	Returns the arctangent of a number.
ATAN2(Value1;Value2)	Returns the arctangent for the specified coordinates.
AVERAGE(Value1; Value2; ...)	Returns the average value of all the parameters. These values may also be arrays. Each element of an array is evaluated to calculate the average.
AVERAGEA(Value1; Value2; ...)	Returns the average value of all the parameters. These values may also be arrays. Each element of an array is evaluated to calculate the average. Text and logical values are included in the calculation too.
COS(Value1)	Returns the cosine of a number.
EVEN(Value)	Rounds the number up to the nearest even integer.
EXP(Value1)	Calculates the exponent for basis e.
INT(Value)	Rounds a number down to the nearest Integer value.
LN(Value1)	Calculates the natural logarithm of a number.
LOG(Value; Base)	Calculates the logarithm to any specified base.
LOG10(Value)	Calculates the base-10 logarithm of a number.
MAX(Value1; Value2; ...)	Returns the maximum value of all the parameters. These values may also be arrays. Each element of an array is evaluated, and the largest value is returned.
MAXA(Value1; Value2; ...)	Returns the maximum value of all the parameters. These values may also be arrays. Each element of an array is evaluated, and the largest value is returned. Text and logical values are included in the calculation too.

Function name	Description
MIN(Value1; Value2; ...)	Returns the minimum value of all the parameters. These values may also be arrays. Each element of an array is evaluated, and the smallest value is returned.
MINA(Value1; Value2; ...)	Returns the maximum value of all the parameters. These values may also be arrays. Each element of an array is evaluated, With and the smallest value is returned.
MOD(Value1; Value2)	Calculates the remainder of division for Value1 divided by Value2.
ODD((Value)	Rounds the number up to the nearest odd integer.
PI()	Returns the value of the number Pi.
POWER(Value; Power)	Computes a number raised to the power by another number.
SIN(Value)	Returns the sine of a number.
SQRT(Value)	Returns the square root of a number.
SUM(Value1; Value2; ...)	Sums two or more values. These values may also be arrays. Every element of a one or two dimensional array will be summed together.
SUMA(Value1; Value2; ...)	Sums two or more values. These values may also be arrays. Every element of a one or two dimensional array will be summed together. Text and logical values are included in the calculation too.
VAR(Value1; Value2; ...)	Calculates the variance based on a sample.

Text functions

These functions work with and manipulate strings.

Function name	Description
EXACT(Text1; Text2)	Returns true if two Text values are exactly equal.
FIND(Search; Text[; Index])	Returns the index of the first occurrence of the search string in the Text, starting at the Index specified. The index parameter is optional.
LEFT(Text; Length)	Returns the left portion of a string up to Length characters.
LEN(Text)	Returns the length of the text.

Function name	Description
LOWER(Text)	Returns the text in all lower case.
MID(Text; Start; Length)	Returns a substring within the Text, starting at Start, and having the length of Length.
REPLACE(Text; Start; Length; New)	Replaces a portion of the Text, starting at Start, and ending at Length with the New text provided.
REPT(Text; Count)	Returns the Text Count times. For instance, if the Text was "test" and the Count was 3, the result would be "testtesttest".
RIGHT(Text; Count)	Returns the right portion of the string up to Length characters.
SUBSTITUTE(Text; Old; New[; Which])	Replaces the Old substring with the New substring in Text. If the Which index is provided, only the Nth Old substring will be replaced.
T(Value)	If the value is of type Text, returns the value, otherwise returns an empty string.
TEXT(Value)	Converts the value to Text. Boolean values are converted to "TRUE" and "FALSE".
TRIM(Text)	Trims any whitespace at the beginning and end of the Text.
UNICHAR(Number)	Converts a code number into a Unicode character or letter.
UNICODE(Text)	Returns the numeric code for the first Unicode character in a text string.
UPPER(Text)	Returns the text in all upper case.
URLENCODE(Text; Encoding)	Encodes the text based on the encoding specified. If no encoding is specified, ISO-8859-1 is used.

Reporting Specific functions

These functions interact with the reporting engine in some way:

Function name	Description
ISEXPORTTYPE(ExportDescriptor)	Returns true if the current export type starts with the provided ExportDescriptor text.
ISEMPTYDATA()	Returns true if the report result set has zero rows.
METADATA(Field; Domain; Name[; Type])	This function returns a metadata value of a Field based on its Domain and Name. This function is demonstrated in Chapter 12.
ROWCOUNT(GroupName)	Returns the current row number of the current group. If no GroupName is specified, returns the global row number.
ENV(Property)	Return the value of a property provided through the ReportEnvironment API. To create a property in your environment, set a configuration property using the format `org.pentaho.reporting.engine.classic.core.environment.<PROPERTY>`

Miscellaneous functions

Many additional functions are available that offer rich capabilities within Pentaho Reporting.

Function name	Description
CHOOSE(Index; Value1; Value2; ...)	Returns the parameter referenced by the index.
COUNT(Value1; Value2; ...)	Returns the number of values. This function will count individual elements within arrays as well.
COUNTA(Value1; Value2; ...)	Returns the number of non-empty values within an array or arrays. This function will count non arrays always, even if they are empty.
COUNTBLANK(Reference)	Returns the number of empty values within a reference that represents an array of values.
HASCHANGED(Text)	Returns true if the field with the name of Text has changed.
ISBLANK(Value)	Returns true if the value is null.

Function name	Description
ISERR(Value)	Returns true if the value is an error, but not the NA error.
ISERROR(Value)	Returns true if the value is an error.
ISEVEN(Value)	Returns true if the value is even.
ISLOGICAL(Value)	Returns true if the value is a logical type.
ISNA(Expression)	Returns true if the expression has generated the NA error object.
ISNONTEXT(Value)	Returns true if the value is not text.
ISNUMBER(Value)	Returns true if the value is a number.
ISODD(Value)	Returns true if the value is odd.
ISREF(Value)	Returns true if the value is a reference.
ISTEXT(Value)	Returns true if the value is a text type.
NA()	Returns the Error NA, or Not Available.
CSVTEXT(Array[; DoQuoting[; Separator[; Quote]]])	Generates a comma separated value list. If DoQuoting is set to true, quote all the strings. By default, the separator is a comma, this can be overridden by setting the Separator parameter. By default, the strings are quoted using a double quote, this can be overridden by setting the Quote parameter.
INDEX(Array; RowNumber; ColumnNumber)	Returns the value at the specified array index.
VALUE(Text)	Converts a Text string to a Numeric value.

As you can see, there are many functions to choose from when defining formulas within reports. In Chapter 3, multiple formulas were used in examples to create rich, dynamic reports.

Internationalization and localization of reports

To internationalize a report, you must use the resource elements available within Pentaho Reporting when creating your report. Each resource element defines a resource base and a resource key reference. Normally, the resource base refers to the name of the message properties file in which localized names are kept. For default handling of resource bundles in Java, please see Java's I18N Tutorial on resource bundles:

http://java.sun.com/docs/books/tutorial/i18n/resbundle/concept.html

Once you've built your report, you'll want to configure your application to access the resource bundle files appropriately. Pentaho Reporting defines a `ResourceBundleFactory` API, which allows you to customize how these files are loaded. By default, a report is configured to use the `DefaultResourceBundleFactory` implementation, which uses Java's `ResourceBundle` implementation. This implementation resolves the provided resource base value on the Java classpath.

Another solution is to use the `LibLoaderResourceBundleFactory`, which uses LibLoader's approach to loading files. `LibLoader` is an extendible framework for loading resources. Utilizing LibLoader's default ResourceLoaders, you may load data from the filesystem, URLs, ZIP files, as well as the classpath.

If neither of these implementations fits your needs, you may implement your own `ResourceBundleFactory`. This factory interface defines the following methods:

- `public ResourceBundle getResourceBundle(String key);`
- `public Locale getLocale();`

If using a factory other than the default, you may specify the factory by calling `setResourceBundleFactory()` on the master report object.

The `ResouceBundleFactory` is also responsible for determining the specific locale to use when rendering the report. The `DefaultResourceBundleFactory` uses the default system locale, but also contains a `setLocale()` method for configuring the locale if necessary.

If you are not planning on implementing your own `ResourceBundleFactory`, the recommended approach for configuring the locale of a report is to provide it through the `ReportEnvironment` API. The `DefaultReportEnvironment` class defines a `setLocale()` method for configuring the report's locale. This is demonstrated in the example below.

Localizing fields

Using the **resource-field** element within your report allows you to localize dynamic data to a certain extent. Instead of providing a static resource key, this element type specifies the field data source where the key is generated from. The only limitation to this approach is that you must have a defined bundle with the key to localized mappings already in place. For a complete solution to dynamic localization, you may want to investigate using the `Indirect Lookup` function, in order to dynamically choose different localized columns in a database for populating a specific dynamic field.

Localization example

Now that you're familiar with the various components involved in setting up an internationalized report, it's time to walk through an example. First, launch the Pentaho Report Designer and create a very basic report with a resource-label in the Report Header. Specify **file:data/localization-example** as the resource-identifier, and use **localizedString** as the **value** attribute. Export this report as `localization-example.prpt`, and place it in the `data` folder for Chapter 2.

You also need to create localized property files. For this example, create a default English message bundle file as `data/localization-example.properties`, with the following text:

```
localizedString=My Localized Report
```

Create a Spanish message bundle file, `localization-example_es.properties`, with the following text:

```
localizedString=Mi Informe Localizar
```

You'll now need to configure the `Chapter2SwingApp`, in order to use the new report, along with the message bundles. First, edit the report reference to use `file:data/localization-example.prpt`. You'll now need to configure the report environment with the correct locale. Add the following lines of code right after creating the MasterReport object:

```
Locale locale = Locale.getDefault();
((DefaultReportEnvironment)report.getReportEnvironment()).
setLocale(locale);
```

Also, make sure to add the following imports:

```
import java.util.Locale;
import org.pentaho.reporting.engine.classic.core.
DefaultReportEnvironment;
```

Run the example by typing `ant run` on the command line. You should see the label "My Localized Report" appearing in the report.

Now change the creation of the Locale object to Spanish:

```
Locale locale = new Locale("es");
```

Execute `ant run` again. This time you should see the new Spanish label in your report.

Summary

In this chapter, you learned the details involved in report parameterization. You also learned about the various ways to dynamically render a report, including learning all the available functions and expressions, as well as learning the LibFormula syntax and function list. Finally, you learned how to internationalize your reports and the static text within a report, so you can build reports that are populated by internationalized data.

8

Adding Sub-Reports and Cross Tabs to Reports

In this chapter, you'll learn the ins and outs of two advanced reporting topics
—sub-reports and cross tabs. Sub-reports allow you to embed reusable reports
within a master report. As you'll see with the help of examples, sub-reports can take
on many forms—from multi-page detail reports to summary sub-reports that include
charts. You'll also learn how to create a side-by-side sub-report example. Along with
sub-reports, you'll learn how to incorporate cross tabs into your reports. Cross tabs
allow you to compare multiple variables in a single table of data values.

Adding sub-reports

In Chapter 3, you created a very simple single data row sub-report that included
details about the current customer for invoicing purposes. In this chapter, you'll
review other scenarios for using sub-reports and learn the technical details involved
in including sub-reports in a master report.

Sub-reports in Pentaho Reporting may be included in any band of a report, except for
the page header and page footer bands. Sub-reports receive a `DataRow` of parameters,
determined by the current state of their parent report when rendering the sub-report.
These parameters may be used when executing a sub-report query or referenced
directly in the sub-report. Within sub-reports, you define named queries that may
reference the `DataRow` of parameters passed in, allowing a sub-report to query only
the currently scoped data, not the entire data set available to the parent report.

Sub-reports may be of any length, may be included in other sub-reports in a nested fashion, and may also be presented side-by-side one another in their parent report. When spanning multiple pages, special considerations must be made, including how to handle the master report's page header, page footer, and group headers. This chapter will cover all of these topics in the examples below.

Multi-page sub-report example

In this first example, you'll build a report, which includes a large sub-report that may span multiple pages. Before you can begin with these examples, you need to create a new folder called chapter8, and copy the JAR files from the chapter3/lib folder into chapter8/lib. Also, copy the chapter2/build.xml file into the chapter8 folder. Finally, copy the chapter3/data folder to chapter8/data, so that you may reuse the already configured ElectroBarn data source.

To begin with the example, you must first define your master report dataset. You'll reuse the ElectroBarn HSQLDB example to build this report. Launch the Report Designer and create a new report. Add a new JDBC dataset. Select the already defined ElectroBarn connection for this example, which was configured in Chapter 3. Now, define the following query:

```
SELECT
        "ENDOFDAY"."SESSIONID",
        "ENDOFDAY"."EMPLOYEEID",
        "ENDOFDAY"."ACTUALCHECKTOTAL",
        "ENDOFDAY"."ACTUALCASHTOTAL",
        "ENDOFDAY"."CHECKOUTTIME"
FROM
        "ENDOFDAY"
ORDER BY
        "ENDOFDAY"."SESSIONID" ASC
```

This simple query selects the high level sales clerk session information. Now that you've configured your dataset, it's time to define your master report. First, create an example page header and footer. Place a **label** in the **Page Header** and add the text Master Report Page Header. For the **Page Footer**, place a **label** and set the text to Master Report Page Footer. For both the header and the footer, check the **sticky** style attribute checkbox, which appears in the **page behavior** group of style attributes. This tells the reporting engine to render the master report's page header and footer on pages generated by the sub-report. Otherwise, these bands would not appear in every page of the generated report.

Finish the master report by dragging and dropping the fields for **SESSIONID** and **EMPLOYEEID** in the **Details** band. Give both of these fields a label as well. Your report should look like the following:

150%		50	·	100	·	150	·	200	·	250	·	300	·	350	·	400	·
Page Header	**Master Report Page Header**																
Report Header																	
Details	**Session ID:** SESSIONID **Employee ID:** EMPLOYEEID																
Report Footer																	
Page Footer	**Master Report Page Footer**																

It's now time to add a sub-report to the master report. Drag-and-drop a **sub-report** [Sub] element from the Palette into the **Details** band, below the **Employee ID**. When prompted, select the **Banded** option for this sub-report. Banded sub-reports act as an independent band within the report and take up the entire width. A Banded sub-report must appear below all other elements within a band. Therefore, if you add additional elements, the sub-report will appear below those added elements.

Now, you're ready to begin editing the sub-report. Double-click on the sub-report element, or right-click and select the **Edit sub-report** menu option, in order to bring up the sub-report for editing.

The first step to setting up the sub-report is to create a new data source query. Create the following ElectroBarn query as part of the sub-report:

```
SELECT
        "PURCHASES"."SESSIONID",
        "PURCHASES"."PAYMENTTYPE",
        "PURCHASES"."PURCHASETIME",
        "PURCHASES"."PURCHASEID",
        "PURCHASEITEMS"."QUANTITY",
        "INVENTORY"."SALEPRICE",
        "INVENTORY"."ITEMNAME"
FROM
        "PURCHASEITEMS" INNER JOIN "INVENTORY" ON
"PURCHASEITEMS"."ITEMID" = "INVENTORY"."ITEMID"
        INNER JOIN "PURCHASES" ON "PURCHASEITEMS"."PURCHASEID" =
"PURCHASES"."PURCHASEID"
WHERE
        "PURCHASES"."SESSIONID" = ${SESSIONID}
ORDER BY
        "PURCHASES"."PURCHASEID" ASC
```

This query selects details for the current **SESSIONID**, and is used by this and subsequent sub-report examples. Now, you must customize the parameters that are available to the sub-report. You can do this by bringing up the sub-report parameters dialog. Right-click on the sub-report's **Parameters** tree item under the **Data** tab and select the **Edit Sub-report Parameters...** menu item. The following dialog will appear:

This example limits the visible fields to the **SESSIONID**. Click the add import parameter button, and edit the table row by typing **SESSIONID** for both the **Outer Name** and **Inner Name**, as displayed above.

The **Outer Name** defines the name of the field within the master report, and the **Inner Name** defines the name as seen by the sub-report. In addition to importing parameters into a sub-report, sub-reports may make parameters available by exporting them to the master report.

You're now ready to style the sub-report. In this sub-report, you'll show the individual sales details with summaries about each sale. To begin, add a **label** element, Sub-Report Page Header, to the sub-report's **Page Header.** Also, add a **label**, Sub-Report Page Footer, to the **Page Footer.**

Second, populate the **Details** band of the sub-report. Drag-and-drop the field for the **ITEMNAME**, as well as for the **SALEPRICE** and **QUANTITY**. Also, add an **Open Formula** function that multiplies **SALEPRICE** by **QUANTITY**, and call this **ITEMPRICE**.

```
=[SALEPRICE] * [QUANTITY]
```

Add **ITEMPRICE** to the **Details** band by dragging and dropping the function into the canvas.

To complete the details band, you'll want to band the detail rows with different colors. Select the **Details** band in the structure tree and name it details. Now, create a **Row Banding Function**, which appears in the **Report** functions group of functions. Set the **Apply Element(s) Named** property to details, along with setting the **Active Banding Color** and **Inactive Banding Color** properties to alternating shades of white and green. The design view of the sub-report **Details** band should look like this:

Now, add some summary information to the sub-report. Right-click on the **Groups** tree and edit the root group, naming it purchaseid and adding the group field **PURCHASEID**. Unselect the **hide-on-canvas** attribute for the **Group Header** and **Group Footer** bands. Drag-and-drop the PURCHASEID and PURCHASETIME fields into the **Group Header**, along with adding a rectangle background to distinguish this from other parts of the report. Also, add header columns for the **Details** band.

Create a **Sum** function called **TotalSale**, which sums the **ITEMPRICE** formula defined earlier. Set the **Group Name** property to purchaseid, which is the name of the group defined earlier.

Drag-and-drop the **TotalSale** function into the far right of the report's **Group Footer**, along with some additional color, in order for the report to look nice.

You're now ready to preview the report to see how the sub-report looks when combined with the master report. Notice that when you preview the sub-report, it also renders the master report.

Also notice that when the sub-report renders, the master report's **Page Header** and **Page Footer** appear alongside the sub-report's **Page Header** and **Page Footer**. Experiment by unselecting the **sticky** style attribute on the **Page Header** and **Page Footer** of the master report, and preview to see that the header and footer do not appear. Save the report as chapter8/data/subreport_multipage.prpt. The sub-report definition is stored as part of the report bundle, so no additional files are necessary for storage.

To complete this example, copy the chapter2/src/Chapter2SwingApp.java file into the chapter8/src folder and rename the class to MultipageSubreportApp.java, creating a simple Java application to demonstrate the sub-report. Update the Java application to reference your new report.

```
Resource res = manager.createDirectly(
    new URL("file:data/subreport_multipage.prpt"), MasterReport.class);
```

Now that you've updated the report definition, you're ready to run the example application. Add the following Ant target to your `build.xml` file:

```
<target name="runmultipagesubreport" depends="compile">
    <java fork="true" classpathref="runtime_classpath" classname="Mult
ipageSubreportApp"/>
</target>
```

Type `ant runmultipagesubreport` to preview the report, which should look something like this:

Master Report Page Header

Session ID: 1

Employee ID: 1

Purchase ID: 1		*Purchase Time:* Tue May 27 10:05:40 EDT 2008	
Item Name	Sale Price	Quantity	Item Price
Green Electronics MP3 Audio Mini Player	75.99	1	75.99
		Total Sale: 75.99	

Purchase ID: 2		*Purchase Time:* Tue May 27 10:26:21 EDT 2008	
Item Name	Sale Price	Quantity	Item Price
Speedy Fly RC UAV Airplane	149.99	1	149.99
12 AA Battery Pack	6.99	2	13.98
		Total Sale: 163.97	

Purchase ID: 3		*Purchase Time:* Tue May 27 10:53:46 EDT 2008	
Item Name	Sale Price	Quantity	Item Price
Tried and True Portable CD Player	24.99	1	24.99
		Total Sale: 24.99	

Purchase ID: 4		*Purchase Time:* Tue May 27 11:15:17 EDT 2008	
Item Name	Sale Price	Quantity	Item Price
Tried and True Radio Alarm Clock	14.99	1	14.99
		Total Sale: 14.99	

Purchase ID: 5		*Purchase Time:* Tue May 27 11:27:44 EDT 2008	
Item Name	Sale Price	Quantity	Item Price
Electro RC Car Racer	59.95	1	59.95
		Total Sale: 59.95	

Purchase ID: 6		*Purchase Time:* Tue May 27 11:43:20 EDT 2008	
Item Name	Sale Price	Quantity	Item Price
Tried and True Radio Alarm Clock	14.99	1	14.99
		Total Sale: 14.99	

Sub-Report Page Footer

Master Report Page Footer

Chart sub-report example

In addition to embedding traditional reports into a master report, sub-reports are also useful for embedding summary or detailed information not available in the initial data source query of a master report. In this example, you'll reuse your previously defined master report, and instead of showing a multi-page sub-report, you'll display a pie chart summarizing the information.

Open the already defined `subreport_multipage.prpt` file. Delete the already defined sub-report element and place a new **Inline** sub-report element in its place. Double-click on the sub-report element to launch the sub-report view. Define a new data source query for the sub-report by re-using the sub-report query defined earlier. Make sure to define `SESSIONID` as a sub-report input parameter.

Now that you've defined the sub-report query, place a **chart** element in the report header of the sub-report. Select the **Pie** chart type. Edit the chart element by setting the **value-column** property to **QUANTITY** and the **series-by-field** property to **PURCHASEID**.

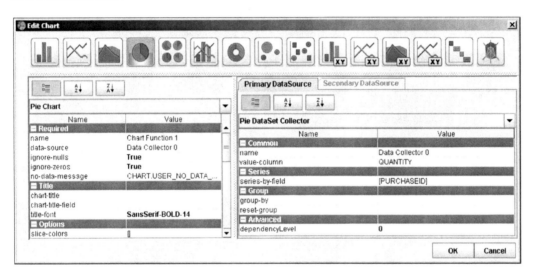

Save this report as `chapter8/data/subreport_chart.prpt`. Note that the sub-report information is stored as part of the PRPT bundle. Copy the `MultipageSubreportApp.java` file to a new class in `chapter8/src` called `ChartSubreportApp.java`. In the class, reference your new chart report.

```
Resource res = manager.createDirectly(
     new URL("file:data/subreport_chart.prpt"), MasterReport.class);
```

Now, add the following Ant target to the `build.xml` file:

```
<target name="runchartsubreport" depends="compile">
    <java fork="true" classpathref="runtime_classpath" classname="Char
tSubreportApp"/>
</target>
```

Type `ant runchartsubreport` to view the results, which should look similar to this:

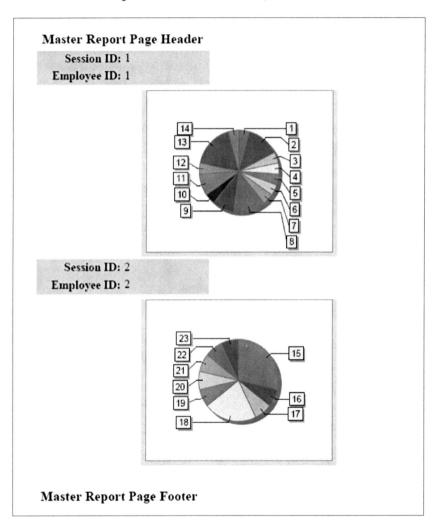

Side-by-side sub-report example

Another capability of sub-reports is to be able to place two or more sub-reports horizontally, beside one another, within a report band. The example below demonstrates this functionality by taking the charting example defined previously, and adding a summary table next to the pie chart for each session.

Open up the `subreport_chart.prpt`, and add a sub-report element next to the chart sub-report:

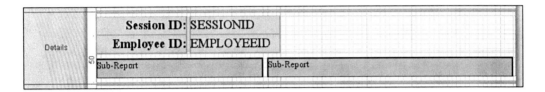

Double-click on the new sub-report to begin editing. You'll use the same data source query as the chart for this sub-report, so define a new JDBC query with the copied SQL. You will also need to define `SESSIONID` as an input parameter to the sub-report.

In this sub-report, you'll want to define a simple summary of each purchase. As in the first sub-report example, define a group with **PURCHASEID** as its field. Make the group's header visible in the report. Also, define the **ITEMPRICE** and **TotalSale** functions as defined in the first example.

Drag-and-drop the **PURCHASEID** and **PURCHASETIME** fields, along with the **TotalSale** function, into the **Group Header**. In the **Report Header**, add the column headers. Finally, add a rectangle to the group header named **GroupBackground**, and add the following **visible** style formula to toggle the rectangle's visibility:

```
=IF( ISODD( [PURCHASEID] ); TRUE(); FALSE() )
```

Toggling the colors acts as a row banding mechanism. The row banding function used earlier works only on the **Details** band, hence the special formula expression.

The report design should look something like this:

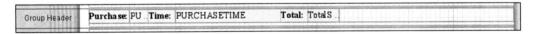

Preview the master report to see side-by-side sub-reports in action. Now, save this report as `chapter8/data/subreport_sidebyside.prpt`. Copy the `MultipageSubreportApp.java` example class to `chapter8/src/SideBySideSubReportApp.java`. Update the class with the new report filename.

```
Resource res = manager.createDirectly(
    new URL("file:data/subreport_sidebyside.prpt"), MasterReport.class);
```

Add the following Ant target to your `build.xml` file:

```
<target name="runsidebysidesubreport" depends="compile">
    <java fork="true" classpathref="runtime_classpath" classname="Side
BySideSubReportApp"/>
</target>
```

Type `ant runsidebysidesubreport` to view the results

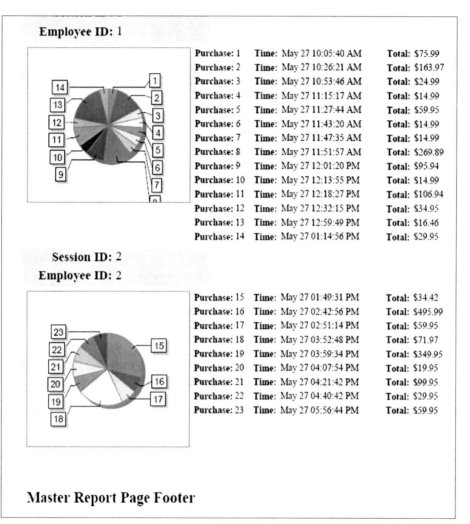

Adding cross tabs

Cross tabs allow you to view dimensional data in a report. Using cross tabs, you can easily view two or more fields and how they relate based on a measure. For instance, you may want to see how much sales each sales person is doing during the course of a week, and a cross tab allows you to present that data easily, as shown in the following table:

	Sales Person 1	**Sales Person 2**
Day 1	$1,240	$1,100
Day 2	$1,400	$1,000

Pentaho Reporting offers the ability to create cross tab-based reports. These are a special type of report that render differently than most standard reports. These reports also expect the data to be in a particular format. Traditionally, cross tab reports are driven by multidimensional queries. As highlighted in Chapter 5, Pentaho Reporting offers a Mondrian and olap4j `DataFactory` for providing multidimensional data to a report. Use the `DenormalizedMDXDataFactory` to populate a cross tab report. This Data Factory flattens out an MDX result set. The following MDX query:

```
select
      [Employee].Members on rows,
      [Time].[All Times].Children on columns
from
      [Sales]
where
      [Measures].[Total Sales]
```

would result in the dataset as shown in the following table:

Employee (All)	**Employee Name**	**Time (All)**	**Time Sale Day**	**Total Sales**
All Employees	—	All Times	Day 1	$2,340
All Employees	—	All Times	Day 2	$2,400
All Employees	Sales Person 1	All Times	Day 1	$1,240
All Employees	Sales Person 1	All Times	Day 2	$1,400
All Employees	Sales Person 2	All Times	Day 1	$1,100
All Employees	Sales person 2	All Times	Day 2	$1,000

Note that the first two rows are the summation of all the employee sales for the first two days.

Pentaho Reporting uses this dataset to populate a cross tab. First, you would define the measure in the Details band of the cross tab. You would then define the Employee dimension as the cross tab column group. Finally, you would define the Time dimension as the cross tab row group.

In MDX, it is possible to select multiple dimensions on the same axis. For each dimension defined on an axis, you may add an additional cross tab row or cross tab column group.

It is also possible to generate the same type of result set with standard SQL. Here is the same data selected as SQL instead of MDX:

```
SELECT
      'All Employees' AS ALLEMPLOYEES,
      "SALES_FACT"."EMPLOYEE",
      "SALES_FACT"."SALEDAY",
      SUM("SALES_FACT"."SALEPRICE") AS TOTAL_SALES
FROM
      "SALES_FACT"
GROUP BY
      "SALES_FACT"."EMPLOYEE",
      "SALES_FACT"."SALEDAY"
ORDER BY
      "SALES_FACT"."EMPLOYEE" ASC,
      "SALES_FACT"."SALEDAY" ASC
```

Note that this query doesn't sum the values at the All Employees level. Grouping sets, an advanced SQL concept, would need to be used to make that possible.

Cross tabs may contain multiple rows and columns. For instance, if you placed both the Employee and Time dimensions in the row group of your cross tab, the results would look identical to the flattened result set displayed above.

Cross tab MDX example

For this example, you'll need a simple Mondrian cube to work with. First define a quick fact table in HSQLDB, along with defining a Mondrian schema that maps to the table. You'll use the example above as the fact table. Add the following DDL to the electrobarn.script file, which is located in the chapter8/data folder:

```
CREATE TEXT TABLE SALES_FACT (EMPLOYEE VARCHAR, SALEDAY
VARCHAR, SALETIME VARCHAR, SALEPRICE DOUBLE)
SET TABLE INVENTORY SOURCE "salesfact.csv;ignore_first=true"
```

The `salesfact.csv` file, along with the `electrobarn.script` file, are provided as part of this book, or you can also download them online at: `http://www.packtpub.com/files/code/3193_Code.zip`

You also need to define the Mondrian Schema. Save the following Mondrian Schema XML in your `chapter8/data` folder as `electrobarn.mondrian.xml`:

```
<Schema name="electrobarn">
    <Cube name="Sales">
            <Table name="SALES_FACT"/>
            <Dimension name="Employee">
                    <Hierarchy hasAll="true">
                            <Level name="Employee Name"
column="EMPLOYEE"/>
                    </Hierarchy>
            </Dimension>
            <Dimension name="Time">
                    <Hierarchy hasAll="true">
                            <Level name="Sale Day" column="SALEDAY"/>
                            <Level name="Sale Time" column="SALETIME"/>
                    </Hierarchy>
            </Dimension>
            <Measure name="Total Sales" column="SALEPRICE"
aggregator="sum"/>
    </Cube>
</Schema>
```

This schema defines the Cube, Dimensions, and Measure discussed earlier.

Now, it's time to build the report in Pentaho Report Designer. To begin, you'll define a Denormalized MDX data source, based on the Sales cube as defined above. Click the **Data** tab, right-click on the **Data Sets** tree item and select **OLAP | Mondrian (Denormalized)**. Select the predefined ElectroBarn HSQLDB Data Source. Edit this data source to point to `chapter8/data/electrobarn`, which contains the recently added `SALES_FACT` table. Now, select the recently saved `electrobarn.mondrian.xml` as the **Mondrian Schema File**.

Define the following MDX Query as part of your Mondrian data set:

```
select [Employee].Members on rows, [Time].[All Times].Children on
columns from [Sales] where [Measures].[Total Sales]
```

This query selects all values from the Employee dimension on rows, and all the members of the first level of the Time dimension on columns. Once the MDX data source is defined, you're ready to build the cross tab report.

Cross tabs are still considered experimental in the Pentaho Report Designer, so to enable cross tab capabilities, you must enter the shortcut key *CTRL-ALT-O*. This adds a new **Add Crosstab Group** menu option to the **Master Report** tree element.

To begin, right-click on the **Master Report** tree element and select **Add Crosstab Group**. This replaces the traditional group hierarchy in the tree with a cross tab group hierarchy, and also changes the canvas view as shown below:

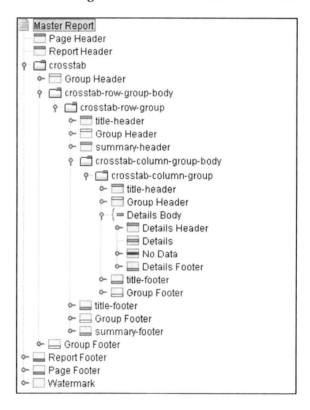

The cross tab report hierarchy consists of cross tab rows, cross tab columns, and finally a details body. You may add additional cross tab rows by right-clicking on the **crosstab-row-group** and selecting **Add Crosstab Row Group**. You can add cross tab columns by right-clicking on the **crosstab-column** group and selecting **Add Crosstab Column Group**.

The next step is to configure the rows of the cross tab. Click on the **crosstab-row-group**, and set the **group** attribute to [Employee].[(All)]. In the **Group Header** tree element within the **crosstab-row-group**, right-click and select **Add Element | string-field**. Set the **field** attribute of the string-field to [Employee].[(All)]. Also, define an empty **label** in the **title-header**. The empty label is used for correct column header spacing. This defines the first row group in the cross tab.

In future versions of Pentaho Report Designer, the canvas will be enabled for cross tab building, so adding elements and editing them through the tree will not be necessary.

Right-click on the **crosstab-row-group** and select **Add Crosstab Row Group**. For this row group, set the **group** attribute to [Employee]. [Employee Name]. In the **Group Header** tree element within the **crosstab-row-group**, right-click and select **Add Element | string-field**. Set the **field** attribute of the string-field to [Employee]. [Employee Name]. Also, define an empty **label** in the **title-header**. The empty label is used for correct column header spacing. This defines the second row group in the cross tab.

Now that you've defined the two necessary row groups, click on the **crosstab-column-group** and set the **group** attribute to [Time]. [Sale Day]. In the **Group Header** tree element within the **crosstab-row-group**, right-click and select **Add Element | string-field**. Set the **field** attribute of the string-field to [Employee]. [Employee Name]. This defines the column group in the cross tab.

To complete the cross tab, add a **number-field** to the **Details** tree element, and select [Measures]. [Total Sales] for the **field** attribute. You may choose to customize the text-field and number-field fonts and styles. Here is the final view of the tree when you've completed, with the **Details number-field** selected:

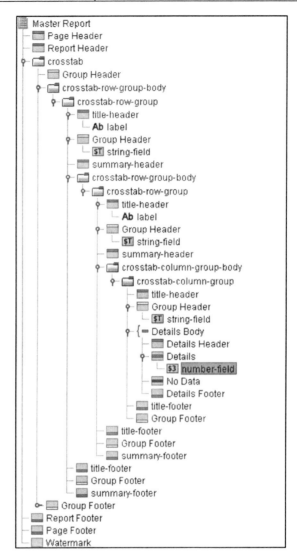

The canvas within Report Designer at this point looks like the following:

Once you've built and previewed the report in Report Designer, you'll need to save the report as `chapter8/data/mdxcrosstab.prpt` and create a Java application to render the report. Update the report reference section of the `onPreview()` method, within a freshly copied `Chapter2SwingApp`, renamed to `MdxCrossTabApp`.

```
Resource res = manager.createDirectly(
        new URL("file:data/mdxcrosstab.prpt"), MasterReport.class);
```

You will also need to copy the necessary Mondrian DataFactory JAR files into the `chapter8/lib` folder. Copy the following JAR files from the Report Designer's `lib` folder:

- `commons-collections.jar`
- `commons-dbcp.jar`
- `commons-math.jar`
- `commons-pool.jar`
- `commons-vfs.jar`
- `eigenbase-resgen.jar`
- `eigenbase-xom.jar`
- `eigenbase-properties.jar`
- `javacup.jar`
- `log4j.jar`
- `mondrian.jar`
- `pentaho-reporting-engine-classic-extensions-mondrian.jar`

Finally, you'll need to add the following Ant target to the `build.xml` file:

```
<target name="runmdxcrosstab" depends="compile">
    <java fork="true" classpathref="runtime_classpath" classname="MdxC
rossTabApp"/>
</target>
```

Type `ant runmdxcrosstab` on the command line to view the results!

		Day 1	Day 2
All Employees		$2,340.00	$2,400.00
All Employees	Sales Person 1	$1,240.00	$1,400.00
All Employees	Sales Person 2	$1,100.00	$1,000.00

Cross tab SQL example

For this exercise, you'll update the previous example to use a SQL query instead of the denormalized OLAP query. Open up the `mdxcrosstab.xml` file in Report Designer and save it as `sqlcrosstab.xml`. You're now ready to modify the data source to use a SQL query. Delete the denormalized MDX data source and create a new JDBC data source.

Now, you need to provide the cross tab SQL statement. The following SQL statement returns nearly identical results to that of the MDX query generated earlier:

```
SELECT
      'All Employees' AS ALLEMPLOYEES,
      "SALES_FACT"."EMPLOYEE",
      "SALES_FACT"."SALEDAY",
      SUM("SALES_FACT"."SALEPRICE") AS TOTAL_SALES
FROM
      "SALES_FACT"
GROUP BY
      "SALES_FACT"."EMPLOYEE",
      "SALES_FACT"."SALEDAY"
ORDER BY
      "SALES_FACT"."EMPLOYEE" ASC,
      "SALES_FACT"."SALEDAY" ASC
```

You'll need to update the cross tab report to reflect the new field names. Change the report element fields **[Employee].[(All)]** to ALLEMPLOYEES, **[Employee].[Employee Name]** to EMPLOYEE, **[Time].[Sale Day]** to SALEDAY, and **[Measures].[Total Sales]** to TOTAL_SALES. Also, make sure to update the **crosstab-row-group** and **crosstab-column-group group** attributes. You're now ready to preview the cross tab example. The result should look similar to the previous MDX-based example, except for displaying the total for all employees.

		Day 1	Day 2
All Employees	**Sales Person 1**	$1,240.00	$1,400.00
All Employees	**Sales Person 2**	$1,100.00	$1,000.00

As you can see from this example, a cross tab report can be driven by both denormalized MDX data, as well as SQL data, given that they return similar result sets. Save the SQL cross tab report as `sqlcrosstab.prpt`. You'll be using it in the next example.

Multiple row and column cross tab example

In this example, you'll update the SQL example with an additional measure, and display both total sales and average sales in the cross tab. Open the `sqlcrosstab.prpt` file in Pentaho Report Designer.

Update the SQL data source query to include the average sale price:

```
SELECT
      'All Employees' AS ALLEMPLOYEES,
      "SALES_FACT"."EMPLOYEE",
      "SALES_FACT"."SALEDAY",
      SUM("SALES_FACT"."SALEPRICE") AS TOTAL_SALES,
      AVG("SALES_FACT"."SALEPRICE") AS AVERAGE_SALES
FROM
      "SALES_FACT"
GROUP BY
      "SALES_FACT"."EMPLOYEE",
      "SALES_FACT"."SALEDAY"
ORDER BY
      "SALES_FACT"."EMPLOYEE" ASC,
      "SALES_FACT"."SALEDAY" ASC
```

You'll now update the cross tab with the necessary report elements, in order to display the average sale, along with labels for the measures. Right-click on the **Details** band in the tree view and select **Add Element | number-field**. Select `AVERAGE_SALES` as the **field** value, and set the **format** to `$#,##0.0`. Because it's not possible to move the report element in the canvas, you'll need to update the size and location attributes to render the cross tab cell correctly. For this element, set the **width** style attribute to `60.0`, and set the **x** style attribute to `60.0`. This places it after the Total Sales **number-field**. Also, select the Total Sales **number-field** and set it's width to `60.0` as well.

You'll also need to update the column header. Select the **SALEDAY string-field** defined in the **crosstab-column-group Group Header**, and set the width to `120.0`. This keeps the column header width in sync with the details body. Now, right-click on the same **Group Header** and add two labels. The first **label** should be given the value `Total Sale` and should have a **width** of `60.0`. It also needs a **y** value of `20.0`. Add a second **label** with the value `Average Sale`, and give this label a **width** of `60.0`, along with an **x** value of `60.0` and **y** value of `20.0`.

The final design time view should look like this:

			SALEDAY	
crosstab			Total Sales	Average Sales
	50	ALLEMPLOYEES	EMPLOYEE	TOTAL_SA AVERAGE_

Click on the preview button. Your report should look something like this:

		Day 1		Day 2	
		Total Sales	Average Sales	Total Sales	Average Sales
All Employees	**Sales Person 1**	$1,240.00	$206.67	$1,400.00	$233.33
All Employees	**Sales Person 2**	$1,100.00	$183.33	$1,000.00	$166.67

Summary

In this chapter, you built from scratch examples of sub-reports and cross tabs, exploring the capabilities offered by Pentaho Reporting. You built a multi-page sub-report, which demonstrated the use of the sticky flag available for managing page headers. You also built a sub-report with a summary chart. You then extended that example as a side-by-side sub-report with a summary chart, as well as a summary table of data retrieved from a different data query than the master report.

You also built cross tab reports based on MDX and SQL queries. These cross tab reports contained multiple row and column headers, and displayed summary data regarding ElectroBarn's sales numbers across multiple days.

Building Interactive Reports

9

In this chapter, you'll learn to enable interactive functionality within reports. Interactive reports are less common, but allow for interesting behaviors within various output formats. Each type of interactive approach covered in this chapter is based on the particular layout engine. You'll learn about Swing and HTML interactive options by creating examples that demonstrate their capabilities. By definition, interactive reports are based on events. Event bindings are defined in the report definition, making it possible to receive event notifications from within a report.

Interactive reports in Swing

In earlier chapters, you learned how to generate a static preview of a report within Swing via Pentaho Reporting's `PreviewDialog` API. This API also allows you to register action, hyperlink, and mouse events, so you can enable interactive reporting within Swing.

Registering event callbacks

The three Java interfaces for retrieving event callbacks from within a report are `ReportHyperlinkListener`, `ReportActionListener`, and `ReportMouseListener`. The `ReportHyperlinkListener` and `ReportActionListener` require special properties defined in your report definition, while the `ReportMouseListener` is a lower level event that is always called within the report `PreviewDialog`.

ReportHyperlinkListener

The `org.pentaho.reporting.engine.classic.core.modules.gui.base.event.` `ReportHyperlinkListener` interface defines the following API callback method:

```
void hyperlinkActivated(ReportHyperlinkEvent event);
```

This method is called whenever someone clicks on an element within a report that has defined the link **url** style attribute. The `ReportHyperlinkEvent` provides additional metadata about the click, including the source node in the report, the hyperlink target definition, as well as the window and title hyperlink definition:

```
// The PreviewPane object
public Object getSource();

// The reporting node object
public RenderNode getSourceNode();

// The defined style attribute url
public String getTarget();

// The defined style attribute window
public String getWindow();

// The defined style attribute title
public String getTitle();
```

`ReportHyperlinkListener` implementations are registered by calling `PreviewPane.addReportHyperlinkListener(listener)`. The `PreviewPane` object is accessible after defining a `PreviewDialog` by calling `PreviewDialog.getPreviewPane()`.

One use case for implementing `ReportHyperlinkListener` is to allow report linking from one high level report to more detailed reports within a Java application.

 Hyperlinks may appear differently when rendering in HTML and Swing. Make sure to preview your report to verify that it renders correctly.

ReportActionListener

In addition to receiving `ReportHyperlinkListener` events, the Swing `PreviewDialog` may also receive special events triggered only in the Swing environment. This is done by specifying the swing `action` attribute on an element. The swing `action` attribute type is a string. When an element within a report defines the `action` attribute, and a user clicks on that element, an event is fired and all registered `ReportActionListener` instances receive an event notification with the specified swing `action` attribute value.

The `org.pentaho.reporting.engine.classic.core.modules.gui.base.event.ReportActionListener` interface defines the following API callback method:

```
public void reportActionPerformed(final ReportActionEvent event);
```

The `ReportActionEvent` object returned in the callback provides the following information:

```
// The PreviewPane object
public Object getSource();

// The reporting node object
public RenderNode getNode();

// The action parameter specified in the report.
public Object getActionParameter();
```

To register a `ReportActionListener`, you must call `PreviewDrawablePanel.addRe`
`portActionListener(listener)`. The `PreviewDrawablePanel` is accessible via the
`PreviewPane.getReportPreviewArea()` API call.

ReportMouseListener

The `org.pentaho.reporting.engine.classic.core.modules.gui.base.event.`
`ReportMouseListener` interface provides the following callbacks:

```
public void reportMouseClicked(ReportMouseEvent event);
public void reportMousePressed(ReportMouseEvent event);
public void reportMouseReleased(ReportMouseEvent event);
```

These are triggered when a user has clicked, pressed, or released their mouse within
a report. Each listener registered is called for every element found at the specific X,
Y location within the report. If there are two or more elements overlapping, multiple
event calls will be made, one for each of the report elements. The `ReportMouseEvent`
provides the following information when a callback occurs:

```
// The PreviewPane object
public Object getSource();

// The reporting node object
public RenderNode getSourceNode();

// The original java.awt.event.MouseEvent
public MouseEvent getSourceEvent();
```

To register a `ReportMouseListener`, you must call `PreviewDrawablePanel.addRe`
`portMouseListener(listener)`. The `PreviewDrawablePanel` is accessible via the
`PreviewPane.getReportPreviewArea()` API call.

By combining these callbacks with additional API calls using the `PageDrawable` API, you can resolve the elements at any particular X, Y location within a report. The `PageDrawable` API defines the following methods:

```
// Retrieves ReportNodes based on x and y location.
// A namespace and name filter may be applied to only
// retrieve nodes that define a certain attribute.
public RenderNode[] getNodesAt (final double x,
final double y, final String namespace, final String name);

// Retrieves nodes within a window, starting at an x,y
// location and stretching out to the defined pixel width
// and height.  A namespace and name filter may be applied
// to only retrieve nodes that define a certain attribute.
public RenderNode[] getNodesAt (final double x,
    final double y, final double width, final double height,
    final String namespace, final String name);
```

The `PageDrawable` object is accessible via the `PreviewDrawablePanel`. `getPageDrawable()` API call.

Interactive Swing example

In this example, you'll combine the three listener interfaces into a simple report that demonstrates the various callbacks. To begin, you need to set up your environment. First, you need to create a new folder called `chapter9`, and copy over the JAR files from the `chapter3/lib` folder into `chapter9/lib`. Also, copy the `chapter3/data` folder to `chapter9/data` so that you may reuse the already configured ElectroBarn data source. Finally, copy the `chapter3/build.xml` file into the `chapter9` folder so that you can build the example.

You'll reuse the `Chapter2SwingApp` class from Chapter 2 as a shell to build from. Copy `chapter2/src/Chapter2SwingApp.java` to `chapter9/src/Chapter9SwingApp.java`, and rename the class to `Chapter9SwingApp`.

Now that you've created the `Chapter9SwingApp` class, you're ready to begin designing the report, along with adding the various Swing event listeners to your Swing `PreviewDialog`. Launch Pentaho Report Designer and create a new report.

For the master report, define the following ElectroBarn SQL query, which you used in Chapter 8:

```
SELECT
       "ENDOFDAY"."SESSIONID",
       "ENDOFDAY"."EMPLOYEEID",
       "ENDOFDAY"."ACTUALCHECKTOTAL",
```

```
        "ENDOFDAY"."ACTUALCASHTOTAL",
        "ENDOFDAY"."CHECKOUTTIME"
FROM
        "ENDOFDAY"
ORDER BY
        "ENDOFDAY"."SESSIONID" ASC
```

In the **Details** band of the master report, place two labels with the text `Session ID` and `Employee ID`, along with dragging and dropping the **SESSIONID** and **EMPLOYEEID** fields into the band. For the **SESSIONID** field, also specify the following formula for the Swing `action` attribute:

```
=[SESSIONID]
```

Later in this example, you'll register a `ReportActionListener`, which will receive the **SESSIONID** as an input parameter, when clicked on the **SESSIONID** field.

Also, enable row banding by adding a background rectangle and setting its **visible** style formula to the following:

```
=IF(ISODD([SESSIONID]);TRUE();FALSE())
```

Now, place an inline sub-report element below the content within the **Details** band. Set the sub-report visible style attribute to the following formula:

```
=AND(NOT(ISNA([REPORT_PARAM_SESSIONID])); [SESSIONID] = [REPORT_PARAM_
SESSIONID])
```

This will evaluate to true if the parameter `REPORT_PARAM_SESSIONID` matches the currently selected session. This parameter will be passed into the report when a user clicks on the **SESSIONID** field.

The **Details** band of the master report should look similar to this:

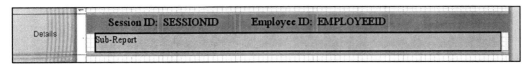

You're now ready to begin editing the sub-report. Double-click on the sub-report element or right-click and select the **Edit sub-report** menu option to bring up the sub-report for editing.

The first step to setting up the sub-report is to create a new data source query. Create the following ElectroBarn SQL query as part of the sub-report:

```
SELECT
    "PURCHASES"."SESSIONID",
    "PURCHASES"."PAYMENTTYPE",
    "PURCHASES"."PURCHASETIME",
    "PURCHASES"."PURCHASEID",
    "PURCHASEITEMS"."QUANTITY",
    "INVENTORY"."SALEPRICE",
    "INVENTORY"."ITEMNAME"
FROM
    "PURCHASEITEMS" INNER JOIN "INVENTORY" ON
"PURCHASEITEMS"."ITEMID" = "INVENTORY"."ITEMID"
    INNER JOIN "PURCHASES" ON "PURCHASEITEMS"."PURCHASEID" =
"PURCHASES"."PURCHASEID"
WHERE
    "PURCHASES"."SESSIONID" = ${SESSIONID}
ORDER BY
    "PURCHASES"."PURCHASEID" ASC
```

This query selects details only for the current **SESSIONID.** You must customize the parameters that are available to the sub-report. You can do this by bringing up the **Sub-report Parameters** dialog by right-clicking on the sub-report's **Parameters** tree item under the **Data** tab and selecting the **Edit Sub-report Parameters...** menu item. The following dialog will appear:

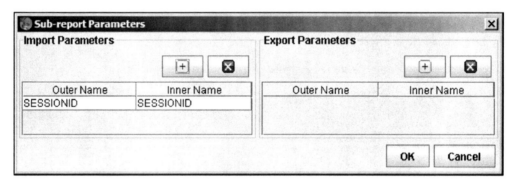

Now that you've defined the sub-report query, place a **chart** element in the report header of the sub-report. Select the **Pie** chart type. Edit the chart element, setting the **value-column** to **QUANTITY** and the **series-by-field** to **PURCHASEID**.

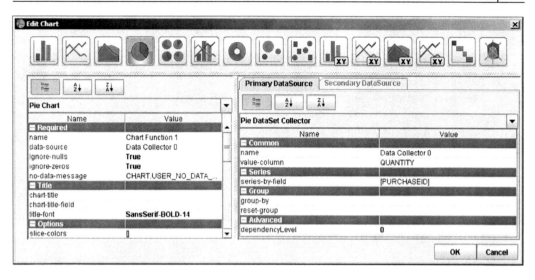

Next to the chart, place two rectangle elements, along with two label elements titled Action 1 and Action 2 within the rectangles. Set the **name** attribute of the rectangles to **Action1** and **Action2** — the names of the rectangles will be used by a ReportMouseListener later in this example. Also, add a **label** below the rectangles titled **Google Reference**. Set the **url** style formula of this label to a Google query, which will search for the first item in the dataset:

```
="http://www.google.com/search?q=" & [ITEMNAME]
```

The & symbol concatenates the **ITEMNAME** to the end of the query string. You'll use this label to demonstrate the ReportHyperlinkListener. The sub-report should look similar to this:

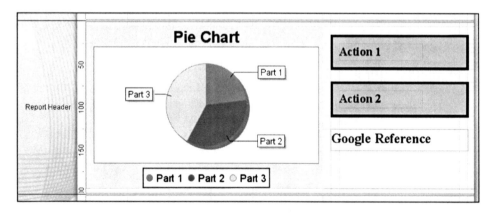

Save the master report as chapter9/data/interactive_swing.prpt. You're now ready to update the Chapter9SwingApp class with event listeners.

First, update the example to render the `interactive_swing.prpt` report in a separate method:

```
public MasterReport createReport() throws IOException,
ResourceException {
    ResourceManager manager = new ResourceManager();
    manager.registerDefaults();
    Resource res = manager.createDirectly(
                    new URL("file:data/interactive_swing.prpt"),
                        MasterReport.class);
    MasterReport report = (MasterReport) res.getResource();
    return report;
}
```

Replace the loading of the report in the `onPreview` method with the following code:

```
MasterReport report = createReport();
```

Now, you'll define three event listeners. The first event listener to be added is a `ReportActionListener`. This listener will re-render the report, displaying the details of the clicked selection. You must first set up a mechanism to pass the current Session ID. Define a class member of type String called `sessionId`:

```
Integer sessionId = null;
```

Add the following code at the end of the `createReport` method, which sets the `sessionId` as an input parameter if it's available:

```
if (sessionId != null) {
report.getParameterValues().put("REPORT_PARAM_SESSIONID", sessionId);
}
```

Now, add the following code right after the `preview.addWindowListener()` call:

```
preview.getPreviewPane().getReportPreviewArea().
addReportActionListener(new ReportActionListener() {

    public void reportActionPerformed(ReportActionEvent event) {
        Integer newSessionId = ((Number)event.getActionParameter()).
                            intValue();
        if (!newSessionId.equals(sessionId)) {
            sessionId = newSessionId;
            SwingUtilities.invokeLater(new Runnable() {
                public void run() {
                    try {
                        preview.setReportJob(createReport());
                    } catch (Exception e) {
                        e.printStackTrace();
```

```
                        }
                   }
              });
         }
    }
});
```

Note that this example uses `SwingUtilities` to update the report once the current event processing is complete.

The second listener to be added is the hyperlink listener. This listener will display a message dialog. In a real application, this might launch a browser window. Add the following code after the previously defined report action listener:

```
preview.getPreviewPane().addReportHyperlinkListener(new
    ReportHyperlinkListener() {
        public void hyperlinkActivated(final ReportHyperlinkEvent event)
        {
            SwingUtilities.invokeLater(new Runnable()
            {public void run() {JOptionPane.showMessageDialog(null,
                            "Link Clicked: " + event.getTarget());}
            });
        }
    });
```

The final listener will determine which rectangle was clicked.

```
preview.getPreviewPane().getReportPreviewArea().addReportMouseListener
(new ReportMouseListener() {
    public void reportMouseClicked(ReportMouseEvent event) {
        if (event.getSourceNode() !=
            null && event.getSourceNode().getName().equals("Action1")) {
        JOptionPane.showMessageDialog(null, "Action 1 Rectangle Clicked");
        } else if (event.getSourceNode() !=
            null && event.getSourceNode().getName().equals("Action2")) {
        JOptionPane.showMessageDialog(null, "Action 2 Rectangle Clicked");
        }
    }
    public void reportMousePressed(ReportMouseEvent event) {}
    public void reportMouseReleased(ReportMouseEvent event) {}
});
```

Remember, the mouse listener is called for every element that you clicked on. In this case, you may have clicked on the label and the rectangle, a scenario which would result in the event handler being called twice.

Also, make sure to add the following imports to the beginning of the class file:

```
import org.pentaho.reporting.engine.classic.core.modules.gui.base.
event.ReportHyperlinkListener;
import org.pentaho.reporting.engine.classic.core.modules.gui.base.
event.ReportHyperlinkEvent;
import org.pentaho.reporting.engine.classic.core.modules.gui.base.
event.ReportActionListener;
import org.pentaho.reporting.engine.classic.core.modules.gui.base.
event.ReportActionEvent;
import org.pentaho.reporting.engine.classic.core.modules.gui.base.
event.ReportMouseListener;
import org.pentaho.reporting.engine.classic.core.modules.gui.base.
event.ReportMouseEvent;
import javax.swing.SwingUtilities;
import javax.swing.JOptionPane;
```

Now that you've added the event listeners, you're ready to build and run the report. Add the following Ant target to the `build.xml` file:

```
<target name="runswinginteractive" depends="compile">
    <java fork="true" classpathref="runtime_classpath" classname="Chap
ter9SwingApp"/>
</target>
```

Type `ant runswinginteractive` on the command line to verify the results. The report should look similar to this:

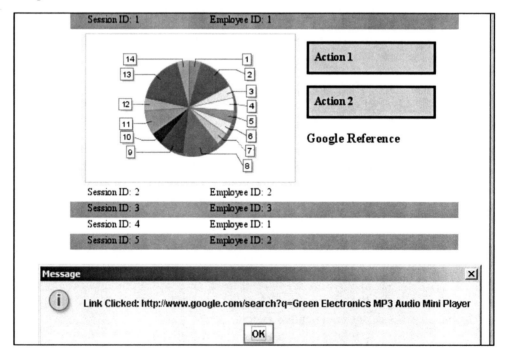

Click on the **Session ID** row to view the details of each session, and click on the action rectangles and **Google Reference** label to view the alerts, triggered by the report listeners.

Interactive reports in HTML

In addition to defining interactive reports in Swing, it is also possible to define highly customized interactive reports within the HTML/JavaScript environment. Pentaho Reporting defines a set of properties, which when specified, allow for rich interactivity between the user and a report. In this section, you will get an overview of these properties, along with a rich example that demonstrates potential uses.

Interactive HTML report properties

All reporting elements share a common set of HTML-related properties that may be used to create a dynamic report. Below is a list of properties and their uses:

HTML Properties	
class	This property sets the class attribute of the current HTML entity to the specified value.
name	This property sets the name attribute of the current HTML entity to the specified value.
title	This property sets the title attribute of the current HTML entity to the specified value.
xml-id	This property allows the naming of the current HTML entity, setting the id attribute, making it possible to reference in outside scripts.
append-body	This property allows the placement of raw HTML within the body of the HTML document, prior to the rendering of the current element.
append-body-footer	This property allows the placement of raw HTML within the body of the HTML document, after the rendering of the current element.
append-header	Defined only at the master report level, this property allows the inclusion of raw HTML within the header of the HTML document generated. This location is traditionally used to load additional CSS files, as well as external JavaScript files.

HTML Events	
on-click	This property renders an `onclick` HTML attribute on the currently defined element. This property is a string of JavaScript that is executed within the browser when a user clicks on the element.
on-double-click	This property renders an `ondblclick` HTML attribute on the currently defined element. This property is a string of JavaScript that is executed within the browser when a user double-clicks on the element.
on-mouse-down	This property renders an `onmousedown` HTML attribute on the currently defined element. This property is a string of JavaScript that is executed within the browser when a user presses a mouse button. This might be used to detect the beginning of a drag operation.
on-mouse-up	This property renders an `onmouseup` HTML attribute on the currently defined element. This property is a string of JavaScript that is executed within the browser when a user releases a mouse button.
on-mouse-move	This property renders an `onmousemove` HTML attribute on the currently defined element. This property is a string of JavaScript that is executed within the browser when a user moves the mouse.
on-mouse-over	This property renders an `onmouseover` HTML attribute on the currently defined element. This property is a string of JavaScript that is executed within the browser when a user moves the mouse over the element.
on-key-down	This property renders an `onkeydown` HTML attribute on the currently defined element. This property is a string of JavaScript that is executed within the browser when a user presses a key down.
on-key-pressed	This property renders an `onkeypressed` HTML attribute on the currently defined element. This property is a string of JavaScript that is executed within the browser when a user presses a key.
on-key-up	This property renders an `onkeyup` HTML attribute on the currently defined element. This property is a string of JavaScript that is executed within the browser when a user releases a key.

Manipulating the reporting HTML DOM

It is possible to alter the HTML document object model dynamically, by combining the `xml-id` property, along with the `on-click` event. For instance, by setting a label's `xml-id` to `example`, and setting the following JavaScript in the `on-click` property, you can toggle between two text values:

```
document.getElementById('example').innerHTML= (document.getElementById
('example').innerHTML == 'Hello') ? 'Goodbye' : 'Hello';
```

Including an external CSS or JavaScript resource

Using the master report object's `append-header` property, it is possible to include CSS or JavaScript in your report. This is useful if you have written a large amount of JavaScript that you would like to keep separate from your report, or if you want to include a useful JavaScript library, as demonstrated in the example that will follow. An example of the `append-header` value might be:

```
<link type="text/css" rel="stylesheet" href="custom.css" />
```

When implementing the server, it's important to make sure that the relative path of the files referenced are accessible from the current document.

Interactive HTML example

As a demonstration of how an interactive report might work, this example walks you through building a dashboard that includes rendering an HTML report with filters and charts, with the ability to view the result in PDF format.

To begin, you'll need to create a standard report. Note that the master report in this example does not require a query. You'll populate only the **Report Header** with two sub-reports. First, add a label to the **Report Header** entitled **Session ID**, and add a text field that references the **SESSIONID** input parameter. Note that you do not need to define the input parameter in Report Designer, as this will be managed by the web application. You'll now add two sub-reports to the **Report Header**. Place two sub-report objects within the report header below the session information. The result should look like this:

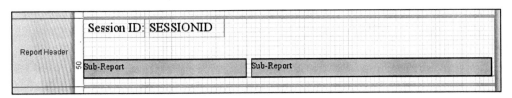

You'll reuse the chart and summary sub-report definitions defined in Chapter 8 as part of the side-by-side sub-report example. Follow the instructions in Chapter 8 for populating these sub-reports.

Also, you must create two identical master reports with the same content and query as the sub-reports. Save these master reports as `chapter9/data/subreport_chart.prpt` and `chapter9/data/subreport_summary.prpt`.

When complete, the chart sub-report should look like this:

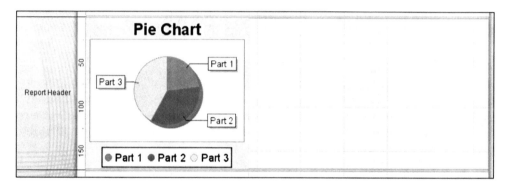

And the summary sub-report should look like this:

| Group Header | | Purchase: PU..Time: PURCHASETIME | Total: TotalS | |

When this dashboard example is complete, the sub-reports will be executed in two different manners. The first is rendered as a sub-report in the master report. The second is an independent report, which will be executed via a call from the browser and embedded within the existing report for dynamic updating. Save your report as `chapter9/data/dashboard.prpt`.

Now that you've defined the basic report without interactive capabilities, you'll set up the server as well. Copy the `chapter3/src/Chapter3Servlet.java` example to `DashboardServlet.java` in the `chapter9/src` folder. Rename the class to `DashboardServlet`. Also, copy `chapter3/war/WEB-INF/web.xml` to `chapter9/war/WEB-INF/web.xml`. Open the `web.xml` file and change all references of `Chapter3Servlet` to `DashboardServlet`.

The new `DashboardServlet` requires the HTTP parameter `reportName` to be passed so that the correct report is rendered. The two changes you'll need to make include updating the Servlet to render reports as HTML, and to pass in the `sessionId` as a report input parameter. First, you'll need to update the Session ID input parameter. Update the `getParameterValues().put()` call to pass the `sessionId` as SESSIONID:

```
report.getParameterValues().put("SESSIONID", sessionId);
```

For the second modification, HTML documents require additional code to render, as external files such as CSS, and images, must be cached and available over HTTP after the report has already been generated. First, add a member variable of type int called reportNum:

```
int reportNum = 0;
```

Now, after the Excel rendering code, add the following lines of code:

```
} else if ("html".equals(outputFormat)) {
    String reportLoc = "report_" + reportNum++;
    String path = this.getServletContext().getRealPath(reportLoc);
    File folder = new File(path);
    folder.mkdir();
    HtmlReportUtil.createDirectoryHTML(report,
                            path + File.separator + "index.html");
    response.sendRedirect(reportLoc + "/index.html");
```

Note that this code creates a new folder with CSS, HTML, and images for every request made to the server. In a production environment, these files would be hosted temporarily while the report loaded, and then cleaned out automatically. Make sure to add the following imports to complete the code changes:

```
import org.pentaho.reporting.engine.classic.core.modules.output.table.
html.HtmlReportUtil;
```

You'll now create the chapter9/war/index.html file with links to the three regular reports:

```
<html>
<body>
<h1>Interactive Dashboard Example</h1>
<p>This is an example application demonstrating how to create an html
based interactive report.</p>
<a href="report?reportName=dashboard&outputFormat=html&sessionId=1">
        Master Report</a> |
<a href="report?reportName=subreport_chart&outputFormat=html&sessionId
        =1">Chart Report</a> |
<a href="report?reportName=subreport_summary&outputFormat=html&session
        Id=1">Summary Report</a>
</body>
</html>
```

You're now ready to test the base set of reports, which you'll use for the interactive example. First, update the `build.xml` to build a `chapter9/war` folder vs. the `chapter2/war` folder. Now, type `ant war`, along with `ant start_tomcat`, and visit `http://localhost:8080/chapter9` in your web browser to view the three reports. The first is the master report.

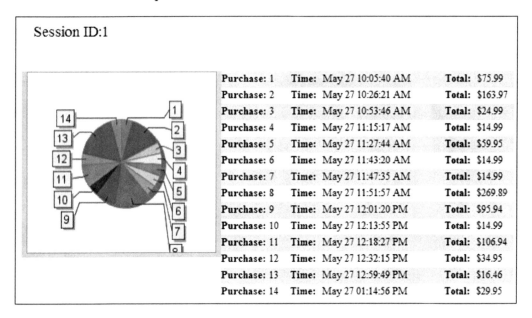

The second is the chart report.

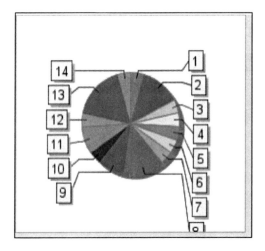

Finally, the last one is the summary report.

Purchase: 1	**Time:** May 27 10:05:40 AM	**Total:** $75.99
Purchase: 2	**Time:** May 27 10:26:21 AM	**Total:** $163.97
Purchase: 3	**Time:** May 27 10:53:46 AM	**Total:** $24.99
Purchase: 4	**Time:** May 27 11:15:17 AM	**Total:** $14.99
Purchase: 5	**Time:** May 27 11:27:44 AM	**Total:** $59.95
Purchase: 6	**Time:** May 27 11:43:20 AM	**Total:** $14.99
Purchase: 7	**Time:** May 27 11:47:35 AM	**Total:** $14.99
Purchase: 8	**Time:** May 27 11:51:57 AM	**Total:** $269.89
Purchase: 9	**Time:** May 27 12:01:20 PM	**Total:** $95.94
Purchase: 10	**Time:** May 27 12:13:55 PM	**Total:** $14.99
Purchase: 11	**Time:** May 27 12:18:27 PM	**Total:** $106.94
Purchase: 12	**Time:** May 27 12:32:15 PM	**Total:** $34.95
Purchase: 13	**Time:** May 27 12:59:49 PM	**Total:** $16.46
Purchase: 14	**Time:** May 27 01:14:56 PM	**Total:** $29.95

Now that you have the three reports rendering, you're ready to add interactive elements, thereby creating a dynamic dashboard.

Adding interactive elements to the dashboard

The first step is to add a commonly used JavaScript library known as `prototype.js` to the `dashboard.prpt` report. You can download `prototype.js` from `http://www.prototypejs.org`. Place the `prototype.js` file in the `chapter9/war` folder. This example uses version 1.6 of `prototype.js`. To include this JavaScript file in your report, add the following text to the `append-header` property of the master report object:

```
<script src="../prototype-1.6.0.3.js"></script>
```

Now, you're ready to add the Session ID select input. Place a label at the top of the **Report Header**, in the space left available. Set the label text to `Select a Session:`. Update the label's **append-body-footer** property to the following HTML and JavaScript:

```
<script>
// this function removes cells and rows from
// the generated HTML report for dynamic rendering
function removeNodes(node) {
 if (node) {
    var next = node.nextSibling;
  node.parentNode.removeChild(node);
  removeNodes(next);
```

```
  }
 }
 // this function is triggered when a change occurs in the
 // selection list
 function filterChanged() {
  var select = $('selection');
  var currentValue = select.options[select.selectedIndex].text;

  // remove cells to allow room for dynamic iframe reports
  var summary = $('summary');
  removeNodes(summary.nextSibling);
  removeNodes(summary.parentNode.nextSibling);
  summary.colSpan = "7";
  summary.className= "";

  // update the chart component with the correct filter
  $('chart').innerHTML = "<iframe width='261' height='240'
   scrolling='no' frameborder='0'
   src='../report?reportName=subreport_chart&outputFormat=
       html&sessionId="+currentValue+"'/>";
  // update the pdf link with the correct filter
  summary.innerHTML = "<iframe width='375' height='300' scrolling='no'
  frameborder='0'
   src='../report?reportName=subreport_summary&outputFormat=
       html&sessionId="+currentValue+"'/>";

  var pdfLink = document.getElementById('pdfLink');
  pdfLink.sessionId.value = currentValue;
 }</script>

<form style="display:inline">
  <select id="selection" name="sessionid" onchange="filterChanged()">
          <option>1</option>
          <option>2</option>
          <option>3</option>
          <option>4</option>
          <option>5</option>
    </select>
</form>
```

This JavaScript references the HTML document object model locations of the sub-reports. In order for this to be successful, you need to specify the xml-id attribute for both the sub-reports as chart and summary.

The above JavaScript first removes cells from the HTML document, and then places two IFRAME elements within the HTML DOM. Pentaho Reporting renders a single HTML table as output, so sub-reports don't get wrapped by a single HTML parent element. The IFRAME elements must be used instead of direct HTML placements. This is to make sure that CSS styles, and relative directory paths of images within sub-reports, are both accessible.

Add a label with a single space to the right side of the report. You'll add a **View As PDF** button at this location. Edit the **append-body** attribute of the empty label with the following HTML and JavaScript:

```
<form style="display:inline" id="pdfLink" action="../report"
method="get">
    <input type="hidden" name="reportName" value="dashboard"/>
    <input type="hidden" name="outputFormat" value="pdf"/>
    <input type="hidden" name="sessionId" value="1"/>
    <input type="submit" value="View As PDF"/>
</form>
```

To demonstrate some of the event callback methods, specify the following JavaScript within the on-click attribute of the chart sub-report element, within the master report:

```
alert("You've clicked on the Chart");
```

Also, specify the following JavaScript within the on-double-click attribute of the chart sub-report element, within the master report:

```
alert("You've double clicked on the chart");
```

The final master report should look like this in design mode within Report Designer:

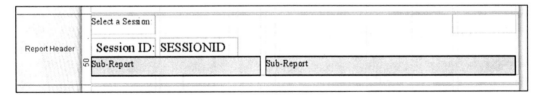

You're now ready to save the changes and deploy them to the server. Note that there are no changes necessary on the server side to enable this interactive report. In your command prompt, type ant war to build the web archive, and ant start_tomcat to restart the server.

When running the interactive report, your browser should show a selection list, as well as a **View As PDF** button:

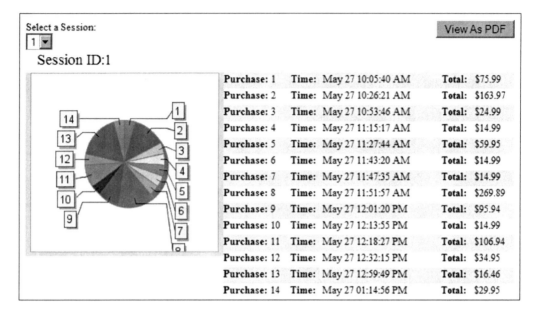

Select another **Session ID**, and notice how the chart and summary sub-reports are dynamically updated. Finally, click the **View as PDF** button. Notice that the append-body attributes defined earlier do not render within the PDF document.

Summary

In this chapter, you learned how to build interactive reports using Swing and HTML as outputs. You learned how to modify report definitions to generate hyperlink events, swing action events, and many different HTML JavaScript events. You built from the ground up a Swing demonstration that selectively shows details of sales sessions from the ElectroBarn data source, along with demonstrating feedback via the ReportMouseListenter API.

You also learned how to render an HTML report on a server, along with including external script files within the HTML rendered report. You learned how to modify the report HTML document object model dynamically when events are triggered from the report. You also learned to view an HTML report as a dashboard, finally allowing the HTML report to be rendered as PDF.

10
API-based Report Generation

In this chapter, you'll learn about Pentaho Reporting's `.prpt` bundle file format, along with the details of Pentaho Reporting's Java API. You'll be introduced to the schemas of the various XML files that persist the data source, parameters, expressions, layout, and style of a report.

With examples of Pentaho's Java API, you'll learn how easy it is to build a report programmatically. You'll walk through a complete example that demonstrates creating different reporting bands, as well as different elements within a report. Finally, you'll be introduced to the Pentaho Wizard Java API.

Understanding the serialized report format

Pentaho Reports are saved as `.prpt` bundle files. This is a ZIP-based file format that includes all the necessary resources to render a report, also referred to as a bundle. The `.prpt` bundle file contains a set of XML files that are crucial to rendering a report, as well as additional resources such as embedded images and sub-reports. This format is based on the OpenDocument format.

This section goes into detail about each of the primary files that make up a report, along with providing a simple example of a report written by hand. With the knowledge of the underlying file format, it is possible to generate reports outside of the Java environment.

The key files that make up a report include `settings.xml datadefinition.xml`, along with individual data source files, `layout.xml` and `styles.xml`.

settings.xml

The `settings.xml` file contains global configuration properties for a report, as well as a placeholder for future runtime information.

```xml
<?xml version="1.0"?>
<settings xmlns="http://reporting.pentaho.org/namespaces/engine/
classic/bundle/settings/1.0">
  <configuration>
    <property name="org.pentaho.reporting.engine.classic.core.
function.LogFormulaFailureCause">true</property>
  </configuration>
  <runtime/>
</settings>
```

One example of a configuration setting is related to the execution of formula expressions. If you set the property `org.pentaho.reporting.engine.classic.core.function.LogFormulaFailureCause` to `true`, and you have your Log4J logging set to debug, you'll receive a stack trace, in addition to an error message, when the formula fails.

Additional configuration properties are available, primarily for use in design tools such as Pentaho Report Designer. Rarely would you need to define a configuration property while generating a report.

datadefinition.xml and the datasources folder

The `datadefinition.xml` file contains information about report input parameters, the report data source, as well as report functions and expressions. The root element in this XML file is `data-definition`, and uses the `http://reporting.pentaho.org/namespaces/engine/classic/bundle/data/1.0` namespace for XML validation.

Parameters

Parameters are defined as children to the `data-definition/parameter-definition` element. There are two types of parameters—plain parameters and list parameters. Plain parameters are represented in XML as a `plain-parameter` element. Plain parameters define four attributes:

XML attribute	Description
name	The parameter name
mandatory	If set to true, a value for this parameter is required before the report is rendered
type	The fully qualified Java type of the parameter
default-value	The default value of the parameter

List parameters are represented in XML as a `list-parameter` element. In addition to sharing the same attributes as the plain parameter, list parameters also define the following attributes:

XML attribute	Description
query	The query name providing the list of values to choose from.
key-column	The key column is returned as the result within a row that was selected.
value-column	The value column is displayed as the selection when presenting data to the user. The `value-formula` attribute may be used in place of the `value-column`.
value-formula	The value formula is displayed as the selection when presenting data to the user. The `value-column` attribute may be used in place of the `value-formula`.
strict-values	If set to true, validation is done on the parameter value to determine if it is part of the query results.
allow-multi-selection	If set to true, this attribute allows multiple selections of parameter values from the query results, creating an array of objects versus a single object.

Sub-reports define a different XML element hierarchy for their parameters. In the context of a sub-report, a parameter is passed in from the master report's context versus user or system input. Instead of using the `parameter-definition` element as a parent, sub-reports use a `parameter-mapping` element. Two sub-report parameter types are defined—import and export. Their XML element tags are `import-parameter` and `export-parameter`. They both define the following two attributes:

XML Attribute	Description
name	The name of the parameter. For imported parameters, this is the name within the master report. For exported parameters, this is the name within the sub-report.
alias	The alias of the parameter. For imported parameters, this is the name within the sub-report. For exported parameters, this is the name within the master report.

Data source reference

A single reference to the report's data source is specified in the `datadefinition.xml` file, as a `data-definition/data-source` XML element. If multiple data sources are used in a single report, you must use a compound data source that combines different data sources. The `data-source` XML element defines the following attributes:

XML attribute	Description
report-query	The named query used by the master report.
limit	If specified, defines the limit to number of rows returned by the primary query of the report.
timeout	If specified, defines the query timeout for the primary query of the report.
ref	A reference to the specified data source definition file.

Functions and expressions

Every function and expression defined in a report is represented by an `expression` XML element. Expression elements have the following five attributes:

XML attribute	Description
name	The name of the function or expression.
class	The class type of the function or expression. This is not required if specifying a formula.
deplevel	The dependency level of the function or expression, which determines the order of execution.
formula	If specified, defines a formula for execution.
initial	If specified, defines a formula for initial execution.

Expressions may also contain properties. These properties appear within a `properties` XML element as child `property` elements. Each `property` XML element contains the following attributes:

XML attribute	Description
name	The name of the property.
class	The class type of the property.

Finally, each `property` XML element contains a text node with the value of the property.

The following is an example of a `datadefinition.xml` file that contains parameters and a data source, as well as an expression:

```
<?xml version="1.0" encoding="UTF-8"?>
<data-definition xmlns="http://reporting.pentaho.org/namespaces/
engine/classic/bundle/data/1.0">

  <!-- define parameters -->

  <parameter-definition>
    <plain-parameter name="Library Size" mandatory="true" type="java.
lang.Integer"/>
  </parameter-definition>

  <!-- define the data source -->

  <data-source report-query="Libraries" limit="0" ref="datasources/
inline-ds.xml"/>

  <!-- define an expression -->

  <expression name="SizeKilobytes" formula="=[Size] / 1024"/>
</data-definition>
```

Data sources folder

For each data source defined in a report, a data source file is created with the necessary information to connect to the data source, usually stored in the `datasources` folder within the `.prpt` bundle file. Defining every data source file is out of the scope of this chapter. The following example XML is of an inline table data source:

```
<?xml version="1.0" encoding="UTF-8"?>
<data:inline-datasource xmlns:data="http://reporting.pentaho.org/
namespaces/datasources/inline/1.0">
  <data:inline-table name="Libraries">
    <data:definition>
      <data:column name="Name" type="java.lang.Object"/>
      <data:column name="Size" type="java.lang.Object"/>
    </data:definition>
    <data:row>
      <data:data type="java.lang.String">libloader</data:data>
```

```
      <data:data type="java.lang.Integer">114287</data:data>
    </data:row>
    <data:row>
      <data:data type="java.lang.String">libformula</data:data>
      <data:data type="java.lang.Integer">331839</data:data>
    </data:row>
  </data:inline-table>
</data:inline-datasource>
```

As mentioned earlier, a compound data source is often used to refer to multiple data sources in a single report. Here is an example of a compound data source definition:

```
<?xml version="1.0" encoding="UTF-8"?>
<data:compound-datasource xmlns:data="http://reporting.pentaho.org/
namespaces/datasources/compound/1.0">
  <data:data-factory href="inline-ds.xml" />
</data:compound-datasource>
```

For each data source type, there is an equivalent XML format. These formats are documented within their XML schema files, which are accessible when downloading the source distribution of the reporting engine and extensions.

layout.xml

The `layout.xml` file defines the primary structure of report bands and elements. Each band is represented as an XML element, and each band's elements are contained within the band. Multiple XML namespaces are used within the context of the layout XML document. The primary namespaces include:

- core, which defines core elements and attributes
- layout, which defines the majority of the elements in this document
- styles, which define inline styles

The styles namespace will be discussed in more detail in the *styles.xml* section that will follow. The core namespace document is located at `http://reporting. pentaho.org/namespaces/engine/attributes/core` The layout namespace, which is specified as the default namespace for this document, is located at `http:// reporting.pentaho.org/namespaces/engine/classic/bundle/layout/1.0`

The layout XML document contains a root `layout` XML element. This element contains root level band information. The layout element may contain attributes defining report level metadata such as the title of the report. The following child XML elements may be specified within the layout element:

XML element	Description
preprocessor	Any number of preprocessor elements may be defined within the report layout element. Preprocessors contain a class attribute that specifies the fully qualified preprocessor Java class, and may contain property elements for the preprocessor. Preprocessors may manipulate a report before it is rendered. You'll see an example of a preprocessor in the *Wizard Java API* section of this chapter.
layout-processors	Certain functions that manipulate the layout of elements may appear within the layout-processors element of the layout document. For instance, the ItemHideFunction is considered a layout processor, so if defined, it will be serialized into this portion of the document.
report-header	The report-header element specifies the layout of the report header. This element contains a child element entitled root-level-content, which contains all references to child elements. Note that the report-header is a report element. Therefore, it may contain general element attributes and child elements, defined later in the *Report elements* section of this chapter.
group	The group element defines the entire hierarchy of groups and detail bands defined in a report. This element hierarchy is defined in more detail in the *Group and detail band hierarchy* section of this chapter.
report-footer	The report-footer element specifies the layout of the report footer. This element contains a child element entitled root-level-content, which contains all references to child elements. Note that the report-footer is a report element. Therefore, it may contain general element attributes and child elements, defined later in the *Report elements* section of this chapter.

Also note that the report itself is represented as a report element. Therefore, in addition to the attributes and child elements defined above, the report may also contain attributes and elements defined in report elements. (These are covered later in the *Report elements* section of this chapter.)

Group and detail band hierarchy

A group may contain either a `group-body` or `data-body` child XML element. A `group-body` contains the XML element `group` to represent a hierarchy of groupings. In addition to containing the `group-body` or `data-body`, a `group` XML element may also contain `group-header` and `group-footer` XML elements. The `group-header` and `group-footer` XML elements may contain a `root-level-content` XML element, which contains child layout elements.

The `data-body` XML element contains the bands relevant to row level data in your report. This XML element may contain `detail-header`, `details`, `no-data`, and `details-footer` child XML elements. Each of these elements may contain a `root-level-content` XML element, which contains child layout elements.

Report elements

Each report element defined in previous chapters is represented in XML, defining its properties, as well as where it is located within a band. The most common elements are highlighted here.

All elements define the `style:element-style` child XML element, which contains styling information for the individual element. The most common style element is `style:spatial-styles`, which defines where in the band the element is located, as well as what size it should render as:

```
<style:element-style>
<style:spatial-styles x="20" y="240" min-width="100" min-height="20"/>
</style:element-style>
```

Here is a list of some of the primary report elements, along with specific details on creating them:

XML element	Description
`label`	The `label` XML element renders a label. This element contains a `core:value` child element, which XML Text is used for the label value.
`text-field`	The `text-field` XML element renders a text field. This element contains a `core:field` attribute, which defines the field to render.
`number-field`	The `number-field` XML element renders a number field. This element contains a `core:field` attribute, which defines the field to render, as well as a `core:format-string` attribute, which defines the number format string to render.

XML element	Description
date-field	The `date-field` XML element renders a date field. This element contains a `core:field` attribute, which defines the field to render, as well as a `core:format-string` attribute, which defines the date format string to render.
message	The `message` XML element renders a message. This element contains a `core:value` child.
resource-label	The `resource-label` XML element renders a resource-label. This element contains a `core:resource-identifier` attribute referencing the message bundle, as well as a `core:value` attribute, which specifies the key to use in the bundle.
resource-field	The `resource-field` XML element renders a resource-field. This element contains a `core:resource-identifier` attribute referencing the message bundle, as well as a `core:field` attribute, which specifies the field that is used to determine the key to be resolved.
resource-message	The `resource-message` XML element renders a resource-message. This element contains a `core:resource-identifier` attribute referencing the message bundle, as well as a `core:value` attribute, which specifies the message.
rectangle	The `rectangle` XML element renders a rectangle. The size of the rectangle is determined by the `style:spatial-sizes` element defined above. A `style:content-styles` XML element may be defined, which specifies attributes such as the boolean attributes `draw-shape` and `fill-shape`, as well as color attributes such as `fill-color`. Colors are represented in RGB hexadecimal notation, for instance #ff3333.
horizontal-line	The `horizontal-line` XML element renders a horizontal line. The length of the line is determined by the `style:spatial-sizes` XML element defined above. A `style:content-styles` XML element is defined to specify line style and color.

XML element	Description
vertical-line	The vertical-line XML element renders a vertical line. The length of the line is determined by the style:spatial-sizes XML element defined above. A style:content-styles XML element is defined to specify line style and color.
sub-report	A sub-report XML element renders a sub-report. The attribute href specifies where the sub-report is located within the .prpt bundle. This XML element may also contain information about its location and style via the style:element-style child XML element, as well as input and output parameter mappings via input-parameter and output-parameter XML elements. These mappings are configured with the master-fieldname and detail-fieldname attributes.
content	A content XML element renders an image. The location of the image binary is determined by the core:value XML element. The scale and aspect ratio properties for a content element may be customized by specifying a style:content-styles element with the attributes scale and keep-aspect-ratio.
content-field	A content-field XML element renders a dynamic image based on a field. The location of the dynamic content to render is determined by the core:field XML element. The scale and aspect ratio properties for a content-field element may be customized by specifying a style:content-styles element, with the attributes scale and keep-aspect-ratio.

Additional report element types are defined within Pentaho Reporting. Those listed in the table are the most common elements, along with some of their primary properties and styles.

Example layout.xml file

The following is a very simple `layout.xml` file, which renders a report header label, as well as a details band text field:

```xml
<?xml version="1.0" encoding="UTF-8"?>
<layout xmlns="http://reporting.pentaho.org/namespaces/engine/
classic/bundle/layout/1.0" xmlns:style="http://reporting.pentaho.
org/namespaces/engine/classic/bundle/style/1.0" xmlns:core="http://
reporting.pentaho.org/namespaces/engine/attributes/core">
  <!-- define the root header -->
  <report-header>
    <root-level-content>
      <!-- define a label element within the report header -->
      <label>
        <style:element-style>
          <style:text-styles bold="true"/>
          <style:spatial-styles x="1" y="1" min-width="100" min-
height="20"/>
        </style:element-style>
        <core:value>Library Information</core:value>
      </label>
    </root-level-content>
  </report-header>
  <!-- define the group header -->
  <group>
    <fields>
    </fields>
    <data-body>
      <details>
        <root-level-content>
          <!-- define a Name text field in the item band -->
          <text-field core:field="Name">
            <style:element-style>
              <style:spatial-styles x="1" y="1" min-width="100" min-
height="20"/>
            </style:element-style>
          </text-field>
          <!-- define a SizeKilobytes text -->
          <text-field core:field="SizeKilobytes">
            <style:element-style>
              <style:spatial-styles x="101" y="1" min-width="100" min-
height="20"/>
```

```
                </style:element-style>
              </text-field>
            </root-level-content>
          </details>
        </data-body>
      </group>
    </layout>
```

styles.xml

The `styles.xml` file defines what page format the report should be rendered as, style rules that dictate how a report should be rendered, global layout processors, a report watermark, and finally the page header and footer sections of a report.

The `styles.xml` file contains the `style` root XML element, and includes namespaces relevant to rendering styles, including the core and layout namespaces defined earlier, as well as the style namespace as the default namespace, which is located at `http://reporting.pentaho.org/namespaces/engine/classic/bundle/style/1.0`. The following child elements may be specified within the `style` XML element:

XML element	Description
page-definition	The `page-definition` XML element contains attributes defining the report's page properties. The attribute `pageformat` specifies the page format type. Examples include "LETTER" and "LEGAL". The attributes `horizontal-span` and `vertical-span` define how many pages a report should span across. The `width` and `height` attributes define the width and height of the paper. The `orientation` attribute defines whether the page should be laid out as portrait, landscape, or reverse-landscape. The attributes `margin-top`, `margin-left`, `margin-bottom`, and `margin-right` define the margin values for the report.
style-rule	Multiple `style-rules` may be defined in the report. A style rule has a `name` and `parent` attribute, which define the inheritance tree of a group of styles. Within the `style-rule`, style elements such as `text-styles` and `spatial-styles` are defined, which contain specific styling information.

XML element	Description
layout:layout-processors	Certain functions that manipulate the layout of the entire report may appear in the layout-processors section of the styles document.
layout:watermark	The watermark XML element is rendered in the background, behind other bands in a report. This element contains a child element entitled root-level-content, which contains all references to child elements. Note that the watermark is a report element, so it may contain general element attributes and child elements, defined earlier.
layout:page-header	The page-header XML element defines the contents of the header for each page. This element contains a child element entitled root-level-content, which contains all references to child elements. Note that the page-header is a report element, so it may contain general element attributes and child elements, defined earlier.
layout:page-footer	The page-footer XML element defines the contents of the header for each page. This element contains a child element entitled root-level-content, which contains all references to child elements. Note that the page-footer is a report element, so it may contain general element attributes and child elements, defined earlier.

Example styles.xml file

Here is a simple styles.xml file that contains a page definition, as well as a label in the page footer:

```
<?xml version="1.0" encoding="UTF-8"?>
<style xmlns="http://reporting.pentaho.org/namespaces/engine/
classic/bundle/style/1.0" xmlns:layout="http://reporting.pentaho.
org/namespaces/engine/classic/bundle/layout/1.0" xmlns:core="http://
reporting.pentaho.org/namespaces/engine/attributes/core">

  <!-- define the page definition -->

  <page-definition horizontal-span="1" vertical-span="1"
pageformat="LETTER" orientation="portrait" margin-top="72" margin-
left="72" margin-bottom="72" margin-right="72"/>

  <!-- define a page footer -->

  <layout:page-footer>

    <!-- define a label in the page footer -->
```

```
    <layout:label>
      <element-style>
        <spatial-styles x="364" y="3" min-width="100" min-
height="20"/>
      </element-style>
      <core:value>Page Footer Label</core:value>
    </layout:label>
  </layout:page-footer>
</style>
```

Additional required files

Additional files are required to complete the `.prpt` bundle file, but are less central to the rendering of the report. This includes the `META-INF/manifest.xml`, `content.xml`, `dataschema.xml`, `meta.xml`, and the `mimetype` files.

The `META-INF/manifest.xml` file contains a listing of all the files in the `.prpt` bundle file, as well as their content types:

```
<?xml version="1.0" encoding="UTF-8"?>
<manifest:manifest xmlns:manifest="urn:oasis:names:tc:opendocument:xml
ns:manifest:1.0">
  <manifest:file-entry manifest:media-type="application/vnd.pentaho.
reporting.classic" manifest:full-path="/"/>
  <manifest:file-entry manifest:media-type="text/xml" manifest:full-
path="content.xml"/>
  <manifest:file-entry manifest:media-type="text/xml" manifest:full-
path="styles.xml"/>
  <manifest:file-entry manifest:media-type="text/xml" manifest:full-
path="meta.xml"/>
  <manifest:file-entry manifest:media-type="text/xml" manifest:full-
path="layout.xml"/>
  <manifest:file-entry manifest:media-type="text/xml" manifest:full-
path="settings.xml"/>
</manifest:manifest>
```

The `content.xml` file is intentionally left empty, and may be used in future for global templates:

```
<?xml version="1.0" encoding="UTF-8"?>
<content xmlns="http://reporting.pentaho.org/namespaces/engine/
classic/bundle/content/1.0">
</content>
```

The `dataschema.xml` file may contain additional metadata used to increase the richness of a data source. Normally, this document is empty.

```
<?xml version="1.0" encoding="UTF-8"?>
<data-schema xmlns="http://reporting.pentaho.org/namespaces/engine/
classic/dataschema/1.0" ></data-schema>
```

The `meta.xml` file is part of the OpenDocument standard, and contains information about the `.prpt` bundle file, including the creation date:

```
<?xml version="1.0" encoding="UTF-8"?>
<office:document-meta xmlns:office="urn:oasis:names:tc:opendocument:x
mlns:office:1.0" xmlns:meta="urn:oasis:names:tc:opendocument:xmlns:me
ta:1.0" xmlns:dc="http://purl.org/dc/elements/1.1/">
  <office:meta>
    <meta:creation-date>Sat Feb 07 20:23:03 EST 2009</meta:creation-
date>
    <meta:initial-creator>Pentaho Reporting Classic</meta:initial-
creator>
    <dc:creator>Pentaho Reporting Classic</dc:creator>
    <dc:date>Sun Feb 08 16:49:16 EST 2009</dc:date>
  </office:meta>
</office:document-meta>
```

The `mimetype` file is a simple text file that contains the mime type of the `.prpt` bundle file.

```
application/vnd.pentaho.reporting.classic
```

Building and running a .prpt bundle example file

Now that you've learned about all the different files that make up a `.prpt` bundle file, combine them to create a single report. First, create a folder and place all the examples above in their appropriate file names. This should include the primary files, `settings.xml` and `datadefinition.xml`, along with the `datasources` folder, `datasources/inline-ds.xml`, `layout.xml`, and `styles.xml`. Also, include the additional required files and folders, the `META-INF` folder, along with the `META-INF/manifest.xml`, `content.xml`, `dataschema.xml`, `meta.xml`, and the `mimetype` files.

Once you've placed these files within the same folder structure, select all the files in Windows Explorer and right-click on them. Select **Send To... Compressed (zipped) Folder...**, and save the file as `example_xml.prpt`.

If you are working in Linux or Mac, you may use the zip command line tool to create the `.prpt` file bundle. Go into the directory where the files were created, and type `zip -r example_xml.prpt *`.

Now, open the `example_xml.prpt` file in Pentaho Report Designer and click the preview button. You should see a report that looks like the following:

Library Information	
libloader	111.6083984375
libformula	324.0615234375

Building a report using Pentaho Reporting's Java API

Now that you've built a report using Pentaho Reporting's XML format, it's time to learn how to do a similar exercise, by building a report using Pentaho Reporting's Java API. To avoid going over the entire Javadoc of Pentaho Reporting, this chapter covers only the essentials. This includes references to important packages, making it easier to find the classes, factories, and interfaces that you need to build your report. Pentaho Reporting's Javadoc is available at `http://javadoc.pentaho.com/reporting/`

The first step in working with Pentaho Reporting's API is to initialize the reporting engine and create an empty `MasterReport` object.

```
// Initialize the reporting engine
ClassicEngineBoot.getInstance().start();
// Create a report object
MasterReport report = new MasterReport();
```

The `ClassicEngineBoot` and `MasterReport` classes are located in the `org.pentaho.reporting.engine.classic.core` Java package.

Once you've created a report object, you're ready to step through the various components that make up an entire report. The following sections demonstrate setting up a data source, adding parameters to a report, including a function, adding layout bands to the report, adding elements to a report, and customizing the report page definition.

Adding a data source

In Chapter 5, you created many different `DataFactory` classes and added them to your reports. Here is a simple example of a `DataFactory` definition, along with code to bind it to the report:

```
// Define a simple TableModel
DefaultTableModel data = new DefaultTableModel(
                new Object[][] {
                                {"libloader", 114287},
                                {"libformula", 331839}
                },
                new String[] {"Name", "Size"}
    );

// create a TableDataFactory
final TableDataFactory dataFactory = new TableDataFactory();

// Add the table model to the factory
dataFactory.addTable("default", tableModel);

// Add the factory to the report
report.setDataFactory(dataFactory);
```

When starting from scratch, you must also tell the report which named data source to use. You can do this by calling the following method:

```
// set the main query to default for this report
report.setQuery("default");
```

The default string is the name of the data source. Additional methods on the report object that relate to data source configuration include `setQueryLimit(int queryLimit)` and `setQueryTimeout(int queryTimeout)`, which allow you to specify the limit of rows returned in the result set, as well as the maximum length of time a result set has to execute before the report engine ends the query.

Defining parameters

By defining parameter types and validation information about parameters, the reporting engine can validate incoming parameters. This information is also available to the system executing the report, allowing for user prompting. Parameters are managed using the `ReportParameterDefinition` API. This API is defined in the package `org.pentaho.reporting.engine.classic.core.parameters`, along with all the other classes and interfaces discussed in this section.

The ReportParameterDefinition API defines individual parameter definitions, as well as the ReportParameterValidator class, which verify that the entries are valid. The following example demonstrates the use of Pentaho Reporting's default implementation, the DefaultParameterDefinition class. Individual parameters use the ParameterDefinitionEntry API. Available implementations of entries include PlainParameter, DefaultListParameter and DefaultFormulaListParameter. The following code demonstrates configuring a PlainParameter called Library Size:

```
// Define a plain parameter
PlainParameter entry = new PlainParameter("Library Size", Integer.
class);

// Make the parameter Mandatory
entry.setMandatory(true);

// Add the parameter to our parameter definition
paramDef.addParameterDefinition(entry);
```

Including functions and expressions

To add a function or expression to a Pentaho Report, simply create the function or expression instance and call report.addExpression(Expression expression). All expressions that get added to a report must implement the Expression interface. All functions added to a report must implement the Function interface, which extends the Expression interface. Most functions discussed earlier in this book, along with the Expression and Function interfaces, are defined within the package org.pentaho.reporting.engine.classic.core.function or a sub-package. Expression implementations use the JavaBean standard getters and setters for configuring their properties. The following code demonstrates creating a FormulaExpression instance and adding it to a report:

```
// create a formula expression
FormulaExpression formula = new FormulaExpression();

// configure the formulas properties
formula.setName("SizeKilobytes");
formula.setFormula("=[Size] / 1024");

// add the expression to the report
report.addExpression(formula);
```

Defining the report's layout

Similar to the `layout.xml` document described earlier in this chapter, defining the JavaBeans that make up the report layout include the common report bands such as the report header and footer, as well as the group band hierarchy that also includes the details band.

Common report bands

For each band defined in a report such as report header, report footer, page header, and page footer, there are equivalent Java classes that are available, all extending from the common abstract class `Band`, located in the `org.pentaho.reporting.engine.classic.core` package. These bands are all located in the same package. Each band defines a set of JavaBean properties, but most simply use those defined in the `Band` abstract class. One of the primary methods defined in this class is `addElement(Element element)`, which you'll use later when creating elements and adding them to their parent bands. A subset of `Band` implementations also implement the `RootLevelBand` interface, which allows the addition of sub-reports to the band via the `addSubReport(SubReport subreport)` method. Bands such as page header, page footer, and watermark do not allow rendering of sub-reports. Here is an example of setting the report header and report footer in a report:

```
// Create report header and footer objects
ReportHeader reportHeader = new ReportHeader();
ReportFooter reportFooter = new ReportFooter();

// add the report header and footer to the report
report.setReportHeader(reportHeader);
report.setReportFooter(reportFooter);
```

It can't get any easier than that!

Group band hierarchy

Group bands also follow this simple JavaBean paradigm. Because it is possible to nest groups, the API is a little bit more advanced. The `RelationalGroup` class is used for regular relational groupings. The `CrosstabGroup` is used for defining cross tabs within a report. The `CrosstabGroup` API is out of the scope of this chapter, but is well documented in Javadoc.

The `RelationalGroup` class may contain a group header and group footer, as well as a `GroupBody` implementation. `GroupBody` is an abstract class that `SubGroupBody` and `GroupDataBody` extend. The `SubGroupBody` allows for nested groups, and the `GroupDataBody` contains the `ItemBand`, as well as three other less used bands, `DetailHeader`, `DetailsFooter`, and `NoDataBand`.

To configure a `RelationalGroup` class, you must provide a set of data row fields that define the grouping. This may be done via the `addField(String field)`, `setFields(List fields)`, or `setFieldsArray(String[] fieldsArray)` method calls. In this example, you'll define a `RelationalGroup` and `ItemBand`, and group by the `Name` field. Note that the `ItemBand` class represents a details band in a report:

```
// Create the root relational group
RelationalGroup group = new RelationalGroup();

// Use "Name" as the root grouping
group.addField("Name");

// Create a group data body
GroupDataBody groupData = new GroupDataBody();

// Create an item band
ItemBand itemBand = new ItemBand();

// place the item band within the group data body
groupData.setItemBand(itemBand);

// place the group data body within the root group
group.setBody(groupData);

// set the root group within the report
report.setRootGroup(group);
```

Adding elements to the report

Now that you've set up all the bands for your report, you're ready to start adding elements. Unlike the previous classes and interfaces introduced for bands, all elements share a single class implementation, `Element`, and are created by element factories. The `Element` class is located in the `org.pentaho.reporting.engine.classic.core` package. The primary set of element factories are located in the `org.pentaho.reporting.engine.classic.core.elementfactory` package.

To use a factory, first instantiate the factory object, and then configure the JavaBean setters of the factory. Once you've built your element within the factory object, call `createElement()` to retrieve the `Element` instance, which you will then add to your report.

As a demonstration of how to use a factory, the following code instantiates an `Element` using the `LabelElementFactory` class:

```
// create a label element factory instance
LabelElementFactory factory = new LabelElementFactory();

// configure the label's text
factory.setText("Library Information");

// instantiate the label element
Element label = factory.createElement();
```

In this example, you instantiated the factory, set a value for the label, and then generated the label `Element` instance. Factories also expose style attributes as JavaBean setters, so it's possible to configure the location, size, and font style of this element.

```
// create a label element factory instance
LabelElementFactory labelFactory = new LabelElementFactory();

// configure the label's text
labelFactory.setText("Library Information");

// configure the label's location and size
labelFactory.setX(1f);
labelFactory.setY(1f);
labelFactory.setMinimumWidth(100f);
labelFactory.setMinimumHeight(20f);

// set the font to bold
labelFactory.setBold(true);

// instantiate the label element
Element label = labelFactory.createElement();
```

Now, add the label to your `ReportHeader` instance defined earlier:

```
// add the label to the report header
reportHeader.addElement(label);
```

It is important to note that for the JavaBean properties not set, elements inherit their default values from their parent band. For instance, you can specify the bold attribute on the `ReportHeader` instance, and all text elements will default to that value.

```
// set the bold property to true, inherited by all
// child text elements
reportHeader.getStyle().setStyleProperty(TextStyleKeys.BOLD, true);
```

Java API example

In this example, you'll take what you've learned and incorporate it into a simple Java Application. You'll build from the Chapter2SwingApp example. Create a new folder, chapter10, along with a src and lib subdirectory. Copy the jar files from chapter2/lib into chapter10/lib. Also, copy Chapter2SwingApp.java to chapter2/src/Chapter10SwingApp.java. Make sure to rename the class to Chapter10SwingApp. Finally, copy the build.xml file from chapter2 to chapter10.

Instead of having Chapter10SwingApp load a report file from disk, create your own. Replace the // load report definition section of the onPreview() method with the following Java source:

```java
// create a new report object
MasterReport report = new MasterReport();

// add a table data source to the report
DefaultTableModel tableModel = new DefaultTableModel(
        new Object[][] {
                    {"libloader", 114287},
                    {"libformula", 331839}
        },
        new String[] {"Name", "Size"}
);
final TableDataFactory dataFactory = new TableDataFactory();
dataFactory.addTable("default", tableModel);
report.setDataFactory(dataFactory);

// add a formula expression to the report
FormulaExpression formula = new FormulaExpression();
formula.setName("SizeKilobytes");
formula.setFormula("=[Size] / 1024");
report.addExpression(formula);

// add the report header and footer
ReportHeader reportHeader = new ReportHeader();
ReportFooter reportFooter = new ReportFooter();
report.setReportHeader(reportHeader);
report.setReportFooter(reportFooter);

// add the item band, with a shortcut that
// handles creating the default group
ItemBand itemBand = new ItemBand();
report.setItemBand(itemBand);

// create a label and add it to the header
```

```
LabelElementFactory labelFactory = new LabelElementFactory();

labelFactory.setText("Library Information");
labelFactory.setX(1f);
labelFactory.setY(1f);
labelFactory.setMinimumWidth(100f);
labelFactory.setMinimumHeight(20f);
labelFactory.setBold(true);

Element label = labelFactory.createElement();
reportHeader.addElement(label);

// Add a text field for the library name, added to
// the item band

TextFieldElementFactory textFactory = new TextFieldElementFactory();
textFactory.setFieldname("Name");
textFactory.setX(1f);
textFactory.setY(1f);
textFactory.setMinimumWidth(100f);
textFactory.setMinimumHeight(20f);
Element nameField = textFactory.createElement();
itemBand.addElement(nameField);

// Add a number field for the library size, added to
// the item band

NumberFieldElementFactory numberFactory = new
NumberFieldElementFactory();
numberFactory.setFieldname("SizeKilobytes");
numberFactory.setX(101f);
numberFactory.setY(1f);
numberFactory.setMinimumWidth(100f);
numberFactory.setMinimumHeight(20f);
Element sizeField = numberFactory.createElement();
itemBand.addElement(sizeField);
```

Make sure to include the necessary imports:

```
import javax.swing.table.DefaultTableModel;
import org.pentaho.reporting.engine.classic.core.Element;
import org.pentaho.reporting.engine.classic.core.ItemBand;
import org.pentaho.reporting.engine.classic.core.MasterReport;
import org.pentaho.reporting.engine.classic.core.ReportFooter;
import org.pentaho.reporting.engine.classic.core.ReportHeader;
import org.pentaho.reporting.engine.classic.core.TableDataFactory;
import org.pentaho.reporting.engine.classic.core.elementfactory.
LabelElementFactory;
```

```
import org.pentaho.reporting.engine.classic.core.elementfactory.
NumberFieldElementFactory;
import org.pentaho.reporting.engine.classic.core.elementfactory.
TextFieldElementFactory;
import org.pentaho.reporting.engine.classic.core.function.
FormulaExpression;
```

As the final step, you must also remove the `try/catch` statement, which no longer applies to the creation of this report.

You're now ready to build and run the example. Update the `build.xml` file, modifying the `run` target.

```
<target name="run" depends="compile">
        <java fork="true" classpathref="runtime_classpath" classname
="Chapter10SwingApp"/>
    </target>
```

Type `ant run` on command line to view the results. You should see a report like this:

Library Information

libloader	111.6083984375
libformula	324.0615234375

Wizard Java API

In addition to building reports via Pentaho Reporting's traditional API, it is also possible to build a report using Pentaho's Wizard API. This API is defined in the wizard-core library, within the `org.pentaho.reporting.engine.classic.wizard` package and sub-packages. The `DefaultWizardSpecification` class, defined in the model package, allows you to quickly populate a report with groupings and details. The Wizard API may incorporate predefined styles, allowing your organization to easily generate dynamic reports that fit your company's style requirements.

Once a `WizardSpecification` is defined, you can easily populate a report with just two lines of code:

```
WizardProcessorUtil.applyWizardSpec(styledReport, wizardSpec);
WizardProcessorUtil.ensureWizardProcessorIsAdded(styledReport, null);
```

The `applyWizardSpec` inserts the `wizardSpec` into the `styledReport`, and the `ensureWizardProcessorIsAdded` method adds a `WizardProcessor` as a `ReportPreProcessor` to the `styledReport`, by calling the `AbstractReportDefinition.addPreProcessor(ReportPreProcessor preprocessor)` method.

In addition to defining a `WizardSpecification` instance, a data source must already be configured before rendering a report.

To learn more about the Wizard API, please review the Javadoc at `http://javadoc.pentaho.com/reporting/org/pentaho/reporting/wizard-core/`

Summary

In this chapter, you walked through Pentaho Reporting's `.prpt` bundle file format, and learned about the various XML documents that combine to render a report. You learned how to define parameters, data sources, and expressions in the `datadefinition.xml` file. You also learned how to lay out and style a report within the `layout.xml` and `styles.xml` files. You combined all the files to generate an example `.prpt` bundle file, and loaded the result in Report Designer to verify that it renders as expected.

This chapter also covered the basics of building a `MasterReport` via Pentaho Reporting's easy to use Java API. You saw examples of defining parameters, adding data sources, and defining expressions. You also learned about how to build the group hierarchy, and add elements to reports via Pentaho Reporting's element factory approach. You then walked through a full example of a simple report, demonstrating how easy it is to build a report from scratch, using just a few lines of code.

Finally, you received a brief introduction to Pentaho's Wizard API, which makes API-based report generation an easy task.

11
Extending Pentaho Reporting

In this chapter, you'll learn how to extend Pentaho Reporting through various APIs available within the reporting engine. You'll first begin with implementing your own report functions and expressions. From there, you'll design your own formula functions, as well as BeanShell expressions. Finally, you'll complete the chapter with an example of writing a custom report element.

Implementing report functions and expressions

As you learned in Chapter 7, Pentaho Reporting comes with many already defined functions and expressions. All expressions implement the `Expression` Java interface, and all functions implement the `Function` Java interface—both are located in the `org.pentaho.reporting.engine.classic.core.function` package. An expression is stateless, and only has access to its current dataset row. Functions are stateful, and may maintain state across rows of data.

Implementing expressions

To implement an expression, you must define a class that implements the `Expression` interface, as well as associated metadata, so the expression may appear in Pentaho's Report Designer.

Defining an expression class

The `Expression` interface defines the methods necessary for an expression to be evaluated. The `Expression` Javadoc, available at `http://javadoc.pentaho.com/reporting/`, provides details on each method within the interface. An `AbstractExpression` class is provided, located in the same Java package as the `Expression` interface, which implements the common interface requirements of all expressions. This includes handling of common properties such as **name**, **dependency level**, and **preserve**, as well as managing the reporting runtime, which includes access to the data row and resource bundle factory.

To implement your own expression, extend the `AbstractExpression` class, add JavaBean getters and setters for the properties you are interested in for configuration of the `Expression`, and implement the `Object getValue()` method, which is part of the `Expression` API. The `getValue` method will be called during report evaluation on every row and band, in order to execute the `Expression`.

Also, you must provide a default constructor for your class. The reporting engine will instantiate a single expression object during report execution.

Note that only certain class types may be used as properties for expressions. For more information on which class types are supported, see the `ConverterRegistry` class, located in the `org.pentaho.reporting.engine.classic.core.util.beans` package, which defines the supported class types along with their converter classes.

Defining expression metadata

If you would like your expression to appear in the Report Designer, you'll need to create additional files that describe your expression. The first file that must be defined is the expression properties bundle. This bundle is a standard Java resource bundle file that contains specific name value pairs. The file should be located in the same directory as the `Expression` implementation, and be named `<Class Name>Bundle.properties`.

Two properties—**display-name** and **grouping**—must be defined for each expression. The **display-name** property defines how the expression is presented in the Report Designer, and the **grouping** property defines which group the expression is located in within the **Add Function** dialog. Each property name must begin with `expression.<package and class name>.<property name>`—for example `expression.ExampleExpression.display-name=Example Expression`.

For each JavaBean property defined within the `Expression` implementation, the **display-name** and **grouping** properties must be defined as well. The names of these properties should appear in the bundle as `expression.<package and class name>.property.<JavaBean property name>.<property name>`—for example `expression.ExampleExpression.property.name.display-name=Name`.

In addition to defining the bundle, you must also provide expression metadata in XML. This is done using Pentaho Reporting's metadata XML namespace. The element should be defined in an XML file as a child element called `expression`, with a root node of `meta-data`. The `expression` XML element should contain the following XML attributes:

Expression attribute	Description
Class	The fully qualified class name of the `Expression` implementation.
Bundlename	The fully qualified path of the resource bundle defined above.
Result	The fully qualified class name of the value returned by the method `getValue()`.
hidden	This attribute can be set to true or false. If true, the element will not appear in the Report Designer.

Also, the expression element should contain a `property` XML element for each JavaBean property defined in the element. The `property` element should contain the following XML attributes:

Property attribute	Description
name	The name of the JavaBean property.
mandatory	Set mandatory to true if this attribute must not be null.
value-role	The role this value is used for. This helps determine the type of editor to display in the Report Designer. The following are valid options—Value, Resource, ElementType, Query, Field, and Group.
hidden	This attribute can be set to true or false. If true, the element will not appear in the Report Designer.

To register the XML file with the reporting engine, you need to define a `Module` class. The `Module` interface is defined in Pentaho Reporting's libbase subproject within the `org.pentaho.reporting.libraries.base.boot` package. The `AbstractModule` class is created to simplify defining a new module. An implemented module should contain a default constructor with a call to the `AbstractModule loadModuleInfo()` method. This loads the necessary module configuration files, which are defined below. To load your expression metadata file, define the following method:

```
public void initialize(final SubSystem subSystem) throws
ModuleInitializeException
```

Within the method, make a call to `ElementMetaDataParser.initializeOptional ExpressionsMetaData(String xmlFile)` with a reference to your metadata XML file defined above.

In addition to defining your `Module` class, you must also define a `module.properties` file that describes your module. This properties file should contain the following properties:

Property name	Description
module.name	The name of the module.
module.producer	The author of the module.
module.description	The description of the module.
module.version.major	The major version number of the module.
module.version.minor	The minor version number of the module.
module.version.patchlevel	The patch level version number of the module.
dependency.core.module	This is the name of the module in which you require to exist before loading. In most cases, this should be set to `org.pentaho.reporting. engine.classic.core. ClassicEngineCoreModule`
dependency.core.dependency-type	This describes the type of dependency, usually set to **required**.
dependency.core.version.major	The major version number of the dependency.
dependency.core.version.minor	The minor version number of the dependency.
dependency.core.version.patchlevel	The `patchlevel` version number of the dependency.

These properties must be defined within the properties file with a colon separating the property and value, as `<Property Name>: <Value>`.

Once you've defined your `Module` implementation, you must also register the module with the reporting engine. To do this, create a properties file at the root of your JAR, containing your module called `classic-engine.properties`, with a property called `org.pentaho.reporting.engine.classic.extensions.modules.<Module Name>.Module`, setting its value to the full module class name including its package.

The reporting engine searches the classpath for this file, and loads the modules listed.

 You may use a single `Module` to define multiple expressions and other extensions within Pentaho Reporting.

An example expression

This example will demonstrate creating an expression by implementing the `RegexExpression` class. This expression will take a data field, run it through a regular expression, and then render a message containing groups from the regular expression.

First, you'll need to set up the Chapter 11 project. Create a folder `chapter11`, and copy the `chapter10/lib` folder into the new project. Also, create an `src` folder. Now, create the file `RegexExpression.java` in the `src` folder, and stub out a class.

```
import org.pentaho.reporting.engine.classic.core.function.
AbstractExpression;
public class RegexExpression extends AbstractExpression {
    public RegexExpression() {
    }
    // add properties here
    // add getValue here
}
```

Now that you've stubbed out the expression class, you're ready to give it a set of properties. Add two properties that are relevant to this expression. The first is `regex`, which will contain a defined regular expression. The second is `field`, which will contain the data field to parse. Add the following lines of code after the `// add properties here` comment:

```
private String regex;
private String field;
public void setRegex(String regex) {
    this.regex = regex;
}
public String getRegex() {
```

```
        return regex;
    }
    public void setField(String field) {
    this.field = field;
    }
    public String getField() {
        return field;
    }
```

It's now time to write the getValue() method of the expression. This method uses the two expression properties and returns a result. Add the following lines of code after the // add getValue here comment:

```
public Object getValue() {
    // wrap the regex code in a try catch, so that an
    // error message can be presented if the parsing failed.
    try {
            // create a pattern based on the regex input
            final Pattern p = Pattern.compile(regex);

            // lookup the field, and if not null, create a matcher
            final Object o = getDataRow().get(getField());
            if (o == null) {
                    return null;
            }
            final Matcher m = p.matcher(o.toString());

            // find the first match in the string
            m.find();

            // return the first group found within the match
            return m.group(1);
    } catch (Exception e) {
            // return the error message instead
            return e.getMessage();
    }
}
```

To complete the RegexExpression class, you must also add the following imports to the beginning of the class:

```
import java.util.regex.Pattern;
import java.util.regex.Matcher;
```

Now that you've defined the `Expression` class, you must also define a properties file describing the expression. Create the `RegexExpressionBundle.properties` file in the `src` folder, and add the following contents:

```
# The name and grouping of the expression
expression.RegexExpression.display-name=Regex Expression
expression.RegexExpression.grouping=Other

# The field property
expression.RegexExpression.property.field.display-name=Field Name
expression.RegexExpression.property.field.grouping=Other

# The regex property
expression.RegexExpression.property.regex.display-name=Regex
expression.RegexExpression.property.regex.grouping=Other

# common properties, name and dependencyLevel
expression.RegexExpression.property.name.display-name=Name
expression.RegexExpression.property.name.grouping=Common
expression.RegexExpression.property.dependencyLevel.display-name=Dependency Level
expression.RegexExpression.property.dependencyLevel.grouping=Common
```

To finish defining all the necessary metadata for the expression, create a `src/meta-expressions.xml` file, which contains details about the expression:

```xml
<meta-data xmlns="http://reporting.pentaho.org/namespaces/engine/classic/metadata/1.0">

    <expression class="RegexExpression"
                bundle-name="RegexExpressionBundle"
                result="java.lang.String" hidden="false">

        <property name="dependencyLevel" mandatory="false"
                value-role="Value" hidden="false"/>

        <property name="field" mandatory="true" value-role="Field"
                hidden="false"/>

        <property name="regex" mandatory="true" value-role="Value"
                hidden="false"/>

        <property name="name" mandatory="true" value-role="Name"
                hidden="false"/>
    </expression>
</meta-data>
```

To complete this example, you need to define a reporting module that will manage the initialization of the expression and other examples that appear later in this chapter. First, create the file `Chapter11Module.java` in the `src` folder, which loads the `meta-expressions.xml` file.

```
import org.pentaho.reporting.engine.classic.core.metadata.
ElementMetaDataParser;
import org.pentaho.reporting.libraries.base.boot.AbstractModule;
import org.pentaho.reporting.libraries.base.boot.
ModuleInitializeException;
import org.pentaho.reporting.libraries.base.boot.SubSystem;

public class Chapter11Module extends AbstractModule {
    // Constructor.  This loads the module specification
    public Chapter11Module() throws ModuleInitializeException {
        loadModuleInfo();
    }

    // initialize the module by loading the expression metadata
    public void initialize(final SubSystem subSystem) throws
ModuleInitializeException {
        ElementMetaDataParser.initializeOptionalExpressionsMetaData(
"meta-expressions.xml");
    }
}
```

Now, create a `src/module.properties` file with the following content:

```
module.name: chapter11module
module.producer: Pentaho Reporting for Java Developers
module.description:  Example classes to demonstrate extending Pentaho
Reporting.
module.version.major: 1
module.version.minor: 0
module.version.patchlevel: 0

dependency.core.module: org.pentaho.reporting.engine.classic.core.
ClassicEngineCoreModule
dependency.core.dependency-type: required
dependency.core.version.major: 3
dependency.core.version.minor: 5
dependency.core.version.patchlevel: 0
```

To register the module with the reporting engine, you must define a properties file that the engine looks for and loads. Create the `classic-engine.properties` file within the `chapter11/src` folder, and add the following property:

```
# Module definition
org.pentaho.reporting.engine.classic.extensions.modules.
chapter11module.Module=Chapter11Module
```

You're now ready to build your module into a JAR file. Create a `build.xml` in the root of the project, and add the following xml:

```xml
<?xml version="1.0" encoding="UTF-8"?>
<project name="Chapter 11 Examples" default="jar">

    <path id="classpath">
            <fileset dir="lib">
                    <include name="*.jar" />
            </fileset>
    </path>

    <target name="clean">
            <delete dir="classes"/>
    </target>

    <target name="compile">
            <mkdir dir="classes"/>
            <javac classpathref="classpath" destdir="classes"
    fork="true" srcdir="src"/>
    </target>

    <target name="jar" depends="compile">
            <mkdir dir="dist"/>
            <copy todir="classes" overwrite="true">
                    <fileset dir="src">
                            <exclude name="**/*.java"/>
                    </fileset>
            </copy>
            <jar destfile="dist/chapter11.jar" basedir="classes"/>
    </target>

</project>
```

After creating the build file, run `ant jar` at the root of the project. The `chapter11.jar` will be created in the `dist` folder. Now copy this JAR file into the Report Designer's `lib` folder, and restart the Report Designer. You should see the function appear in the designer:

Now it's time to create a very basic report to demonstrate the **Regex Expression**.
Create a report with a table data source, with the following values:

Field
Please call 513-523-1222 at your earliest convenience.
The number 518-123-5555 is unlisted.
To place an order, call 941-563-1324.

Drag-and-drop the **Field** into the details band. Also, add a label with the text "**Fields**"
in the report header. Now, add a **Regex Expression** to the report. Set the **Field
Name** equal to Field, and the **regex** equal to (\d{3}-\d{3}-\d{4}). This regular
expression will find the first phone number in the field. Drag the expression into
the details band, and run a preview of the report. Also, add a label in the report
header called **Phone Number**. Your results should look something like the following:

Field	Phone Number
Please call 513-523-1222 at your earliest convenience.	513-523-1222
The number 518-123-5555 is unlisted.	518-123-5555
To place an order, call 941-563-1324.	941-563-1324

Save this report as chapter11.prpt — you'll be using it later in this chapter.

Implementing functions

As mentioned earlier, functions are stateful expressions. The `Function` interface extends the `Expression` interface, as well as the `ReportListener` interface defined in the `org.pentaho.reporting.engine.classic.core.event` package. Functions receive event notifications while the report is being generated, allowing functions to detect progress in report generation. See the `ReportListener` Javadoc for the various callbacks that the `Function` interface receives.

An additional class called `FunctionUtilities`, located in the `org.pentaho.reporting.engine.classic.core.function` package, provides useful methods for accessing elements within a report, as well as determining the exact state of report generation. Knowing that the report is in the prepare run state is important for functions calculating values. This is possible with the `FunctionUtilities.isDefinedPrepareRunLevel()` method call. Please see the `FunctionUtilities` Javadoc for additional information on the utility functions available.

Functions must provide the same exact metadata that an expression defines, as described above. There are many examples of `Function` and `Expression` implementations in the reporting engine core project that demonstrate everything from row banding to open formula evaluation.

Implementing a formula function

As described in Chapter 7, formulas are used in many places within a report for dynamic evaluation. Pentaho Reporting allows the definition of custom formula functions so that developers may extend the capability of the formula subsystem.

To define a formula function, you must implement the `Function` interface located in the `org.pentaho.reporting.libraries.formula.function` package, as well as a `FunctionDescription` defined in the same package. Note that this is a different `Function` interface as described earlier. The two methods a formula function must implement are:

```
// This is the name of the function as it appears in the formula
public String getCanonicalName();

// this method evaluates a result based on the incoming parameters
public TypeValuePair evaluate(FormulaContext context,
                             ParameterCallback parameters)
     throws EvaluationException;
```

The `TypeValuePair` class simply contains a variable value and its type. The `FormulaContext` class provides access to the formula system, and the `ParameterCallback` class provides information about the parameters being passed into the current function.

The `FunctionDescription` interface describes details about the function, including its inputs and output type. The `AbstractFunctionDescription` class is available to simplify the implementation of your `FunctionDescription` class. When using the `AbstractFunctionDescription`, you must implement the following methods in your description class, along with a properties bundle file:

Method	Description
Default Constructor	The default constructor of your description class must call `AbstractFunctionDescription`'s `super(String canonicalName, String messageBundle)` parent constructor to initialize properly.
FunctionCategory getCategory()	Defines which `FunctionCategory` the formula function should appear in. Normally, custom functions should return `UserDefinedFunctionCategory.CATEGORY`.
int getParameterCount()	Defines the number of parameters accepted by this function.
Type getParameterType(int position)	Returns the parameter type of a parameter expected at a specific position.
public Type getValueType()	Returns the result value type.
public boolean isParameterMandatory(int position)	Returns true if a parameter is required at a specific position.

The properties bundle contains information about the function. Required properties include:

Property	Description
display-name	The canonical name of the formula function.
Description	The description of the formula function.
parameter.<N>.display-name	The display name of the Nth parameter.
parameter.<N>.description	The description of the Nth parameter.

Finally, to register the function with libformula, you need to create a libformula.
properties file at the root of the module JAR, and add the property org.pentaho.
reporting.libraries.formula.functions.information.<Function Name>.
class, which references the implemented Formula class, as well as org.pentaho.
reporting.libraries.formula.functions.information.<Function Name>.
description, which references the implemented FormulaDescription class.

Regex formula function example

In this example, you'll define a function called regex, which takes a regular
expression and an input string, returning the first matching group of the regular
expression. To begin the example, create a class named RegexFunction.java in
the src folder, and add the following content to the file:

```
import java.util.regex.Matcher;
import java.util.regex.Pattern;

import org.pentaho.reporting.libraries.formula.EvaluationException;
import org.pentaho.reporting.libraries.formula.FormulaContext;
import org.pentaho.reporting.libraries.formula.LibFormulaErrorValue;
import org.pentaho.reporting.libraries.formula.function.Function;
import org.pentaho.reporting.libraries.formula.function.
ParameterCallback;
import org.pentaho.reporting.libraries.formula.lvalues.TypeValuePair;
import org.pentaho.reporting.libraries.formula.typing.TypeRegistry;
import org.pentaho.reporting.libraries.formula.typing.coretypes.
TextType;

public class RegexFunction implements Function {

    // This method evaluates the regular expression function
    public TypeValuePair evaluate(FormulaContext context,
                ParameterCallback parameters) throws
EvaluationException {
            // throw an exception if the function doesn't have
            // both parameters
        if (parameters.getParameterCount() != 2) {
            throw new EvaluationException(
                    LibFormulaErrorValue.ERROR_ARGUMENTS_VALUE);
        }

        final TypeRegistry typeRegistry = context.getTypeRegistry();
        final String param1 = typeRegistry.convertToText(parameters.
getType(0), parameters.getValue(0));
        final String param2 = typeRegistry.convertToText(parameters.
getType(1), parameters.getValue(1));
```

```
        try {
                // create a pattern based on the regex input
                final Pattern p = Pattern.compile(param1);
                final Matcher m = p.matcher(param2);
                // find the first match in the string
                m.find();
                // return the first group found within the match
                return new TypeValuePair(TextType.TYPE, m.group(1));
        } catch (Exception e) {
                // return the error message as the result
                return new TypeValuePair(TextType.TYPE, e.getMessage());
        }
    }

    public String getCanonicalName() {
        return "REGEX";
    }
  }
```

Now that you've defined an implementation of the `Function` class, you must also provide a `FunctionDescription` class. Create a `RegexFunctionDescription.java` file in your `src` folder, and enter the following text:

```
import org.pentaho.reporting.libraries.formula.function.
AbstractFunctionDescription;
import org.pentaho.reporting.libraries.formula.function.
FunctionCategory;
import org.pentaho.reporting.libraries.formula.function.userdefined.
UserDefinedFunctionCategory;
import org.pentaho.reporting.libraries.formula.typing.Type;
import org.pentaho.reporting.libraries.formula.typing.coretypes.
TextType;

public class RegexFunctionDescription extends
AbstractFunctionDescription {

    public RegexFunctionDescription() {
            // make sure to call the super constructor, with
            // the function name and the function resource bundle
        super("REGEX", "Regex-Function");
    }

    // place this function in the user defined category
    public FunctionCategory getCategory() {
            return UserDefinedFunctionCategory.CATEGORY;
    }
```

```
// this function requires two parameters,
// regex and input string
public int getParameterCount() {
    return 2;
}
// both of the parameters are of type text
public Type getParameterType(int position) {
    return TextType.TYPE;
}
// the output type is of type text
public Type getValueType() {
    return TextType.TYPE;
}

// both parameters are required for execution
public boolean isParameterMandatory(int position) {
    return true;
}
}
```

You must also define a resource bundle for the function. Create a `Regex-Function.properties` file in the `src` folder, and enter the following text:

```
display-name=REGEX
description=Executes a regular expression on a string, returning the
first found group
parameter.0.display-name=Regular Expression
parameter.0.description=A Java Regular Expression string, with a
grouping defined within the string.
parameter.1.display-name=String Input
parameter.1.description=A string to parse.
```

To register the formula function with libformula, you must also provide a `libformula.properties` file in the `src` folder, with the following information:

```
org.pentaho.reporting.libraries.formula.functions.information.Regex.
class=RegexFunction
org.pentaho.reporting.libraries.formula.functions.information.Regex.de
scription=RegexFunctionDescription
```

You're now ready to build the `chapter11` project with the new formula function. Type `ant jar`, and place the generated JAR file in the Report Designer's classpath. Launch the Report Designer, and use the earlier defined report example. Add an **Open Formula** function with the following formula:

```
=REGEX("(\d{3}-\d{3}-\d{4})";[Field])
```

In the Details band, drag-and-drop the expression below the already defined
RegexExpression. Congratulations! Your new formula results should look
identical to the regex expression example defined earlier.

Implementing BeanShell expressions

Another approach to implementing your own report expressions is using the
BSHExpression report expression, which uses BeanShell to evaluate an expression.
BeanShell is a Java code interpreter, so you can write Java for direct execution
within a report with this expression. The **BSHExpression** contains a property called
expression, which should contain the necessary BeanShell script. This script must
contain the `Object getValue()` method, which is called to evaluate the expression.
Imports and additional functions may be included in the expression. The expression
also has access to the `DataRow` class instance named `dataRow`. This allows for easy
access to the current row of data for the expression to use.

Example BSHExpression

Open up the already defined `chapter11.prpt`, defined earlier in this chapter,
within Report Designer. Now add a **Bean-Scripting-Host (BSH)** expression, which
is located within the **Script** function group. Set the expression property to the
following BeanShell syntax:

```
import java.util.regex.*;
Object getValue() {
   try {
        final Pattern p = Pattern.compile("(\\d{3}-\\d{3}-\\d{4})");
        final Matcher m = p.matcher(dataRow.get("Field"));
        // find the first match in the string
        m.find();
        // return the first group found within the match
        return m.group(1);
   } catch (Exception e) {
        // appropriate way to log a error / warning message?
        return e.getMessage();
   }
}
```

Drag-and-drop the expression onto the details band, below the other expressions.
You should see results similar to the first and second examples above. To learn
more about BeanShell, please visit `http://www.beanshell.org/`.

Implementing a report element

With Pentaho Reporting's API, it is possible to implement your own report elements. In this section, you'll walk through the necessary steps to implement a basic report element. You'll learn how to define an `ElementType`, XML read and write handlers, as well as all the metadata necessary to have your report element appear in the Report Designer.

Defining an ElementType class

The first step in defining a new report element is implementing the `ElementType` interface, located in the `org.pentaho.reporting.engine.classic.core.metadata` package. This interface defines a set of methods that allow the creation and rendering of an element within a report.

```
// the getMetaData method returns the element type's
// metadata, including the element name, attributes and styles
public ElementMetaData getMetaData();

// Inherited from the DataSource interface, the getValue
// method generates a renderable object that will appear
// in a report.
public Object getValue(final ExpressionRuntime runtime, final Element
element)

// the getDesignValue returns a design time rendering of the
// element.  This is useful if you have an element
// without access to its source data.
public Object getDesignValue(ExpressionRuntime runtime, final Element
element);

// the configureDesignTimeDefaults method is used in
// designers when an element is first added to a report.
public void configureDesignTimeDefaults(Element element, Locale
locale);
```

The `getValue` method must return a Java object that the report engine knows how to process for rendering. This includes the types `java.lang.String`, `java.awt.Shape`, `org.pentaho.reporting.engine.classic.core.util.ReportDrawable`, along with any class that defines the following method, which is executed via introspection:

```
public void draw(Graphics2D, Rectangle2D)
```

The `ReportDrawable` interface defines the draw method, as well as additional methods providing access to the report configuration, the current stylesheet, and the resource bundle factory. Also defined is the `getImageMap` method, which allows the `ReportDrawable` implementation to define a clickable map over the content.

The Report Engine renders in multiple formats, and each format handles the rendering of Java graphics differently. For instance, PDF rendering, which uses iText, translates the rendered items within the Graphics2D context into PDF elements.

In the `getValue` method, the current element instance is provided for access to its attributes and styles. See the `org.pentaho.reporting.engine.classic.core.Element` Javadoc API for details on how to access attributes and styles.

Defining element metadata

Now that you've defined the main `ElementType` class, you need to define the metadata to go along with the element. Element metadata is similar to expression metadata defined earlier. The element should be defined in an XML file with a root node of `meta-data`, as a child XML element called `element`. This XML file should use the namespace: `http://reporting.pentaho.org/namespaces/engine/classic/metadata/1.0`. The `element` XML element should contain the following attributes:

XML attribute	Description
Name	The name of the element type.
Hidden	This attribute can be set to true or false. If true, the element will not appear in the Report Designer.
Deprecated	This attribute can be set to true or false. This attribute is not used at this time.
container	This attribute can be set to true or false. If true, the element is recognized as a container type element.
bundle-name	The fully qualified location of the resource bundle.
implementation	The fully qualified class name of the `ElementType` implementation.

The `element` XML may also contain child elements, defining attributes and styles. The `attribute` XML element contains the following XML attributes:

Attribute	Description
Namespace	The namespace of the attribute.
Name	The name of the attribute.
Mandatory	This attribute can be set to true or false. This attribute is not used at this time.

Attribute	Description
Hidden	This attribute can be set to true or false. If true, the attribute will not appear in the Report Designer.
Computed	This attribute can be set to true or false. If true, this attribute will not be serialized.
design-time-value	If computed, and design-time-value is set, the attribute will still be serialized.
Deprecated	This attribute can be set to true or false. This attribute is not used at this time.
prefer-bulk	This attribute determines where in the element XML the attribute is serialized.
value-type	The fully qualified Java class name of the attribute value.
value-role	The role this value is used for. This helps determine the type of editor to display in the Report Designer. The following are valid options—Value, Resource, ElementType, Query, Field, and Group.
propertyEditor	Defines the java.beans.PropertyEditor class for this attribute.
bundle-name	Defines the fully qualified bundle name for this attribute.

In addition to defining custom attributes and styles, defined elements may also import existing groups of attributes and styles. To reference these groups, first you must include the global XML file within the root meta-data XML element:

```
<include-globals src="res://org/pentaho/reporting/engine/classic/
core/metadata/global-meta-elements.xml"/>
```

Within the child element, you must specify an attribute-group-ref child XML element, or a style-group-ref XML element, to include a group. Set the ref XML attribute to the named group. Examples of common attribute groups include common-attributes and interactivity. Examples of common styles include borders, common, layout, and replaced-content. See the global-meta-elements. xml for additional groups.

Elements, along with their attributes and styles, may refer to resource bundles for defining localized property information. For element properties, the syntax is element.<ELEMENT_NAME>.<PROPERTY>=<VALUE>. For attributes and styles, the syntax is element.<ELEMENT_NAME>.attribute.<ATTRIBUTE_ NAMESPACE>.<ATTRIBUTE_NAME>.<PROPERTY>. Localized properties for elements, styles, and attributes include:

Property	Description
display-name	The name displayed in the Report Designer.
grouping	The group in which the item appears.
grouping.ordinal	The defined group location relative to other groups.
ordinal	The ordinal location of this item related to other items in the Report Designer.
description	The description of the item.
deprecated	A deprecation message if the item is deprecated.
icon	A reference to the element icon, displayed in the Report Designer. This property does not apply to attributes and styles.

Once you've defined the `meta-elements.xml` file, as well as its resource bundle, you must inform the reporting engine that these elements are available. You may do this by calling the following method within your module's initialize method:

```
ElementMetaDataParser.initializeOptionalElementMetaData("meta-
elements.xml");
```

Defining read and write handlers

Now that you've defined the `ElementType` class, as well as the metadata relating to the element, you're ready to define the element's read and write handlers, so you can serialize the element state to XML. You'll do this by defining an `ElementReadHandler`, as well as a `BundleElementWriteHandler`. The `ElementReadHandler` interface is located in the `org.pentaho.reporting.engine.classic.core.modules.parser.bundle.layout` package, and the `BundleElementWriteHandler` is located in the `org.pentaho.reporting.engine.classic.core.modules.parser.bundle.writer` package. Luckily for us, the reporting engine defines abstract classes that do most of the serialization work, based on the metadata you defined for your element.

Read and write handlers are registered through the module's `configuration.properties` file. A demonstration using the `AbstractElementReadHandler` and the `AbstractElementWriteHandler` class is provided in the following section.

An example report element

This example will demonstrate what you just learned by walking through a full implementation of a new `ElementType`, a star shape, and seeing it run within the Report Designer.

The first step is defining the `StarType` class, which implements the `ElementType` interface. Create `StarType.java` in the `chapter11/src` folder, with the following code:

```
import java.awt.Polygon;
import java.util.Locale;

import org.pentaho.reporting.engine.classic.core.Element;
import org.pentaho.reporting.engine.classic.core.function.
ExpressionRuntime;
import org.pentaho.reporting.engine.classic.core.metadata.
ElementMetaData;
import org.pentaho.reporting.engine.classic.core.metadata.ElementType;
import org.pentaho.reporting.engine.classic.core.metadata.
ElementTypeRegistry;
import org.pentaho.reporting.engine.classic.core.style.
ElementStyleKeys;
import org.pentaho.reporting.engine.classic.core.util.StringUtil;

// This ElementType implementation renders a Star in a report
public class StarType implements ElementType {

    // the default namespace for this element
    private static String NAMESPACE =
                    "http://reporting.pentaho.org/namespaces/pr4jd";

    // a reference to the element metadata, defined in the
    // meta-elements.xml file
    private transient ElementMetaData elementType;

    // a default constructor
    public StarType() {
    }

    // load the default metadata about the star element type
    public ElementMetaData getMetaData() {
        if (elementType == null) {
            elementType = ElementTypeRegistry.getInstance().
                    getElementType("star");
        }
        return elementType;
    }

    // renders a star, using inner-percent, start-angle,
    // and points as custom attributes
    public Object getValue(final ExpressionRuntime runtime,
            final Element element) {
        if (element == null) {
```

```java
                    throw new NullPointerException(
                                    "Element must never be null.");
        }
        // read in the star's custom parameters
        final float innerPercent = parseParam(element,
                                "inner-percent", 0.5f);
        final float startAngle = parseParam(element, "start-angle",
                                    0f);
        final int points = (int) parseParam(element, "points", 5);

        // render a star based on the parameters
        int outerRadius = 100;
        int innerRadius = (int) (outerRadius * innerPercent);
        double startingRotation = (startAngle - 90) * Math.PI / 180;
        double angleIncrement = 2.0 * Math.PI / points;
        double currRadians = startingRotation;
        int minX = Integer.MAX_VALUE;
        int minY = Integer.MAX_VALUE;
        final Polygon p = new Polygon();
        for (int i = 0; i < points; i++) {
                // gotta love trig
                double outerX = outerRadius + outerRadius * Math.
                                cos(currRadians);
                double outerY = outerRadius + outerRadius * Math.
                                sin(currRadians);
                double innerX = outerRadius + innerRadius
                            * Math.cos(currRadians + angleIncrement
                                    / 2);
                double innerY = outerRadius + innerRadius
                            * Math.sin(currRadians + angleIncrement
                                    / 2);
                p.addPoint((int) outerX, (int) outerY);
                p.addPoint((int) innerX, (int) innerY);
                currRadians += angleIncrement;
    // keep track of the smallest x and y values
                minX = Math.min((int)outerX, minX);
                minY = Math.min((int)outerY, minY);
        }
        // move the star's points to 0,0 for
        // appropriate rendering
        if (minX > 0 || minY > 0) {
                final Polygon p2 = new Polygon();
                for (int i = 0; i < p.npoints; i++) {
                        p2.addPoint(p.xpoints[i] - minX, p.ypoints[i]
                        - minY);
```

```
                }
                return p2;
        } else {
                return p;
        }
}

// returns the design time value of this element, rendered
// in the Report Designer
public Object getDesignValue(final ExpressionRuntime runtime,
            final Element element) {
        return getValue(runtime, element);
}

// this method is called when a star is first added to
// a report within the Report Designer.  Set up
// the default values here.
public void configureDesignTimeDefaults(final Element element,
            final Locale locale) {
        element.getStyle().setStyleProperty(ElementStyleKeys.SCALE,
                Boolean.TRUE);
        element.getStyle().setStyleProperty(
                ElementStyleKeys.DRAW_SHAPE, Boolean.TRUE);
        element.getStyle().setStyleProperty
                (ElementStyleKeys.MIN_WIDTH, new Float(100));
        element.getStyle().setStyleProperty(
                ElementStyleKeys.MIN_HEIGHT, new Float(100));

        element.setAttribute(NAMESPACE, "inner-percent", 0.5f);
        element.setAttribute(NAMESPACE, "start-angle", 0f);
        element.setAttribute(NAMESPACE, "points", 5);
}

// this is a utility function that parses the
// custom attributes
private float parseParam(final Element element,
            final String attrName,
            final float defaultValue) {
        final float val;
        final Object attrib = element.getAttribute(
                            NAMESPACE, attrName);
        if (attrib != null) {
                if (attrib instanceof Number) {
                        final Number n = (Number) attrib;
```

```
                                     val = n.floatValue();
                    } else {
                              val = StringUtil.parseFloat(
                                      String.valueOf(attrib),defaultValue);
                    }
            } else {
                    val = defaultValue;
            }
            return val;
      }

      // clone is required, because the reporting engine may
      // create new instances of the StarType when new reports
      // are rendered.
      public Object clone() throws CloneNotSupportedException {
            return super.clone();
      }
}
```

Note that you've defined three custom attributes—inner-percent, start-angle, and points. These three attributes combine to define any shape of star the report may need.

Now you need to define the element metadata, defining the three custom attributes, as well as including groups of attributes that are common across elements. Create a meta-elements.xml file in the src folder with the following content:

```
<meta-data xmlns="http://reporting.pentaho.org/namespaces/engine/
classic/metadata/1.0">

  <include-globals src="res://org/pentaho/reporting/engine/classic/
core/metadata/global-meta-elements.xml"/>

  <element name="star" hidden="false" bundle-name="metadata"
           implementation="StarType">

    <attribute-group-ref ref="common-attributes"/>
    <attribute-group-ref ref="interactivity"/>

    <attribute namespace="http://reporting.pentaho.org/namespaces/
pr4jd"
                name="inner-percent"
                mandatory="true"
                hidden="false"
                value-type="java.lang.Number"
                value-role="Value"/>
```

```
    <attribute namespace="http://reporting.pentaho.org/namespaces/
pr4jd"
                name="start-angle"
                mandatory="true"
                hidden="false"
                value-type="java.lang.Number"
                value-role="Value"/>
    <attribute namespace="http://reporting.pentaho.org/namespaces/
pr4jd"
                name="points"
                mandatory="true"
                hidden="false"
                value-type="java.lang.Number"
                value-role="Value"/>
  <style-group-ref ref="borders"/>
  <style-group-ref ref="common"/>
  <style-group-ref ref="layout"/>
  <style-group-ref ref="replaced-content"/>
  </element>

</meta-data>
```

You must also define a localized bundle that describes the element and its attributes. Create a `metadata.properties` file in the `src` folder with the following content:

```
element.star.display-name=star
element.star.grouping=s
element.star.grouping.ordinal=1100
element.star.ordinal=98
element.star.description=
element.star.deprecated=
element.star.icon=star.png

element.star.attribute.pr4jd.inner-percent.display-name=inner-percent
element.star.attribute.pr4jd.inner-percent.grouping=star
element.star.attribute.pr4jd.inner-percent.grouping.ordinal=350
element.star.attribute.pr4jd.inner-percent.ordinal=10
element.star.attribute.pr4jd.inner-percent.description=
element.star.attribute.pr4jd.inner-percent.deprecated=

element.star.attribute.pr4jd.start-angle.display-name=start-angle
element.star.attribute.pr4jd.start-angle.grouping=star
element.star.attribute.pr4jd.start-angle.grouping.ordinal=350
element.star.attribute.pr4jd.start-angle.ordinal=20
element.star.attribute.pr4jd.start-angle.description=
element.star.attribute.pr4jd.start-angle.deprecated=
```

```
element.star.attribute.pr4jd.points.display-name=points
element.star.attribute.pr4jd.points.grouping=star
element.star.attribute.pr4jd.points.grouping.ordinal=350
element.star.attribute.pr4jd.points.ordinal=30
element.star.attribute.pr4jd.points.description=
element.star.attribute.pr4jd.points.deprecated=
```

You'll need to place the `star.png` image file referenced in the resource bundle in the `src` folder so that the Report Designer displays an icon next to the star element. This file is provided on the book's web site, or you can make your own file using a program such as Gimp. The image should be 14 by 14 pixels and should be saved in the PNG format.

Now you need to define XML read and write handlers for the star element. You'll first define the read handler. Create the file `StarReadHandler.java` in the `src` folder, with the following contents:

```java
import org.pentaho.reporting.engine.classic.core.modules.parser.
bundle.layout.elements.AbstractElementReadHandler;
import org.pentaho.reporting.libraries.xmlns.parser.ParseException;

// this class handles reading in of the star element

public class StarReadHandler extends AbstractElementReadHandler {

  // all you need to do is pass the name of the element
  // to the parent class
  public StarReadHandler() throws ParseException {
    super("star");
  }
}
```

The `AbstractElementReadHandler` does the work of loading in all the report element's attributes and styles. You now need to create the file `StarWriteHandler.java` in the `src` folder with the following code:

```java
import java.io.IOException;

import org.pentaho.reporting.engine.classic.core.Element;
import org.pentaho.reporting.engine.classic.core.modules.parser.
bundle.writer.BundleWriterException;
import org.pentaho.reporting.engine.classic.core.modules.parser.
bundle.writer.BundleWriterState;
import org.pentaho.reporting.engine.classic.core.modules.parser.
bundle.writer.elements.AbstractElementWriteHandler;
import org.pentaho.reporting.libraries.docbundle.
WriteableDocumentBundle;
```

```
import org.pentaho.reporting.libraries.xmlns.common.AttributeList;
import org.pentaho.reporting.libraries.xmlns.writer.XmlWriter;
import org.pentaho.reporting.libraries.xmlns.writer.XmlWriterSupport;

// manages writing the star element type to .prpt bundle
public class StarWriteHandler extends AbstractElementWriteHandler {
    // namespace for XML elements
    private static final String NAMESPACE = "http://reporting.pentaho.
                                         org/namespaces/pr4jd";

    // default consructor
    public StarWriteHandler() {
    }
    // writes the star element to the xmlWriter
    public void writeElement(final WriteableDocumentBundle bundle,
                final BundleWriterState state, final XmlWriter
                xmlWriter,final Element element) throws IOException,
                BundleWriterException {
        if (bundle == null) {
            throw new NullPointerException();
        }
        if (state == null) {
            throw new NullPointerException();
        }
        if (xmlWriter == null) {
            throw new NullPointerException();
        }
        if (element == null) {
            throw new NullPointerException();
        }
        // add the attribute namespace if not already there
        final AttributeList attList = createMainAttributes(element,
                                   xmlWriter);
    if (xmlWriter.isNamespaceDefined(NAMESPACE) == false) {
      attList.addNamespaceDeclaration("pr4jd", NAMESPACE);
    }
        // write the star element, within the pr4jd namespace
        xmlWriter.writeTag(NAMESPACE, "star", attList,
                    XmlWriterSupport.OPEN);
        writeElementBody(bundle, state, element, xmlWriter);
        xmlWriter.writeCloseTag();
    }
}
```

It's now time to update the earlier defined `Chapter11Module` to initialize the element, and notify the reporting engine about the read and write handler classes. Open up `Chapter11Module.java`, and add the following line to the initialize method:

```
ElementMetaDataParser.initializeOptionalElementMetaData("meta-
elements.xml");
```

You also need to create the module's `configuration.properties` file with the information regarding the read and write handlers. This file should be created in the `src` folder. Add the following text to the configuration file:

```
# define the prefix for this configuration
org.pentaho.reporting.engine.classic.core.modules.parser.bundle.
element-factory-prefix.pr4jd=pr4jd.

# define the pr4jd namespace for this configuration
pr4jd.namespace.pr4jd=http://reporting.pentaho.org/namespaces/pr4jd

# define the pr4jd namespace for the metadata
org.pentaho.reporting.engine.classic.core.metadata.namespaces.
pr4jd=http://reporting.pentaho.org/namespaces/pr4jd

# define the star read handler
pr4jd.tag.pr4jd.star=StarReadHandler

# define the star write handler
org.pentaho.reporting.engine.classic.core.modules.parser.bundle.
writer.element-write-handler.star=StarWriteHandler
```

You're now ready to build the project and see some stars. Type `ant jar` to build the `chapter11.jar` file. Place the `chapter11.jar` file in the `lib` folder of the Report Designer, and start the Report Designer. You should see the star element within the list of elements. Drag-and-drop a star element into the report header.

In addition to adjusting the star's custom properties, you may also use the built-in styles to configure the border and colors, as well as properties such as aspect ratio. These capabilities are available because you defined a `Shape` object as the element value.

Set the star's **inner-percent** to **0.75**, and **points** to **16**. Under the **Style** tab, set **fill** to **true** and **fill-color** to **yellow**. Add a label over the star, and preview the report in PDF. You should see something like this:

Pentaho Reporting

Save your report, and reopen it. The star was saved into the `.prpt` file with the defined XML write handler, and reopened using the defined XML read handler.

> Due to the table rendering technique used when generating HTML, Excel, and RTF outputs, by default Shape objects are not rendered during report generation. You may enable Shape rendering by setting the report configuration property `org.pentaho.reporting.engine.classic.core.modules.output.table.html.ShapeAsContent` to `true` via a JVM system setting. Table renderers do not allow overlapping of elements, so in the previous example, the Pentaho Reporting label would be hidden until it was moved below the star.

Summary

In this chapter, you learned a great deal about Pentaho Reporting Engine extension points. You learned the details of implementing a report expression, including defining the `Expression` class, as well as all of the necessary metadata to view the expression in the Report Designer. With the `RegexExpression` example, you were able to execute your own expression in the Report Designer. You also learned about report functions and how they differ from expressions.

Next, you learned how to implement your own formula functions, as well as the necessary metadata to execute the formula function within the Report Designer. You took the same regex example and placed it within the formula system. You then used the `BSHExpression` to add your own custom code directly into a report within the Report Designer.

The chapter ended with an introduction to building report elements, and you created a star element that defines its own set of properties and renders different types of stars within reports.

12
Additional Pentaho Reporting Topics

This chapter covers a potpourri of useful, short Pentaho Reporting subjects that couldn't fit into earlier chapters. You'll start off by learning about Pentaho's Business Intelligence Server, which acts as a centralized reporting server where users can publish, schedule, and create ad hoc reports. From there, you'll learn how to use Pentaho Reporting for mobile reporting. The chapter continues with a look at the `MetaTableModel` API, which provides data source metadata to a report. Also included in this chapter is a brief introduction to Pentaho Reporting's `OutputProcessor` API for generating custom report output types. The chapter concludes with additional information about the Pentaho Reporting community and where to go for help.

Using Pentaho Reporting with Pentaho's Business Intelligence Server

As part of Pentaho's suite of products, Pentaho offers an open source Business Intelligence Server. The BI Server is a web application which allows users to publish and manage reports within an enterprise Business Intelligence system. The BI Server offers many capabilities, including the management and execution of Pentaho Reports. Combining Pentaho Reporting and Pentaho's BI Server, information technologists may utilize Pentaho Reporting in their environment without writing any code. In addition to the publishing and execution of reports, the open source BI Server allows for scheduling, background execution, security, and much more. With Pentaho's Enterprise BI Server, additional capabilities are available, including enterprise auditing as well as server management.

In this section, you'll get a taste of the capabilities within the BI Server related to Pentaho Reporting.

Downloading and Installing the BI Server

To download Pentaho's open source BI Server, go to `http://sourceforge.net/projects/pentaho` and download version 3.5 of the Business Intelligence Server. The file to download begins with `biserver-ce-`. Pentaho Reporting 3.5 is included in this release of the BI Server. The BI Server is a large download, and comes bundled with much more than Pentaho Reporting. The download includes an Apache Tomcat web server, which includes the Pentaho web application, a sample HSQLDB database, as well as an administration console for managing users and database connections.

Before you start the server, you need to enable a publish password so that you can send reports from the Report Designer application to the server. Unzip the distribution, and go into the `bi-server-ce/pentaho-solutions/system` folder. Edit the `publisher_config.xml` file, updating the empty `publisher-password` XML element with a password such as:

```
<publisher-password>password</publisher-password>
```

Now go back to the `bi-server-ce` folder and execute `start-pentaho.bat`. This will start the sample HSQLDB database, as well as Tomcat.

Once you've started the server, you may visit `http://localhost:8080/pentaho` in your browser to view the **Pentaho User Console**, where BI related content is hosted, created, and executed.

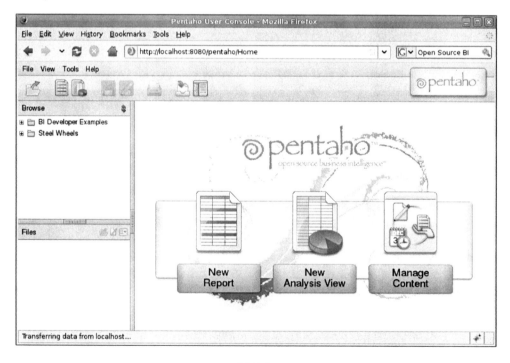

To complete starting up the BI Server, go into the `administration-console` folder and run `startup.bat`. This starts the administration console application, which is hosted within a Jetty web server. It is accessible by visiting `http://localhost:8099` in your browser. The default username and password are **admin** and **password**.

Publishing a report to the BI Server

Now that you have the BI Server running, you're ready to publish a report to the server. Open one of the example reports within Pentaho Report Designer. You can access the sample reports through the main menu by going to the **Help | Welcome** screen and double clicking on a report in the samples tree. All of these reports are based on the same sample database provided in the BI Server. Select **File | Publish**. You'll see the following dialog:

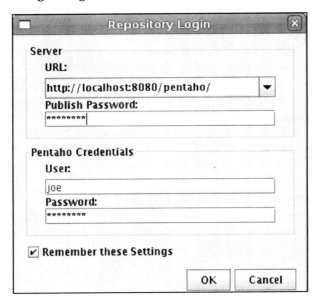

Make sure the URL is set to `http://localhost:8080/pentaho`. Enter your user credentials for the BI Server. The example user **joe** with the default password **password** is provided. Click **OK**. You should see a repository browser dialog:

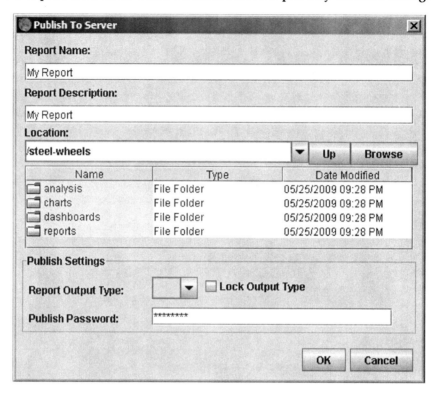

Name the report, and traverse into the `steel-wheels` folder. Note that you cannot publish reports in the root of the repository. Enter your recently created publish password and click the **OK** button. The report is sent to the server via HTTP. You can now log into the BI Server and execute the report.

Report definitions published to the server are stored in the server's solution repository, and are given default author read and write permissions. Report definitions may be deleted by going to the BI Server's solution navigator, right-clicking on the file, and selecting **Delete**.

Scheduling reports

Once a report has been published, you may choose to create a recurring schedule for the report to execute. This feature is even more useful if you configure the report for email, which is described below. To schedule a report, right-click on the report within the **Pentaho User Console** solution navigator and select **Schedule....** This brings up the following dialog:

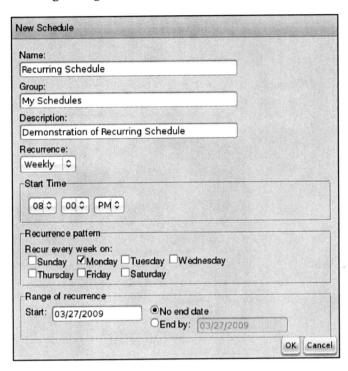

Enter a name, group, and description. Groups allow you to organize your schedules, so you can enter any group name that you prefer. You may choose from a set of recurrence options. As an example, choose **Weekly**, and check **Monday** at 8PM, beginning with the current date.

Now that you've created a schedule based on a published report, you should expect to see the generated report in your workspace after execution. Select **View | Workspace** from the main menu. The workspace contains all of your schedules, including results generated from those schedules:

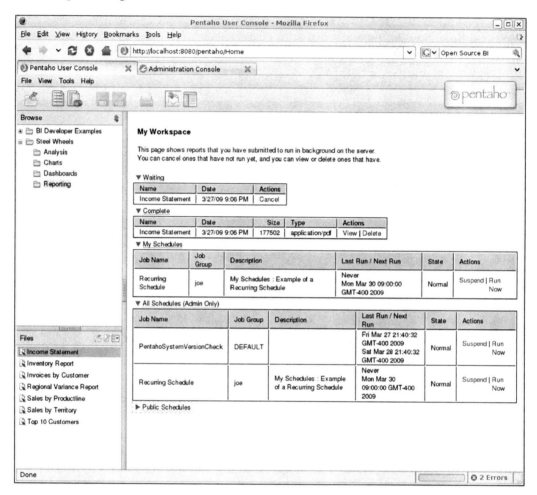

In addition to defining custom schedules, administrators may define a public recurring schedule and attach reports to that schedule, so business users may easily register for pre-canned reports.

Configuring permissions

As an administrator of the Pentaho BI Server, you may choose to limit a user's usage of the BI Server. This is possible by configuring permissions on folders and individual published reports. Right-click on a folder or a report and select **Properties**. Now select the **Share** tab:

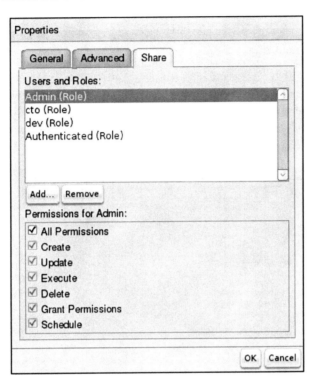

From this view, you can manage individual users and role permissions for the file or folder selected. Each item in the repository has a set of permissions for various actions such as **Execute, Create,** and **Schedule.** Later in this section you'll learn how to add and manage roles and users for the BI Server.

Report emailing and bursting

To enable advanced features within the BI Server such as report bursting and emailing, you must wrap your report in an action sequence. Action sequences are created using the Pentaho Design Studio, and can be thought of as a simple programming environment for advanced business users. The Pentaho Design Studio is based on the Eclipse project. You can download the Design Studio from Pentaho's SourceForge project page.

Once you've downloaded and unzipped the Design Studio, you'll walk through creating a simple emailed report. Launch the Design Studio by executing `PentahoDesignStudio.bat`. This brings up a design environment. To begin, you need to create a project that will host your action sequences. Select **File | New | Project...**, and create a project using the **General | Project** wizard.

> For Linux users, you will also need to create a workspace directory before defining your project.

Once you've created your new project, create a new action sequence by selecting **BI Platform | New Action Sequence** in the main menu. Select your recently created project as the container, and name your action sequence. Finally, select **Send Email** as the template for the action sequence and click **OK**. This will open the new action sequence on the **Define Process** tab.

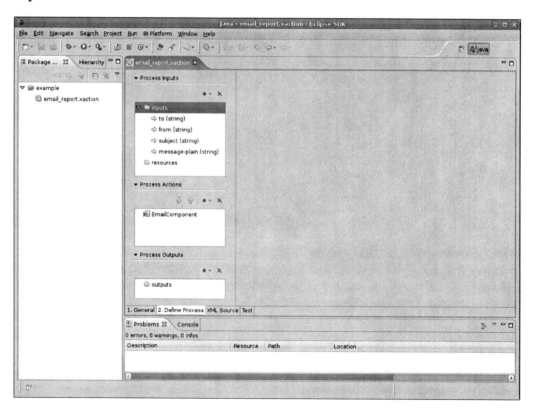

The action sequence is created with predefined action inputs, along with an **EmailComponent** ready to send out an email. You'll need to update the inputs with your own values, and add a report to the action sequence to complete the example.

Click the **to** input parameter, and enter in the default email ID you'd like the report to be sent to. You may also adjust the **from**, **subject**, and **message** input parameters, which define who the report will be sent from, along with email details.

Now you need to add a report component to the action sequence, which generates a report from the PRPT file. Select the add image-button under **Process Actions**, and select **Report | Pentaho Report**. Click the **Browse...** button under the **Report Specification** text field, and locate your PRPT file. Also, enter "pdf" as the **Report Format**. Finally, set the **Output Report Name** for reference later. The configured report component should look something like this:

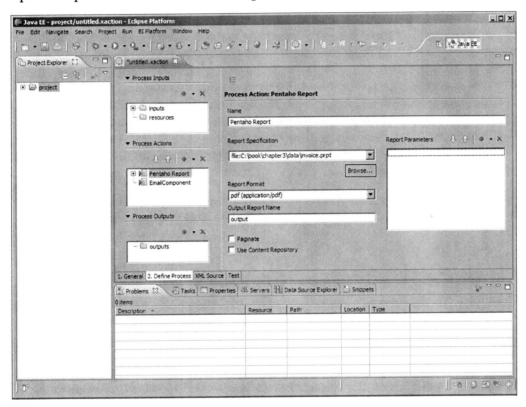

Make sure that your report component appears above the **EmailComponent** in the process list. To complete the action sequence, click on the **EmailComponent**, and scroll to the bottom of the component screen. Click the **Attachments** add image-button and select the **Output Report Name** defined in the previous step. Now save your changes. The file is saved with an .xaction extension.

You're now ready to deploy the action sequence to the server. To do this, copy the .xaction file along with the PRPT file into the bi-server/pentaho-solutions/steel-wheels folder.

Before executing the report on the server, you need to configure the BI Server's email settings. Open the `bi-server/pentaho-solutions/system/smtp-email/email_config.xml` file, and update the SMTP configuration with your SMTP server settings. Once you've made your changes, run **Tools | Refresh | System Settings** in the user console as an admin user. Also, to have the action sequence appear in the solution navigator, you will need to run **Tools | Refresh | Repository Cache**.

Once you've successfully published the new action sequence to the server, log into the BI Server and browse to the solution location where the report was saved. Execute the action sequence. You should see a success message, as well as receiving the email.

To broaden this example to burst the report to multiple individuals, you would need to set up a method for accessing multiple email addresses, as well as adding a loop within the action sequence to email the report multiple times. The email list might be stored as an action sequence string-list input parameter, or possibly stored in a database accessible through the use of an action sequence **SQLLookupRule** component, which you can add to an action sequence in Design Studio by selecting **Get Data From | Relational** in the **Process Actions** menu. To add the loop within the Design Studio, select **Loop** in the **Process Actions** menu, and select your list or result set as the **loop on** field.

To learn more about the Design Studio, please see the Design Studio documentation located on Pentaho's wiki: `http://wiki.pentaho.com/display/ServerDoc2x/Design+Studio`.

Managing database connections and users

Managing database connections and users for the Pentaho BI Server is done through the Pentaho Administration Console. This application appears in the BI Server under the `administration-console` folder. If you haven't already, you can launch the Administration Console by typing `startup.bat`. This starts a web server on port 8099. Open a browser and go to `http://localhost:8099`. A basic authentication dialog will appear. The default username and password for the administration console are **admin** and **password**.

The home page of the **Administration Console** looks like this:

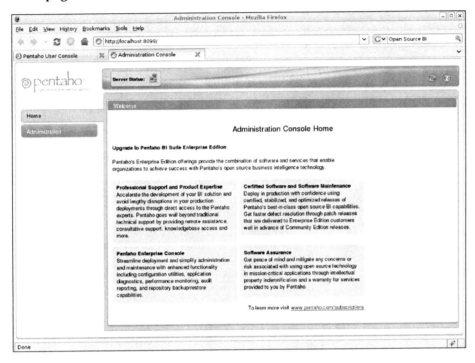

Now that you've started the **Administration Console**, click on the **Administration** section. This section of the **Administration Console** contains the **User and Roles** tab, as well as the **Database Connections** tab. Click on the **User and Roles** tab. From this screen, you can easily add and remove users and roles to be used within the BI Server:

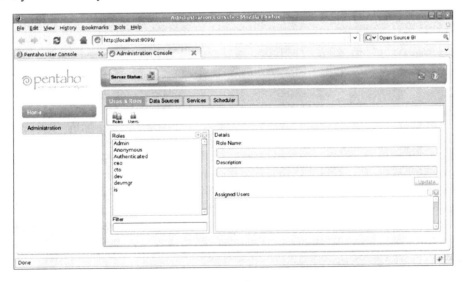

Now click on the **Database Connections** tab. On this page, you can add, manage, and remove configured JDBC database connections.

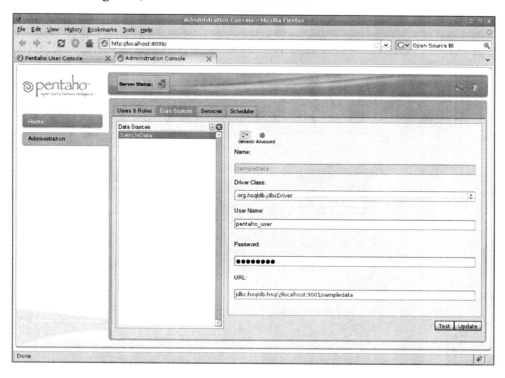

The BI Server comes pre-configured with the **SampleData** database connection, which connects to the HSQLDB sample data database provided with the application. If you are using a JDBC driver that isn't already packaged with the BI Server, you'll need to install it before configuring your database connection. Place the JDBC driver in the `administration-console/jdbc` folder, as well as within the `tomcat/webapps/pentaho/WEB-INF/lib` folder, and restart your web server for the driver to be recognized.

Creating ad hoc reports

In addition to publishing reports made in Report Designer, the BI Platform allows users to create reports on the fly based on predefined Pentaho Metadata models, as well as SQL Queries and CSV files. In order to enable Pentaho Metadata functionality, a DBA or IT Expert would need to use Pentaho Metadata Editor as described in the data sources chapter, and publish the model to the BI Server. Once published, users are able to define their own reports without requiring knowledge of SQL and table relationships. The ad hoc reporting tool appears in the user console when users click on the new report toolbar icon:

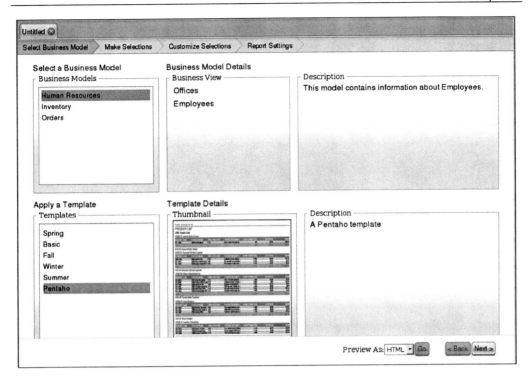

To learn more about many of the other capabilities of the BI Server, please visit
`http://www.pentaho.com`.

Mobile reporting

When discussing mobile reporting, there are multiple factors involved in providing a robust reporting solution. This section focuses on discussing issues with building a mobile reporting solution for the latest smart phone platforms. Most of these platforms have some capability around viewing rich document formats such as PDF, Excel, and HTML. Also, most of these platforms have the ability to create basic navigation HTML web pages or install a custom application that allows navigation.

Mobile report server

The first step in building a mobile reporting solution is developing a report server that can support mobile clients. Due to the differences in smart phone technologies, it's important that the reporting server has the ability to detect the phone technology that is making the request, and proxy to the correct service for providing a mobile user interface. For instance, if your reporting server was using a rich HTML Javascript client, you may not want to attempt to render that on a mobile phone. Instead, you would redirect the request to a simpler version of the user interface.

Because most smart phones provide PDF rendering capabilities with similar results, it's most likely that your reporting server will default to rendering the reports as PDF. Various smart phone technologies also support Excel viewing, so making this an option for a general reporting server is also valuable.

Another consideration when hosting a report server meant for mobile use is mobile phone access to Intranets and wireless networks. Not all mobile phone platforms provide VPN access, so it may be necessary to provide access outside your Intranet to your report server. This increases the need to verify that your web server hosting the report server is secure, and that only authorized business users from your organization have access to the server.

Another option to consider when building a report server that works with multiple smart phone technologies is providing an XML-based web service layer, implementing smart phone native applications for browsing reports instead of relying on the smart phone's browser as a delivery platform. The disadvantage to this approach is the need to implement and maintain one or many custom phone applications. Advantages to this approach include offline browsing of cached reports, as well as richer integration with the platform for things such as ad hoc report generation and event-driven report generation. Imagine a scenario where a report is automatically requested and stored locally on a smart phone when a business user arrives at the office on Monday morning. This type of capability is possible today only by implementing a custom application on a specific smart phone platform that offers geo-location capabilities.

At this time, there are no known mobile platforms that can execute Pentaho's reporting engine natively within a phone's operating system, but as smart phone technology evolves, this could become possible. Having the ability to generate reports directly on a phone opens up even more possibilities for the future of mobile reporting. Business application developers who are moving more capabilities to the mobile phone may consider rendering PDF and Excel based reports directly on the phone itself, instead of relying on a reporting server.

Mobile report design

While any report designed as a PDF should render on a smart phone, it's important to consider the implications of mobile reporting when designing reports. Mobile phones have less memory, and may have a difficult time rendering a large report with many pages of data. For this scenario, designing summary reports and enabling drill through into sub-reports might be useful.

Also when designing a report, it's important to consider the screen size in which the report will be rendered. Font size and style become important when building a report specifically designed for the phone. Because of potential incompatibilities with fonts and layout, make sure to test designed reports on the mobile platform before releasing it out to business users.

Example: Pentaho's iPhone BI extension

Pentaho offers an open source extension to the BI Server, which allows easy navigation and report execution on the iPhone. The following link describes the steps for configuring the BI Server:

```
http://wiki.pentaho.com/display/COM/Enabling+the+iPhone+BI+Extension.
```

When browsing the Pentaho BI Server, a user would see screens such as these:

This example uses Java Servlet Filters to detect the iPhone client, and redirects requests to a customized navigation system designed specifically for the iPhone interface. A similar approach could be used for designing navigation for Google's Android, Windows Mobile, Palm, and Blackberry smart phone technologies.

Data source metadata in Pentaho Reporting

As described in Chapter 5, data sources implement the `DataFactory` interface which returns a `TableModel`, representing the data used to populate the report. Pentaho Reporting defines an extension to `TableModel`, called `MetaTableModel`. This extension to `TableModel` allows the report to query column and cell-level metadata, allowing for customization of styles dynamically based on the data source.

One example of this implementation is the Pentaho Metadata `DataFactory`. As described in Chapter 5, Pentaho Metadata allows business users to build queries and select data without requiring knowledge of SQL or the underlying database schema. Along with those capabilities, it is also possible to attach style attributes to business columns. For example, metadata information can be fed into Pentaho Reporting to manage the formatting of a number within a report, or to adjust the font styles of a column within a report.

Most implementations of metadata define their metadata differently. Pentaho Reporting provides a method for mapping external metadata values to known Pentaho Reporting attributes and styles.

MetaTableModel API

The `MetaTableModel` interface defines four additional methods to the `TableModel` interface. The `MetaTableModel` interface is located within the `org.pentaho.reporting.engine.classic.core` package. Following are the four methods and descriptions of each:

```
// getTableAttributes returns a list of table wide attributes.

public DataAttributes getTableAttributes();

// getColumnAttributes returns a list of attributes
// per column.

public DataAttributes getColumnAttributes(final int column);

// isCellDataAttributesSupported returns true if
// the implementation supports cell level data attributes.
// The OLAP data factories are an implementation example
// of cell level data attributes.

public boolean isCellDataAttributesSupported();

// getCellDataAttributes returns a list of attributes
// related to a specific cell in the table model.

public DataAttributes getCellDataAttributes(final int row,
                                            final int column);
```

The `DataAttributes` interface, located within the `org.pentaho.reporting. engine.classic.core.wizard` package, defines the following methods, used to access individual metadata:

```
// getMetaAttributeDomains returns the namespaces of
// metadata attributes available.

public String[] getMetaAttributeDomains();

// getMetaAttributeNames returns the list of attributes
```

```
// under a particular domain.
public String[] getMetaAttributeNames(String domainName);
// getMetaAttribute returns the value of an attribute.
public Object getMetaAttribute(String domain,
                               String name,
                               Class type,
                               DataAttributeContext context);
// getMetaAttribute returns the value of an attribute,
//  returning a default value if not set
public Object getMetaAttribute(String domain,
                               String name,
                               Class type,
                               DataAttributeContext context,
                               Object defaultValue);
// getMetaAttributeMapper returns the defined concept
// query mapper for a particular attribute.
public ConceptQueryMapper getMetaAttributeMapper(
                                        String domain,
                                         String name);
```

The `ConceptQueryMapper` interface is related to mapping external metadata, and will be described in the next section.

For a real world example of a `MetaTableModel` implementation, please see the `PmdMetaTableModel` class, located in the `org.pentaho.reporting.engine.classic.extensions.datasources.pmd` package within Pentaho Reporting's `extension-pentaho-metadata` project.

Mapping external metadata

Pentaho Reporting manages the mapping from external metadata through the use of the data schema XML specification. The `dataschema.xsd` XML schema file is located in Pentaho Reporting's `engine-core` project.

To register a data schema XML file with mappings, a reporting module must specify a property starting with `org.pentaho.reporting.engine.classic.core.DataSchemaDefinition` within its configuration properties file. Once registered, the reporting engine manages the mapping of its named attributes and styles to the external system's metadata.

Your data schema XML file should consist of a root element `data-schema`, with a default namespace of `http://reporting.pentaho.org/namespaces/engine/classic/dataschema/1.0`. The three supported mapping types that appear as child XML elements are—`direct-mapping`, `indirect-mapping`, and `global-mapping`.

The `direct-mapping` element requires a `field` attribute, which specifies the `TableModel` column name in which to map a property. The direct mapping may contain `data-attributes` and `data-attribute-mapping` elements as children. The `data-attributes` element may contain XML attributes that map directly to a style or attribute within Pentaho Reporting.

The `data-attribute-mapping` element defines the mapping between Pentaho Reporting's attributes and the specific `MetaTableModel` attribute namespace, also referred to as a domain. The attributes—`source-domain` and `source-name`—define the `MetaTableModel` class's attribute instance. The `target-domain` and `target-name` attributes define the reporting engine's attribute instance. If the attribute `concept-mapper` is defined, the value is used as the `ConceptQueryMapper` class to be used for conversion from the `MetaTableModel` class's attribute type to the reporting engine's attribute type.

The `indirect-mapping` element contains a `match` XML element, which contains a `domain` and `name` attribute describing the external attribute to match. Optionally, you may specify a `type` and `value` attribute. The `type` attribute defines what Java class type the value is, and the `value` attribute is the specific value required for matching. These `match` elements are used to determine if the `indirect-mapping` applies to the current `MetaTableModel` implementation. The `indirect-mapping` elements also specify the `data-attributes` and `data-attribute-mapping` elements defined above. The `indirect-mapping` element is more widely used over the other two element types for integrating metadata into the reporting engine.

The `global-mapping` XML element defines the same `data-attributes` and `data-attribute-mapping` as the previous mapping elements, and requires no additional configuration. All `data-attribute` and `data-attribute-mapping` elements contained within `global-mapping` elements are passed into the final data schema used by the report.

The `ConceptQueryMapper` interface allows conversion from external metadata system Java types to Pentaho Reporting's expected attribute types. This interface defines a single method:

```
// getValue converts an external metadata value to the
// expected Pentaho reporting object type.

public Object getValue(final Object value, final Class type, final
DataAttributeContext context);
```

The DataAttributeContext object provides access to the running report's context such as the locale of the report.

Using metadata attributes in a report

Only a subset of attributes and styles defined in Pentaho Reporting support external MetaTableModel metadata without the use of OpenFormula. The MetaDataStyleEvaluator class, located in the org.pentaho.reporting.engine. classic.core.function.sys, manages updating the individual supported elements within a report. Only those elements that define the field attribute located in the core namespace, or the labels-detail-header attribute located in the wizard namespace, support these metadata attributes.

In addition to defining these attributes, the element must also have the sstyle-format attribute, located in the query-metadata name space, set to true. Otherwise metadata attributes are ignored. The following is a list of all the style attributes that are currently supported:

- font-family
- font-size
- bold
- italic
- underline
- strikethrough
- color
- background-color
- horizontal-alignment
- vertical-alignment

It is also possible for the metadata to set the format-string, as well as the value attribute of a report element, as long as the data-format attribute located in the query-metadata namespace is set to true within the element. An example of this might be to set a report label's value based on metadata. You would need to set the label's labels-detail-header attribute to the MetaTableModel column containing the value metadata, as well as setting the label's data-format attribute to true. This would allow the label's value to be set to the MetaTableModel class's label attribute, located in the formatting namespace.

If the `format-string` isn't explicitly set by the `MetaTableModel`, the reporting engine uses the `AutoGeneratorUtility`, located in the `org.pentaho.reporting.engine.classic.core.wizard` package, to determine a correct format string. Additional metadata is accessed to determine the correct format, including the `type`, `currency`, `scale`, and `precision` attributes. A format string is generated if the type is of `java.util.Date`, `java.sql.Date`, `java.sql.Time`, or `java.lang.Number`.

Another method for applying metadata from a `MetaTableModel` is to use the `METADATA` formula function. This function takes three parameters and returns a metadata value. The first parameter is the column name in which to extract metadata, the second parameter is the namespace of the metadata value, and the third parameter is the metadata name for the value being accessed.

Current MetaTableModel implementations

A few working examples are available within reporting to demonstrate the use of `MetaTableModel`. The first, already discussed, is Pentaho Metadata. Pentaho Metadata allows easy configuration of the supported style attributes. Additional column metadata is used during wizard report generation such as `display-size`, which is used to calculate relative column widths.

Another working example is the `SQLReportDataFactory`. The `MetaTableModel` implementation exposes `ResultSet` metadata, including column names as well as column types.

The other working examples of the `MetaTableModel` are the olap4j and Mondrian set of `DataFactory` classes. Using OLAP allows for cell-level metadata, not just column level metadata.

All existing implementations of `MetaTableModel` only use `indirect-mapping` with `data-attribute-mapping` elements. There are no existing examples of `global-mapping` or `direct-mapping` in use within the reporting engine today.

The metadata and OLAP projects can be found within Pentaho Reporting's SVN repository under `engines/classic/trunk/extensions-pentaho-metadata`, `engines/classic/trunk/extensions-mondrian`, and `engines/classic/trunk/extensions-olap4j`.

Metadata example: DefaultMetaTableModel

To demonstrate how to build your own `MetaTableModel` implementation, along with applying mappings to the metadata, you'll go through a simple example, defining a `DefaultMetaTableModel`, which wraps a TableModel `instance` and implements the `MetaTableModel` API. You'll define a report that utilizes data source metadata attributes, and build a `DefaultMetaTableModel` that provides those attributes.

Instead of building a new workspace for this chapter, reuse the Chapter 11 project, so you can easily reuse the module configuration for this example. First, you'll need to define a `MetaTableModel` implementation. Create the file `src/DefaultMetaTableModel.java`, with the following source code. The inline comments describe the key areas of functionality.

```
import java.util.HashMap;
import java.util.Map;

import javax.swing.event.TableModelListener;
import javax.swing.table.TableModel;

import org.pentaho.reporting.engine.classic.core.MetaTableModel;
import org.pentaho.reporting.engine.classic.core.wizard.
DataAttributes;
import org.pentaho.reporting.engine.classic.core.wizard.
DefaultDataAttributes;
import org.pentaho.reporting.engine.classic.core.wizard.
EmptyDataAttributes;

public class DefaultMetaTableModel implements MetaTableModel {

// wrap an existing table model instance

    TableModel model;

// Define a map of column attributes that map to each
// column index.

    Map<Integer, DefaultDataAttributes> columnAttributes = new
HashMap<Integer, DefaultDataAttributes>();

// This constructor wraps a given model and provides
// column attributes as well

    public DefaultMetaTableModel(TableModel model) {
        this.model = model;
    }

// The getColumnAttributes method returns a list of column
// attributes for a particular column.  This should never
// return null, so return an empty list if one doesn't
// already exist.
```

```
    public DataAttributes getColumnAttributes(int column) {
        DefaultDataAttributes attribs = columnAttributes.
get(column);
        if (attribs == null) {
            return EmptyDataAttributes.INSTANCE;
        } else {
            return attribs;
        }
    }
// Allow setting of column attributes.

    public void setColumnAttribute(int column, String domain, String
name, Object value) {
// First find the attribute list for this column.
        DefaultDataAttributes attribs = columnAttributes.
get(column);
        if (attribs == null) {
// If an attribute list doesn't exist, create one and add
// it to the map.
            attribs = new DefaultDataAttributes();
            columnAttributes.put(column, attribs);
        }
// Set the attribute.  Note that a null ConceptMapper
// results in the default mapping behavior.
        attribs.setMetaAttribute(domain, name, null, value);
    }
// Support for table attributes is not provided in
// this example.
    public DataAttributes getTableAttributes() {
        return EmptyDataAttributes.INSTANCE;
    }
// Support for cell attributes is not provided in
// this example.
    public DataAttributes getCellDataAttributes(int row, int column) {
        return null;
    }
    public boolean isCellDataAttributesSupported() {
        return false;
    }
// Wrap the public API of TableModel
```

```
        public void addTableModelListener(TableModelListener listener) {
            model.addTableModelListener(listener);
        }

        public Class<?> getColumnClass(int col) {
            return model.getColumnClass(col);
        }

        public int getColumnCount() {
            return model.getColumnCount();
        }

        public String getColumnName(int col) {
            return model.getColumnName(col);
        }

        public int getRowCount() {
            return model.getRowCount();
        }

        public Object getValueAt(int row, int col) {
            return model.getValueAt(row, col);
        }

        public boolean isCellEditable(int row, int col) {
            return model.isCellEditable(row, col);
        }

        public void removeTableModelListener(TableModelListener listener)
    {
            model.removeTableModelListener(listener);
        }

        public void setValueAt(Object value, int row, int col) {
            model.setValueAt(value, row, col);
        }
    }
```

Now that you've created a `MetaTableModel` implementation, you need to build a report using it. For this example, you'll take a shortcut. Open the Report Designer, and build a very simple report. Create a static table of data, with a single column named `Value` with data `Row 1`, `Row 2`, and `Row 3`. Name the static table `default`.

Now add the **Value** field to the report **Details** band. Modify the background color style formula for this field, which appears in the **Style** tab as **text | bg-color**. Set it to:

```
=METADATA("Value"; "exampleDomain"; "bg-color")
```

This executes the metadata formula function described earlier, looking for the metadata attribute `bg-color` in the `exampleDomain` namespace. Now place a report label in the report header. Set the label's **labels-detail-header** value to the Value field. The **labels-detail-header** value can be found as part of the **Attributes** tab under the **wizard** category. This informs the engine that the label should use column-level metadata from the **Value** column in the table data source. Also set the label's **data-format** and **style-format** metadata attributes to `true`. Both of these attributes can be found as part of the **Attributes** tab under the **query-metadata** category. This informs the reporting engine to look for the value metadata attribute for the **Value** column, which is located in the engine's formatting namespace.

Preview your report. At this point, there is no metadata feeding the label or the background color, so you should see a report like this:

Row 1

Row 2

Row 3

Save your report as `metadata_table.prpt` in the `chapter11/data` folder. You'll now write a simple application that loads the report definition and renders a PDF. Before rendering the report, you'll update the report's `TableModel`, named **default**, defined earlier with metadata from your `DefaultMetaTableModel` implementation, including your two metadata attributes—`bg-color` and `label`. Create the `src/MetaTableModelDemo.java` file with the following source code:

```
import java.net.URL;

import javax.swing.table.TableModel;

import org.pentaho.reporting.engine.classic.core.ClassicEngineBoot;
import org.pentaho.reporting.engine.classic.core.CompoundDataFactory;
import org.pentaho.reporting.engine.classic.core.MasterReport;
import org.pentaho.reporting.engine.classic.core.TableDataFactory;
import org.pentaho.reporting.engine.classic.core.modules.output.
pageable.pdf.PdfReportUtil;
import org.pentaho.reporting.libraries.resourceloader.Resource;
import org.pentaho.reporting.libraries.resourceloader.ResourceManager;

public class MetaTableModelDemo {

// The main method generates a PDF based on the defined
```

```
                    // report along with the DefaultMetaTableModel implementation.
                        public static void main(final String[] args) throws Exception {
                    // Boot the engine and load the report.
                            ClassicEngineBoot.getInstance(). start();
                                ResourceManager manager = new ResourceManager();
                                manager.registerDefaults();
                                Resource res = manager.createDirectly(new
                    URL("file:data/metadata_table.prpt"), MasterReport.class);
                                MasterReport report = (MasterReport) res.getResource();
                    // Get a reference to the default TableModel defined in
                    // the Report Designer.

                                CompoundDataFactory factory = (CompoundDataFactory)
                    report.getDataFactory();
                                TableDataFactory tableFactory = (TableDataFactory)
                    factory.getReference(0);
                                TableModel tableModel = tableFactory.
                                            queryData("default", null);
                    // create a MetaTableModel based on the regular table model
                                DefaultMetaTableModel metaTableModel =
                                        new DefaultMetaTableModel(tableModel);
                    // Add bg-color and exampleLabel metadata values as part of
                    // the exampleDomain for the first column of data.

                                metaTableModel.setColumnAttribute(0, "exampleDomain",
                    "bg-color", "#abcdef");
                                metaTableModel.setColumnAttribute(0, "exampleDomain",
                    "exampleLabel", "Field Label");

                    // Overwrite the earlier table model with the new
                    // MetaTableModel.
                                tableFactory.addTable("default", metaTableModel);
                    // Generate a PDF output of the report.

                                PdfReportUtil.createPDF(report,
                                            "metadata_table.pdf");
                        }
                    }
```

You'll need to update the Ant file with a new `runmeta` target, as well as a new path reference. Add the following XML to the `chapter11/build.xml` file:

```
<path id="runtime_classpath">
    <fileset dir="lib">
            <include name="*.jar" />
    </fileset>
    <dirset dir="classes"/>
</path>

<target name="runmeta" depends="jar">
    <java fork="true" classpathref="runtime_classpath" classname="Meta
TableModelDemo"/>
</target>
```

Now type `ant runmeta` on the command line. The PDF file `metadata_table.pdf` will be created in the root of the project. Open the PDF. Your results should look something like this:

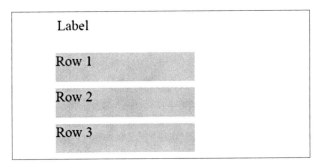

Note that the background `bg-color` attribute is taking effect, but the report header label is still not updating. Before this will work, you need to map the `exampleLabel` metadata attribute to the reporting engine's `label` attribute. To do this, you'll need to create a mapping between the two domains. Create the file `src/dataschema.xml` and add the following XML:

```
<data-schema xmlns="http://reporting.pentaho.org/namespaces/engine/
classic/dataschema/1.0">

  <indirect-mapping>
    <match domain="exampleDomain"
           name="exampleLabel"/>

      <data-attribute-mapping target-domain="http://reporting.pentaho.
org/namespaces/engine/meta-attributes/formatting"
                              target-name="label"
                              source-domain="exampleDomain"
                              source-name="exampleLabel"/>
  </indirect-mapping>
</data-schema>
```

This defines an indirect mapping from `exampleLabel` to the reporting engine's `label` attribute. Finally, you'll need to tell the reporting engine about this data schema file. Add the following property to `configuration.properties`, which already exists in the `chapter11/src` folder:

```
# specify the data schema location
org.pentaho.reporting.engine.classic.core.DataSchemaDefinition.
exampleDomain=res://dataschema.xml
```

The reporting engine looks for all properties that begin with `org.pentaho. reporting.engine.classic.core.DataSchemaDefinition`, loading all the mappings defined in those files. Now re-run the report by typing `ant runmeta`, and re-open the `metadata_table.pdf` file. Your report should now look like this:

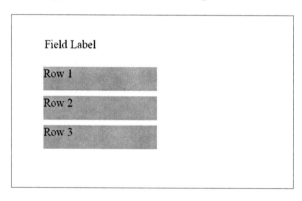

The report is now fully utilizing the attributes defined in the `DefaultMetaTableModel` implementation.

Working with Pentaho Reporting's output layer

One of the core APIs deep within Pentaho Reporting is the set of output layer interfaces. These interfaces, along with abstract class implementations, make it possible to write your own custom output generator. In this section, you'll discover the main interfaces within the API, learn about some of the key classes involved in rendering a report, as well as walk through a very simple example demonstrating how to render a report to your own custom format.

The OutputProcessor API is used during the last stage in general report processing. Before the calls are made to the OutputProcessor API, a ReportProcessor implementation generates an internal logical model of the report to be rendered. This includes executing all the functions defined, calculating all the locations and sizes of individual components within the report, and in the case of a paged report, determining which content goes on what page.

Once a ReportProcessor has completed the internal calculations necessary for rendering, it then proceeds to making calls into the provided OutputProcessor implementation. When implementing your own output layer, you must implement the OutputProcessor interface, as well as the OutputProcessorMetaData interface. The OutputProcessor and OutputProcessorMetaData interfaces are located in the org.pentaho.reporting.engine.classic.core.layout.output package.

The OutputProcessorMetaData interface

The OutputProcessorMetaData interface provides a general metadata interface for the OutputProcessor, including which features and content are supported, as well as providing access to the report configuration along with access to font metric details. The class AbstractOutputProcessorMetaData is available, which implements the common set of functionality across the various output implementations. As an example, the Excel implementation of OutputProcessorMetaData configures the various features of Excel rendering based on configuration properties, while the PDF implementation also overrides some of the default font behavior for translation into the PDF format.

The OutputProcessor interface

The OutputProcessor interface defines callbacks so that the ReportProcessor may trigger rendering of the output. During the processing of a report and after it is complete, a call is made to the processContent method for each logical page generated by the Renderer implementation, described later. The class AbstractOutputProcessor is available, which implements common state management tasks. Two subclass implementations — AbstractPageableOutputProcessor and AbstractTableOutputProcessor — are available for the different output rendering types. Pageable outputs include documents such as PDF, while table outputs include documents such as Excel and HTML.

The AbstractPageableOutputProcessor traverses the logical page, providing direct access to each physical page within the page grid. The AbstractTableOutputProcessor provides a flattened two dimensional structure of the report, useful for rendering cell based formats. The AbstractTableOutputProcessor also implements the IterativeOutputProcessor interface, an extension to the OutputProcessor interface, which allows for iterative rendering.

RenderNode Document Object Model

The OutputProcessor receives the report model in a RenderNode Document Object Model, which it translates to a specific output. The RenderNode class, located in the org.pentaho.reporting.engine.classic.core.layout.model package, is the base of the RenderNode DOM and defines a set of core attributes. Child classes add additional metadata. For instance, the RenderBox class provides a linked list of children, and acts as a container object. The RenderableText and SpacerRenderNode contain the text-related information within a report, while the RenderableReplacedContentBox contains references to content such as images and Java Shape and Drawable objects.

The RenderNode objects are generated during the rendering process. The Renderer implementations within the reporting engine manage the creation of the RenderNode DOM. The two primary rendering implementations are PageableRenderer, which manages generating individual pages, and StreamingRenderer, which ignores pages.

Updating Report Designer

To expose a custom output format in Report Designer, you must implement a `DesignerContextAction` located in the `org.pentaho.reporting.designer.core.actions` package of Report Designer. The `org.pentaho.reporting.designer.core.actions.report.preview` package contains the default implementations as examples. These examples contain the user interface and report generation code, allowing previews in the various supported formats.

To add the action to Report Designer's menu system, edit the `designer-frame.xul` file located in the `org.pentaho.reporting.designer.core.xul` package. Find the `file-preview-popup` menu pop up element in the XUL file, and add a new menu item with reference to the action class name.

Under the covers, the Report Designer uses its own `OutputProcessor`, the `DesignerOutputProcessor`, which only works with the logical page model, for rendering of the report in design mode. This guarantees compatibility between the Report Designer and the reporting engine, reusing the same layout algorithms for both rendering and designing a report.

Example: PojoObject output

In this example, you'll implement your own `OutputProcessor` and `OutputProcessorMetaData` classes that will generate a list of `PojoObject` instances, containing their text and location within the report. To keep the example simple, you'll write a `main` method within a `PojoUtil` class that executes the simple report `metadata_table.prpt` defined in the earlier `MetaTableModel` example.

First, create the `PojoOutputMetaData` class, which must provide an export descriptor. This descriptor is accessible by report functions, allowing the report to know which context it is rendering in. The expected syntax of the export descriptor is `[output class]/[output type]/[output sub type]`. Create the file `chapter11/src/PojoOutputMetaData.java` with the following source code:

```
import org.pentaho.reporting.engine.classic.core.layout.output.
AbstractOutputProcessorMetaData;
import org.pentaho.reporting.libraries.base.config.Configuration;

public class PojoOutputMetaData extends
AbstractOutputProcessorMetaData {

// Define a basic constructor that calls its super.
    public PojoOutputMetaData(final Configuration configuration) {
            super(configuration);
    }
```

```
// Provide an export descriptor.

   public String getExportDescriptor() {
          return "stream/pojo";
   }
}
```

Now you'll begin to build the `PojoOutputProcessor` class. This class implements the `OutputProcessor` interface, and manages the creation of the list of plain old Java objects, which will contain an x and y coordinate, along with the text associated with that location. Comments have been placed in the source that describe the inner workings of this very simple example. Create the file `chapter11/src/ PojoOutputProcessor.java` with the following source code:

```
import java.util.ArrayList;
import java.util.List;

import org.pentaho.reporting.engine.classic.core.layout.model.
LogicalPageBox;
import org.pentaho.reporting.engine.classic.core.layout.model.
ParagraphPoolBox;
import org.pentaho.reporting.engine.classic.core.layout.model.
RenderBox;
import org.pentaho.reporting.engine.classic.core.layout.model.
RenderNode;
import org.pentaho.reporting.engine.classic.core.layout.model.
RenderableText;
import org.pentaho.reporting.engine.classic.core.layout.model.
SpacerRenderNode;
import org.pentaho.reporting.engine.classic.core.layout.output.
AbstractOutputProcessor;
import org.pentaho.reporting.engine.classic.core.layout.output.
ContentProcessingException;
import org.pentaho.reporting.engine.classic.core.layout.output.
LogicalPageKey;
import org.pentaho.reporting.engine.classic.core.layout.output.
OutputProcessorMetaData;
import org.pentaho.reporting.libraries.base.config.Configuration;

// The PojoOutputProcessor extends the
// AbstractOutputProcessor, which manages the
// processing state.

public class PojoOutputProcessor extends AbstractOutputProcessor {

// Define a pojo object which you'll populate when
// rendering the report

   public static class PojoObject {

// Define the x location of the PojoObject.
```

```
        int x;
// Define the y location of the PojoObject.
        int y;
// Define the text extracted during report rendering.
        String text = "";
    }


// Define a reference to the PojoOutputMetaData class.
    PojoOutputMetaData metadata;
// Define a list of the pojo objects you're about to generate.
    List<PojoObject> pojoObjects = new ArrayList<PojoObject>();
// The constructor creates a new metadata object.
    public PojoOutputProcessor(final Configuration configuration) {
        metadata = new PojoOutputMetaData(configuration);
    }
// The processPageContent callback renders a report page from
// a LogicalPageBox.  This method is called by
// the ReportProcessor when the page content is ready
// for rendering.
    protected void processPageContent(LogicalPageKey logicalPageKey,
                LogicalPageBox logicalPage) throws
ContentProcessingException {
// Call into the recursive handle method, which
// traverses the logical page DOM.
        handle(logicalPage);
    }
// The handle method loops through the child nodes of
// a specified RenderBox, either recursing into child nodes
// or rendering ParagraphPoolBox nodes.
    public void handle(RenderBox box) {
        RenderNode node = box.getFirstChild();
        while (node != null) {
            if (node instanceof ParagraphPoolBox) {
// The ParagraphPoolBox contains the text within a report.
                ParagraphPoolBox ppb = (ParagraphPoolBox)node;
                handleParagraph(ppb);
            }
            if (node instanceof RenderBox) {
// Recurse into the DOM.
```

```
                    handle((RenderBox)node);
                }
                node = node.getNext();
            }
        }

// The handleParagraph method generates a PojoObject based
// on a ParagraphPoolBox, which contains text and spacer
// nodes.
    public void handleParagraph(ParagraphPoolBox box) {
            RenderNode node = box.getFirstChild();

// Create a PojoObject with x and y coordinates.
            PojoObject object = new PojoObject();
            object.x = (int)node.getX() / 1000;
            object.y = (int)node.getY() / 1000;

// Populate the PojoObject's text appropriately.
            while (node != null) {
                if (node instanceof RenderableText) {
                        object.text += ((RenderableText)node).
getRawText();
                } else if (node instanceof SpacerRenderNode) {
                        for (int i = 0; i < ((SpacerRenderNode)node).
getSpaceCount(); i++) {
                            object.text += " ";
                        }
                }
                node = node.getNext();
            }

// Add the PojoObject to the list.
            pojoObjects.add(object);
        }

// Return a reference to the custom OutputProcessorMetaData
// instance.
    public OutputProcessorMetaData getMetaData() {
            return metadata;
        }

// Allow access to the generated PojoObject list.
    public List<PojoObject> getPojoObjects() {
            return pojoObjects;
        }
    }
```

The final class you must define is `PojoUtil`. This class provides a helper method for generating the output, binding all the necessary report components together. This class also contains an example `main` method, which prints out the final object model to the command line. Create the file `src/PojoUtil.java` with the following source code:

```java
import java.io.IOException;
import java.net.URL;
import java.util.List;

import org.pentaho.reporting.engine.classic.core.ClassicEngineBoot;
import org.pentaho.reporting.engine.classic.core.MasterReport;
import org.pentaho.reporting.engine.classic.core.
ReportProcessingException;
import org.pentaho.reporting.engine.classic.core.modules.output.table.
base.StreamReportProcessor;
import org.pentaho.reporting.libraries.resourceloader.Resource;
import org.pentaho.reporting.libraries.resourceloader.ResourceManager;

public class PojoUtil {

// The createPojoReport method generates a PojoObject
// list from a report.

    public static List<PojoOutputProcessor.PojoObject>
createPojoReport(final MasterReport report)
        throws ReportProcessingException, IOException {

// Instantiate a target PojoOutputProcessor class,
// passing in the report configuration.

        final PojoOutputProcessor target = new
PojoOutputProcessor(report.getConfiguration());

// Instantiate a StreamReportProcessor with references
// to the report and the OutputProcessor.

        final StreamReportProcessor reportProcessor = new
StreamReportProcessor(report, target);

// Process the report.

        reportProcessor.processReport();

// Close the report after processing.

        reportProcessor.close();

// Return a list of the plain old Java objects
// generated from this report.

        return target.getPojoObjects();
    }

// The main method generates a plain old Java object
// output from the simple report defined earlier.
```

```
     public static void main(final String[] args) throws Exception {
// Boot the reporting engine.
        ClassicEngineBoot.getInstance().start();
// Load the report PRPT file.
     ResourceManager manager = new ResourceManager();
     manager.registerDefaults();
     Resource res = manager.createDirectly(
       new URL("file:data/metadata_table.prpt"), MasterReport.class);
     MasterReport report = (MasterReport) res.getResource();
// Generate the PojoObject list.
     List<PojoOutputProcessor.PojoObject> objs =
                         PojoUtil.createPojoReport(report);
// Write the PojoObject list to System.out as an example.
     for (PojoOutputProcessor.PojoObject obj : objs) {
        System.out.println("" + obj.x + "," + obj.y + ": "
                     + obj.text);
     }
  }
}
```

You're now ready to build and run the simple `PojoOutputProcessor` example. Add the following target to the `chapter11/build.xml` Ant file:

```
<target name="runpojo" depends="jar">
   <java fork="true" classpathref="runtime_classpath"
classname="PojoUtil"/>
</target>
```

Type `ant runpojo` to see the results. You should see a printout that looks something like this:

```
4,21: Row 1
4,42: Row 2
4,63: Row 3
```

In this example, you created the simplest of output formats, the plain old Java object `OutputProcessor`, demonstrating the implementation and use of an `OutputProcessor` within the reporting engine.

The Pentaho community—getting help and contributing

As an open source project, Pentaho Reporting has a community of people and organizations who contribute through answering questions, contributing translations, filing and fixing bugs, writing documentation, and of course, contributing code. To make sure you can find what you need to engage the Pentaho Reporting community. The following is the list of online places and tools to help you get started.

Asking questions, helping others

Today, there are two primary methods of communication within the Pentaho Reporting community. The first and most widely used are the Pentaho Reporting forums. These forums are located at `http://forums.pentaho.org/` under the main category Reporting. **Thomas Morgner**, the founder and primary architect of Pentaho Reporting, also known as **Taqua** in the forums, has over 4,800 posts and is always helping out folks with their questions. You can search and read forum discussions, or sign up for an account and ask your own questions.

Another method of communication is Pentaho's IRC channel, set up by Pentaho community members. This channel is located on the `chat.freenode.net` server, as channel `##pentaho`. A large number of active Pentaho community members are available to answer technical questions.

Online documentation

Pentaho hosts a wiki, which contains community documentation for Pentaho's various projects. You can find the wiki at `http://wiki.pentaho.com`, which contains links to Pentaho Reporting documentation, as well as tech tips that walk through specific use cases. As a wiki, community members may contribute their own tech tips or documentation around any of the Pentaho projects.

Pentaho also hosts a sub-domain dedicated to the Pentaho Reporting community at `http://reporting.pentaho.org`, which contains information about the latest releases and download links. Also, Javadoc for the latest versions of Pentaho's open source projects is hosted online at `http://javadoc.pentaho.com`. Pentaho Reporting Javadoc can be found at http://javadoc.pentaho.com/reporting/.

Submitting bugs and viewing backlogs

To submit a bug, or view Pentaho Reporting's backlog, you can visit Pentaho's JIRA bug tracking system at `http://jira.pentaho.com`.

Pentaho Reporting is broken out into two main projects—the **Pentaho Reporting Engine** and the **Pentaho Report Designer**. Each project contains a **Road Map** link, containing a list of prioritized activities that Pentaho and the open source community are working on.

Contributing code

If you'd like to add a new feature to Pentaho Reporting or fix a bug, the source code for the reporting engine and Report Designer is easily accessible. Pentaho hosts the reporting project's SVN server at `http://source.pentaho.org/pentaho-reporting`. The reporting engine's core source code is located in the `engines/classic` sub-folder, and the Report Designer is located in the `tools/report-designer` sub-folder. By going to `http://source.pentaho.org/viewvc/pentaho-reporting/`, you can browse the source and version changes using your browser.

Once you've made your change, you can submit your patch to Pentaho's JIRA system. If you become a regular contributor, often Thomas will grant you direct commit access to SVN.

One of the many types of contributions Pentaho receives includes translated message bundles. These message bundles are located within the reporting projects, and can be found by searching for `messages.properties` files within each project. For instance, there are many of these files within the engine-core project.

Enterprise support

Pentaho offers an Enterprise Edition of Pentaho Reporting, which includes direct customer support, as well as additional functionality such as enterprise auditing within Pentaho's Business Intelligence Server. If you are working within an enterprise and would like to purchase an enterprise license, you can contact Pentaho directly by visiting `http://www.pentaho.com`. Subscription customers have access to Pentaho's Knowledge Base, which contains many articles and enterprise documentation on all of Pentaho's products.

Pentaho also offers online and in-person training courses, which include hands on tutorials of the Pentaho Report Designer, as well as the Pentaho Business Intelligence Server. Pentaho works with a large set of partners to offer consulting, which may include everything from setting up your reporting server to writing custom functionality that your business requires.

Summary

In this chapter, you learned about a broad range of topics. You began with an introduction to Pentaho's open source Business Intelligence Server, which allows organizations to publish, schedule, and build reports from a web application. You learned about action sequences for emailing and bursting reports, along with learning where to set up database connections and add users to the BI Server. You also were introduced to mobile reporting, which included a reference to Pentaho's iPhone BI Extension.

Also in this chapter, you discovered Pentaho Reporting's data source metadata capabilities by implementing your own `MetaTableModel` class. You were introduced to Pentaho Reporting's output rendering API through a simple plain old Java object output example.

Finally, you learned more about the Pentaho Reporting community, including where to go to ask questions, file bugs, and how to contribute back to Pentaho's open source reporting projects.

Thank you for taking the time to read this book. I hope you learned a lot along the way, and are excited about using Pentaho Reporting to solve your business reporting needs!

Index

Thank you for buying
Pentaho Reporting 3.5 for Java Developers

Packt Open Source Project Royalties

When we sell a book written on an Open Source project, we pay a royalty directly to that project. Therefore by purchasing Pentaho Reporting 3.5 for Java Developers, Packt will have given some of the money received to the Pentaho project.

In the long term, we see ourselves and you — customers and readers of our books — as part of the Open Source ecosystem, providing sustainable revenue for the projects we publish on. Our aim at Packt is to establish publishing royalties as an essential part of the service and support a business model that sustains Open Source.

If you're working with an Open Source project that you would like us to publish on, and subsequently pay royalties to, please get in touch with us.

Writing for Packt

We welcome all inquiries from people who are interested in authoring. Book proposals should be sent to author@packtpub.com. If your book idea is still at an early stage and you would like to discuss it first before writing a formal book proposal, contact us; one of our commissioning editors will get in touch with you.

We're not just looking for published authors; if you have strong technical skills but no writing experience, our experienced editors can help you develop a writing career, or simply get some additional reward for your expertise.

About Packt Publishing

Packt, pronounced 'packed', published its first book "Mastering phpMyAdmin for Effective MySQL Management" in April 2004 and subsequently continued to specialize in publishing highly focused books on specific technologies and solutions.

Our books and publications share the experiences of your fellow IT professionals in adapting and customizing today's systems, applications, and frameworks. Our solution-based books give you the knowledge and power to customize the software and technologies you're using to get the job done. Packt books are more specific and less general than the IT books you have seen in the past. Our unique business model allows us to bring you more focused information, giving you more of what you need to know, and less of what you don't.

Packt is a modern, yet unique publishing company, which focuses on producing quality, cutting-edge books for communities of developers, administrators, and newbies alike. For more information, please visit our website: www.PacktPub.com.

Java EE 5 Development with NetBeans 6

ISBN: 978-1-847195-46-3   Paperback: 400 pages

Develop professional enterprise Java EE applications quickly and easily with this popular IDE

1. Use features of the popular NetBeans IDE to improve Java EE development

2. Careful instructions and screenshots lead you through the options available

3. Covers the major Java EE APIs such as JSF, EJB 3 and JPA, and how to work with them in NetBeans

4. Covers the NetBeans Visual Web designer in detail

DWR Java AJAX Applications

ISBN: 978-1-847192-93-6   Paperback: 228 pages

A step-by-step example-packed guide to learning professional application development with Direct Web Remoting

1. Learn Direct Web Remoting features from scratch and how to apply DWR practically

2. Topics such as configuration, testing, and debugging are thoroughly explained through examples

3. Demonstrates advanced elements of creating user interfaces and back-end integration

Please check **www.PacktPub.com** for information on our titles

LWUIT 1.1 for Java ME Developers

ISBN: 978-1-847197-40-5   Paperback: 364 pages

Create great user interfaces for mobile devices

1. Make your applications stand out with dazzling graphics that look and behave the same on different mobile devices

2. Log information on the runtime behavior of your program

3. Write applications with attractive visual effects like transitions and animations

3. Use localization so that your applications can adapt to different languages and locales

Flex 3 with Java

ISBN: 978-1-847195-34-0   Paperback: 304 pages

Develop rich internet applications quickly and easily using Adobe Flex 3, ActionScript 3.0 and integrate with a Java backend using BlazeDS 3.2

1. A step-by-step tutorial for developing web applications using Flex 3, ActionScript 3.0, BlazeDS 3.2, and Java

2. Build efficient and seamless data-rich interactive applications in Flex using a combination of MXML and ActionScript 3.0

3. Create custom UIs, Components, Events, and Item Renders to develop user friendly applications

Please check **www.PacktPub.com** for information on our titles

LaVergne, TN USA
13 November 2009

163950LV00003B/49/P

9 781847 193193